Lecture Notes of the Institute for Computer Sciences, Social Informatics and Telecommunications Engineering 487

The LNICST series publishes ICST's conferences, symposia and workshops.

LNICST reports state-of-the-art results in areas related to the scope of the Institute. The type of material published includes

- Proceedings (published in time for the respective event)
- Other edited monographs (such as project reports or invited volumes)

LNICST topics span the following areas:

- General Computer Science
- E-Economy
- E-Medicine
- Knowledge Management
- Multimedia
- Operations, Management and Policy
- Social Informatics
- Systems

Hamid Reza Karimi · Ning Wang
Editors

Sensor Systems and Software

13th EAI International Conference, S-Cube 2022
Dalian, China, December 7–9, 2022
Proceedings

 Springer

Editors
Hamid Reza Karimi
Politecnico di Milano
Milan, Italy

Ning Wang
Dalian Maritime University
Dalian, China

ISSN 1867-8211 ISSN 1867-822X (electronic)
Lecture Notes of the Institute for Computer Sciences, Social Informatics
and Telecommunications Engineering
ISBN 978-3-031-34898-3 ISBN 978-3-031-34899-0 (eBook)
https://doi.org/10.1007/978-3-031-34899-0

This Springer imprint is published by the registered company Springer Nature Switzerland AG
The registered company address is: Gewerbestrasse 11, 6330 Cham, Switzerland

Preface

We are delighted to introduce the proceedings of the thirteenth edition of the European Alliance for Innovation (EAI) - International Conference on Sensor Systems and Software (EAI S-CUBE 2022). The aim of this conference was to provide an ideal venue to disseminate state-of-the-art research in the broad area of system development and software support for control systems and cyber-physical systems (CPS) over networks. The technological revolution occurring in sensorization and digitalization is pushing the way we must engineer solutions by considering robustness, efficiency, scalability, flexibility, sustainability, and security in the product development.

The scope of the conference covers all aspects and dimensions of sensors, control technologies, and networks applied to smart applications, including, but not restricted to: Sensors and Actuators; Networked control systems; Complex networks; Intelligent systems; IoT sensors and networks; Smart and efficient sensors (environmental, infrastructure, others); Cyber-physical systems; Digital Twins; Wireless sensor networks; Resilience control; Data processing, storage, and management; Distributed algorithms for reasoning and signal processing; Disaster (pandemics, earthquakes, etc.) monitoring, sensing, and control; Environmental Monitoring; Security and privacy in sensor systems (security and privacy by design); Health monitoring of cyber-physical systems; Smart-Homes, Smart-Cities, and Building automation; Tools and platforms for sensor systems planning, deployment, monitoring, and maintenance; Case studies (Healthcare, Vehicles, Robotics, Marine systems, Public Services, Surveillance, Education, Sport, and Leisure).

The technical program of S-CUBE 2022 consisted of 16 full papers. The conference tracks were: Track 1 - Sensor Technology for Marine Systems; Track 2 - Resilience Control Systems; Track 3 - Applications. Aside from the high-quality technical paper presentations, the technical program also featured three keynote speeches. The three keynote speakers were Xinping Yan from Wuhan University of Technology, China; Kai Cheng from Brunel University London, UK and Md Atiqur Rahman Ahad from University of East London, UK.

Coordination with the steering committee members was essential for the success of the conference. We sincerely appreciate their constant support and guidance. It was also a great pleasure to work with such an excellent organizing committee team for their hard work in organizing and supporting the conference. In particular, the Technical Program Committee members completed the peer-review process of technical papers and made a high-quality technical program. We are also grateful to the Conference Manager, Kristina Havlickova, for her support and to all the authors who submitted their papers to the S-CUBE 2022 conference.

We strongly believe that the S-CUBE conference series provides a good forum for all researchers, developers and practitioners to discuss all science and technology aspects that are relevant to sensors, software, and systems. We also expect that future S-CUBE conferences will be as successful and stimulating, as indicated by the contributions presented in this volume.

June 2023   Hamid Reza Karimi
                                                                        Ning Wang

Organization

Steering Committee

Ning Wang	Dalian Maritime University, China
Witold Pedrycz	University of Alberta, Canada
Qingguo Wang	University of Johannesburg, South Africa

Organizing Committee

General Chair

Hamid Reza Karimi	Politecnico di Milano, Italy

General Co-chairs

Yongjun Gong	Dalian Maritime University, China
Weidong Zhang	Shanghai Jiaotong University, China
Shiji Song	Tsinghua University, China

TPC Chair and Co-chairs

Ning Wang	Dalian Maritime University, China
Len Gelman	University of Huddersfield, UK
Xudong Zhao	Dalian University of Technology, China
Mohd Rizal Arshad	Universiti Sains Malaysia, Malaysia
Jianchuan Yin	Guangdong Ocean University, China
Defeng Wu	Jimei University, China

Sponsorship and Exhibit Chairs

Zhengtian Wu	Suzhou University of Science and Technology, China
Hongde Qin	Harbin Engineering University, China

Local Chair

Yejin Lin   Dalian Maritime University, China

Publications Chairs

Josep Maria Rossell   Universitat Politècnica de Catalunya (UPC), Spain
Dongsheng Yang   Northeastern University, China

Posters and PhD Track Chair

Yuanqing Wu   Guangdong University of Technology, China

Panels Chair

Yi Wei   Dalian Maritime University, China

Demos Chair

Jundong Zhang   Dalian Maritime University, China

Tutorials Chairs

Yancheng Liu   Dalian Maritime University, China
Baoping Jiang   Suzhou University of Science and Technology,
                                     China

Technical Program Committee

Ömer Nezih Gerek   Eskisehir Technical University, Turkey
Yusuf Ozturk   San Diego State University, USA
Xiao-Zhi Gao   University of Eastern Finland, Finland
Liu Jun   Singapore University of Technology and Design,
                                     Singapore
Kalyana Veluvolu   Kyungpook National University, South Korea
B.D. Parameshachari   GSSSIET for Women, India
Jing Jin   East China University of Science and Technology,
                                     China
Gisela Pujol   Universitat Politècnica de Catalunya, Spain
Alessandro do Nascimento Vargas   Universidade Tecnológica Federal do Paraná,
                                     Brazil

Contents

Applications

Sensor Technology for Marine Systems

Way Points and Reference Speed Based Trajectory Generator for an Unmanned Surface Vehicle

Hongkun He[1]([✉])[ID] and Ning Wang[2][ID]

[1] School of Marine Electrical Engineering, Dalian Maritime University,
Dalian 116026, China
`hehongkun4@163.com`
[2] School of Marine Engineering, Dalian Maritime University, Dalian 116026, China
`n.wang@ieee.org`

Abstract. On the basis of successive way points (WPs) and piecewise reference speed, a trajectory generator (TG) is elaborately devised to generate a smooth trajectory for an unmanned surface vehicle (USV) in this paper. Firstly, the seventh-order polynominal is exclusively deployed to fit foregoing WPs, resulting in the parameterized path with sufficient differentiability. Then, the reference speed passes through the second-order filter, such that the speed command is uniformly continuous. Together with the parameterized path and speed command, the path speed is readily designed, and thereby contributing to the continuously differentiable trajectory. Certainly, the desired trajectory is much easier for users to predesignate in the electronic chart, and is more favorable to be exactly tracked by the USV in practice. Eventually, the model-based controller for the USV is synthesized to asymptotically track the generated trajectory in the absence of unmodeled dynamics and external disturbances. Comprehensive simulations are conducted on the benchmark prototype CyberShip II, so as to validate the effectiveness of both the proposed TG and trajectory-tracking controller.

Keywords: Unmanned surface vehicle (USV) · Trajectory generator (TG) · Way points (WPs) · Seventh-order polynominal · Second-order filter

1 Introduction

As an ocean robot, the unmanned surface vehicle (USV) can replace humans to execute dangerous and repetitive tasks, and thereby playing an increasingly important role in the marine community [3,16–18]. In some cases, the USV should reach the desired position with the prescribed time and course angle, e.g.,

This work is supported by the National Natural Science Foundation of China (Grant 52271306) and Innovative Research Foundation of Ship General Performance (Grant 31422120).

H. R. Karimi and N. Wang (Eds.): S-Cube 2022, LNICST 487, pp. 3–16, 2023.
https://doi.org/10.1007/978-3-031-34899-0_1

the hydrographic survey of restricted access areas [11]. Therefore, the trajectory tracking control of the USV involving both spatial and temporal constraints, has great application potential in engineering [5,15,22]. Naturally, the trajectory-tracking problem has also attracted extensive attention from researchers, investigating challenges and sharing latest results from different perspectives [14,23,25].

Note that, the USV moves on the water to track the desired trajectory, and would suffer from complex uncertainties arising from itself and surrounding environments, including unmodeled dynamics and external disturbances[13]. With respect to the parameter perturbation problem, a new guidance law has been constructed for an underactuated USV in [4], wherein nonlinear tracking differentiators are introduced to obtain derivative signals instead of the first-order filter, achieving satisfactory differential performance and fast trajectory-tracking response. In addition to internal uncertainties of the USV, external disturbances have been exactly observed by the disturbance estimator [8], and the resultant controller is derived from the backstepping technique, rendering trajector-tracking errors globally exponentially stable. To further enhance the ability of disturbance rejection, the finite-time control scheme has been created in [19], whereby the finite-time disturbance observer and nonsingular fast terminal sliding-mode manifold are combined, such that both disturbance observation and trajectory-tracking errors can be finite-time stable. Since the settling time of the finite-time control method is related to initial states, a novel fixed-time nonsingular sliding mode manifold [24] has been developed according to the bi-limit homogeneous theory, and thereby resulting in the fixed-time trajectory-tracking scheme for the USV, making both position and velocity errors converge to the origin within a fixed settling time, certainly in the presence of model uncertainties and external disturbances.

Besides the disturbance rejection, other prominent problems behind the trajectory tracking control of the USV have been also widely researched in the existing literature. In [6], both error constraints and input saturation have been taken into account, thereby the tan-type barrier Lyapunov function is used to remain trajectory-tracking errors within the prescribed regions, and the hyperbolic tangent function to deal with the saturation problem. Since the control execution is often periodic, the computational cost is rather expensive. Aiming at both faster convergence rate and lower computational burden, a novel event-triggered adaptive practical fixed-time fuzzy controller has been proposed in [10]. When working for a long time at sea, the USV may suffer from the actuator fault problem. In [7], an adaptive neural network-based fault-tolerant trajectory-tracking controller has been proposed in combination with the parameter adaptive method and the radial basis function neural networks. Furthermore, the actuator dead-zone problem has been elegantly solved by a finite-time trajectory-tracking control method [2], wherein time-varying input coefficients are also regarded as system uncertainties, and are exactly observed by a robust homogeneous differentiator.

Although a lots of challenges have been skillfully overcome by aforementioned works, a practically fundamental problem has not been sufficiently touched, i.e., how to generate a feasibly desired trajectory. In [10], the reference trajectory and its derivatives have been assumed to be available, but how to obtain it is not mentioned. In [4, 6–8, 24, 25], sine and cosine functions have been used to directly predefine the sinusoidal, circular or straight trajectories. Since the trigonometric function is sufficiently differentiable, the resultant trajectory is absolutely continuous [21]. Clearly, the reference signal can be smoothly tracked by the USV, and thereby resulting in a simple trajectory-generation method. Moreover, another prevailing method is adopting a virtual ship to generate the desired trajectory [2, 5, 12, 19, 20, 22]. In fact, the trajectory is driven by the nominal model of the USV, whereby unmodeled dynamics and external disturbances are reasonably neglected. Since the desired and actual systems are in the same form, the resultant trajectory is feasible to be tracked by the USV. It should be highlighted that, it is rather difficult to determine setup parameters of both trigonometric function and virtual ship methods, such that the configuration of generated trajectory can be arbitrarily changed according to human intentions. In this context, foregoing methods are infeasible in practice.

To solve the trajectory-generation problem from a practical viewpoint, a trajectory generator (TG) is devised on the basis of successive way points (WPs) and reference speed in this paper. Actually, it is not hard for users to predesignate these WPs in the electronic chart. Furthermore, the reference speed can be allowed to be piecewisely constant, such that it is easy for users to assign values. To guarantee sufficient differentiability, a seventh-order polynominal is exclusively deployed to fit WPs in sequence, and thereby resulting in a parameterized path. To smooth the reference speed, a second-order filter is employed, making the speed command uniformly continuous. In combination with the parameterized path and speed command, the desired trajectory is readily generated by designing the path speed. Based on the model information, a PD-like controller is also synthesized for the USV to track the generated trajectory, and the closed-loop system is strictly proven to be asymptotically stable. Comprehensive simulations are conducted on the CyberShip II, so as to validate the effectiveness of both the proposed TG and trajectory-tracking controller.

The remainder of this paper is arranged as follows. Section 2 formulates the concerned problem. The proposed TG and trajectory-tracking controller is presented in Sect. 3. Simulation results are given in Sect. 4. This paper is concluded in Sect. 5.

2   Problem Formulation

The USV is assumed to move in a calm water when tracking a desired trajectory, and thus magnitudes of pith, roll and heave motions are quiet small, such that they can be reasonably neglected. To facilitate the problem formulation, as shown in Fig. 1, the earth-fixed coordinate frame EXY is built with X and Y axes pointing towards the north and east, respectively. In addition, the frame BX_bY_b is fixed to the USV, wherein the point B is the geometric center, X_b and Y_b axes are directing to the fore and starboard, respectively. In this context, the USV can be modeled in EXY and BX_bY_b for kinematics and dynamics, respectively,

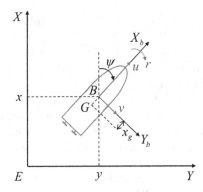

Fig. 1. Earth- and body-fixed coordinate frames of the USV.

which is presented as follows [1]

$$\dot{\boldsymbol{\eta}} = \boldsymbol{R}(\psi)\boldsymbol{\nu} \tag{1a}$$

$$\boldsymbol{M}\dot{\boldsymbol{\nu}} = -\boldsymbol{C}(\boldsymbol{\nu})\boldsymbol{\nu} - \boldsymbol{D}(\boldsymbol{\nu})\boldsymbol{\nu} + \boldsymbol{\tau} \tag{1b}$$

where $\boldsymbol{\eta} = [x, y, \psi]^T$ is the pose vector consisting of position coordinates (x, y) and yaw angle $\psi \in (-\pi, \pi]$ in EXY, $\boldsymbol{\nu} = [u, v, r]^T$ denotes the velocity vector including surge/sway velocities (u, v) and angular rate r in BX_bY_b, and $\boldsymbol{\tau} = [\tau_u, \tau_v, \tau_r]^T$ represents the control input vector.

Moreover, $\boldsymbol{R}(\psi)$ denotes the rotation matrix from EXY to BX_bY_b, $\boldsymbol{M}$ represents the inertia matrix including hydrodynamic added masses, $\boldsymbol{C}(\boldsymbol{\nu})$ and $\boldsymbol{D}(\boldsymbol{\nu})$ are Coriolis/centripetal and damping matrices, respectively. For readability, aforementioned matrices are intensively given by

$$\boldsymbol{M} = \begin{bmatrix} m_{11} & 0 & 0 \\ 0 & m_{22} & m_{23} \\ 0 & m_{32} & m_{33} \end{bmatrix} \tag{2a}$$

$$\boldsymbol{R}(\psi) = \begin{bmatrix} \cos\psi & -\sin\psi & 0 \\ -\sin\psi & \cos\psi & 0 \\ 0 & 0 & 1 \end{bmatrix} \tag{2b}$$

$$\boldsymbol{D}(\boldsymbol{\nu}) = \begin{bmatrix} d_{11}(\boldsymbol{\nu}) & 0 & 0 \\ 0 & d_{22}(\boldsymbol{\nu}) & d_{23}(\boldsymbol{\nu}) \\ 0 & d_{32}(\boldsymbol{\nu}) & d_{33}(\boldsymbol{\nu}) \end{bmatrix} \tag{2c}$$

$$\boldsymbol{C}(\boldsymbol{\nu}) = \begin{bmatrix} 0 & 0 & -m_{11}v - m_{23}r \\ 0 & 0 & -m_{11}u \\ m_{11}v + m_{23}r & m_{11}u & 0 \end{bmatrix} \tag{2d}$$

where $m_{11} = m - X_{\dot{u}}$, $m_{22} = m - Y_{\dot{v}}$, $m_{23} = mx_gY_{\dot{r}}$, $m_{32} = mx_g - N_{\dot{v}}$, $m_{33} = I_z - N_{\dot{r}}$, $d_{11}(\boldsymbol{\nu}) = -X_u - X_{|u|u}|u| - X_{uuu}u^2$, $d_{22}(\boldsymbol{\nu}) = -Y_v - Y_{|v|v}|v| - Y_{|r|v}|r|$, $d_{23}(\boldsymbol{\nu}) = -Y_r - Y_{|v|r}|v| - Y_{|r|r}|r|$, $d_{32}(\boldsymbol{\nu}) = -N_v - N_{|v|v}|v| - N_{|r|v}|r|$, and $d_{33}(\boldsymbol{\nu}) = -N_r - N_{|v|r}|v| - N_{|r|r}|r|$. Here, m is the mass of the USV, I_z is the movement inertia about yaw motions, and x_g is the distance between B

and the gravity center G as shown in Fig. 1. Besides, all terms X_*, Y_* and N_* consistently represent hydrodynamic derivatives.

In engineering, the USV is deployed to explore some waters by simply tracking the desired trajectory $\boldsymbol{\eta}_d = [x_d, y_d, \psi_d]^T$. In the existing literature, the trigonometric function method [4,6–8,24,25] predefines the time-varying signal as follows

$$\boldsymbol{\eta}_d(t) = \boldsymbol{f}(\cos(t), \sin(t), t) \tag{3}$$

where $\boldsymbol{f}(\cdot)$ is sufficiently differentiable. Derived from (1), the virtual ship method [2,5,12,19,20,22] is formulated by

$$\dot{\boldsymbol{\eta}}_d = \boldsymbol{R}(\psi_d)\boldsymbol{\nu}_d \tag{4a}$$
$$\boldsymbol{M}\dot{\boldsymbol{\nu}}_d = -\boldsymbol{C}(\boldsymbol{\nu}_d)\boldsymbol{\nu}_d - \boldsymbol{D}(\boldsymbol{\nu}_d)\boldsymbol{\nu}_d + \boldsymbol{\tau}_d \tag{4b}$$

where $\boldsymbol{\tau}_d$ is the desired input vector, $\boldsymbol{\eta}_d$ and $\boldsymbol{\nu}_d$ are desired outputs.

Clearly, both trigonometric function and virtual ship methods are rather abstract, since it is difficult to intuitively determine setup parameters of (3) and (4), such that the resultant trajectory can be arbitrarily changed, so as to satisfy practical requirements. In this context, it seems like a big barrier between the theory and practice for trajectory tracking of the USV. From a practical viewpoint, it is pretty easier for practitioners to plan the trajectory-tracking task in the electronic chart by prescribing a sequence of WPs as follows

$$\boldsymbol{p}_{d_i} = [x_{d_i}, y_{d_i}]^T \tag{5}$$

where $i = 1, 2, \cdots, n$, and n is the number of WPs. Therefore, how to generate a feasibly desired trajectory based on prescribed WPs (5) are exclusively taken into account in this paper.

To clearly demarcate the edge of our concerned problem, a assumption is reasonably made as follows.

Assumption 1. *All model parameters in (1) have been previously identified to facilitate controller designs, in addition that unmodeled dynamics and external disturbances are sufficiently small such that they can be reasonably neglected.*

Instead of both the trigonometric function method (3) and virtual ship approach (4), the main objective of this paper is to invent a generalized method that can generate a smooth trajectory passing through successive WPs (5) with programmable course and velocities. Besides, another objective is to design the control input $\boldsymbol{\tau}$ in (1) such that the generated trajectory can be tracked by the USV.

3   Trajectory Generation and Control Design

3.1   Trajectory Generation

As shown in Fig. 2, a series of WPs are predesignated by users in the electronic chart. Certainly, it is not easy to generate a trajectory passing these WPs by

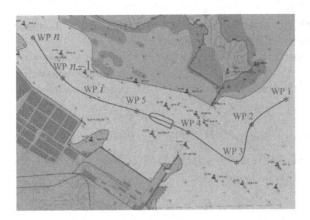

Fig. 2. The USV is maneuvering from WP to WP along a smooth trajectory.

virtue of the trigonometric function (3) or virtual ship (4). In the proposed TG, a parameterized path is firstly planned on the basis of spacial constraints, then it is transformed into the desired trajectory by applying temporal constraints. In contrast, our method is more intuitive and practical in engineering.

To be specific, an unique parameterized value θ_i is attached to each WP in (5), i.e.,

$$\boldsymbol{p}_d(\theta_i) = [x_d(\theta_i), y_d(\theta_i)]^T. \tag{6}$$

Without loss of generality, θ_i is simply determined by

$$\theta_i = i - 1. \tag{7}$$

In other words, these successive WPs are starting at WP 1 with $\theta_1 = 0$ and are ending at WP n with $\theta_n = n - 1$.

In the sequel, a seventh-order polynomial is employed to interpolate foregoing data, and thereby the parameterized subpath from WP i to WP $i + 1$ can be mathematically formulated by

$$\boldsymbol{p}_d(\theta) = \boldsymbol{B}\boldsymbol{\theta}_7 \tag{8}$$

with

$$\boldsymbol{B} = \begin{bmatrix} b_{x_7}, b_{x_6}, \cdots, b_{x_1}, b_{x_0} \\ b_{y_7}, b_{y_6}, \cdots, b_{y_1}, b_{y_0} \end{bmatrix} \tag{9a}$$

$$\boldsymbol{\theta}_7 = [(\theta - \theta_i)^7, (\theta - \theta_i)^6, \cdots, (\theta - \theta_i), 1]^T \tag{9b}$$

where θ is the parameterized variable.

Note that the coefficient matrix $\boldsymbol{B}$ in (8) is inherently unknown, and it needs sixteen constraint equations at least to solve these coefficients. To guarantee both the continuity and differentiability of $\boldsymbol{p}_d(\theta)$ at WP i, spacial constraints are required as follows

$$\boldsymbol{p}_d(\theta_i) = \boldsymbol{p}_{d_i} \tag{10a}$$

$$\left.\frac{\partial \boldsymbol{p}_d(\theta)}{\partial \theta}\right|_{\theta=\theta_i} = \begin{cases} \boldsymbol{p}_d(\theta_{i+1}) - \boldsymbol{p}_d(\theta_i) & i = 1 \\ k\left(\boldsymbol{p}_d(\theta_{i+1}) - \boldsymbol{p}_d(\theta_i)\right) & i \in (1, n) \\ \boldsymbol{p}_d(\theta_i) - \boldsymbol{p}_d(\theta_{i-1}) & i = n \end{cases} \tag{10b}$$

$$\left.\frac{\partial^2 \boldsymbol{p}_d(\theta)}{\partial \theta^2}\right|_{\theta=\theta_i} = \begin{cases} \left.\frac{\partial \boldsymbol{p}_d(\theta)}{\partial \theta}\right|_{\theta=\theta_{i+1}} - \left.\frac{\partial \boldsymbol{p}_d(\theta)}{\partial \theta}\right|_{\theta=\theta_i} & i = 1 \\ k\left(\left.\frac{\partial \boldsymbol{p}_d(\theta)}{\partial \theta}\right|_{\theta=\theta_{i+1}} - \left.\frac{\partial \boldsymbol{p}_d(\theta)}{\partial \theta}\right|_{\theta=\theta_i}\right) & i \in (1, n) \\ \left.\frac{\partial \boldsymbol{p}_d(\theta)}{\partial \theta}\right|_{\theta=\theta_i} - \left.\frac{\partial \boldsymbol{p}_d(\theta)}{\partial \theta}\right|_{\theta=\theta_{i-1}} & i = n \end{cases} \tag{10c}$$

$$\left.\frac{\partial^3 \boldsymbol{p}_d(\theta)}{\partial \theta^3}\right|_{\theta=\theta_i} = \begin{cases} \left.\frac{\partial^2 \boldsymbol{p}_d(\theta)}{\partial \theta^2}\right|_{\theta=\theta_{i+1}} - \left.\frac{\partial^2 \boldsymbol{p}_d(\theta)}{\partial \theta^2}\right|_{\theta=\theta_i} & i = 1 \\ k\left(\left.\frac{\partial^2 \boldsymbol{p}_d(\theta)}{\partial \theta^2}\right|_{\theta=\theta_{i+1}} - \left.\frac{\partial^2 \boldsymbol{p}_d(\theta)}{\partial \theta^2}\right|_{\theta=\theta_i}\right) & i \in (1, n) \\ \left.\frac{\partial^2 \boldsymbol{p}_d(\theta)}{\partial \theta^2}\right|_{\theta=\theta_i} - \left.\frac{\partial^2 \boldsymbol{p}_d(\theta)}{\partial \theta^2}\right|_{\theta=\theta_{i-1}} & i = n \end{cases} \tag{10d}$$

where $k > 0$ is used to design the curvature at WP i, and thereby $\boldsymbol{B}$ can be determined by (10).

In essence, the desired position of the USV is predefined by the path (8), and thereby the desired course angle can be naturally determined by its tangent angle, i.e.,

$$\psi_d(\theta) = \text{atan2}\left(\frac{\partial y_d(\theta)}{\partial \theta}, \frac{\partial x_d(\theta)}{\partial \theta}\right) \tag{11}$$

where atan2($\cdot$) is the four-quadrant arc-tangent function. Therefore, the desired configuration of the USV can be given by

$$\boldsymbol{\eta}_d(\theta) = [\boldsymbol{p}_d^T(\theta), \psi_d(\theta)]^T. \tag{12}$$

In addition, users should also prespecify the reference speed $u_r > 0$ as the temporal constraints to generate the desired trajectory. Certainly, it is easier for users to assign piecewise constant values to u_r. However, such a reference signal is not sufficiently smooth and can not be tracked immediately by the USV. As a result, the second-order low-pass filter can be exploited as follows

$$\ddot{u}_d + 2\iota\varsigma\dot{u}_d + \varsigma^2 u_d = \varsigma^2 u_r \tag{13}$$

where $u_d \geq 0$ is the continuous speed command, $\iota > 0$ and $\varsigma > 0$ are the damping ratio and natural frequency of the filter, respectively.

Eventually, the desired trajectory $\boldsymbol{\eta}_d(t)$ can be obtained from (12) by designing the path speed

$$\dot{\theta} = \frac{u_d(t)}{\sqrt{\left(\frac{\partial y_d(\theta)}{\partial \theta}\right)^2 + \left(\frac{\partial x_d(\theta)}{\partial \theta}\right)^2}} \tag{14}$$

and the desired dynamics are given by

$$\dot{\boldsymbol{\eta}}_d = \frac{\partial \boldsymbol{\eta}_d}{\partial \theta} \dot{\theta} \tag{15a}$$

$$\ddot{\boldsymbol{\eta}}_d = \frac{\partial^2 \boldsymbol{\eta}_d}{\partial \theta^2} \dot{\theta}^2 + \frac{\partial \boldsymbol{\eta}_d}{\partial \theta} \left(\frac{\partial \dot{\theta}}{\partial \theta} \dot{\theta} + \frac{\partial \dot{\theta}}{\partial t} \right). \tag{15b}$$

Note that $\ddot{\boldsymbol{\eta}}_d$ is expected to be continuous, which implies that $\frac{\partial^3 \boldsymbol{p}_d(\theta)}{\partial \theta^3}$ should be continuous as shown in (11). That is why we choose the seventh-order polynomial at least to fit given WPs as demonstrated in (10d).

3.2   Control Design

From (1a), we redefine a new variable $\boldsymbol{\omega} = \boldsymbol{R}(\psi)\boldsymbol{\nu}$, which represents the USV velocity vector expressed in EXY. As usual, the trajectory-tracking and velocity-tracking errors are defined by $\boldsymbol{e}_\eta = \boldsymbol{\eta} - \boldsymbol{\eta}_d$ and $\boldsymbol{e}_\omega = \boldsymbol{\omega} - \dot{\boldsymbol{\eta}}_d$, respectively. Taking the time derivative of $\boldsymbol{e}_\eta$ along (1) and (15) yields

$$\dot{\boldsymbol{e}}_\eta = \boldsymbol{e}_\omega \tag{16a}$$

$$\dot{\boldsymbol{e}}_\omega = \boldsymbol{S}(\omega_\psi)\boldsymbol{\omega} - \boldsymbol{R}(\psi)\boldsymbol{M}^{-1}(\boldsymbol{C}(\boldsymbol{\nu})\boldsymbol{\nu} + \boldsymbol{D}(\boldsymbol{\nu})\boldsymbol{\nu} - \boldsymbol{\tau}) - \ddot{\boldsymbol{\eta}}_d \tag{16b}$$

where $\boldsymbol{e}_\eta := [e_{\eta_1}, e_{\eta_2}, e_{\eta_3}]^T$, $\boldsymbol{e}_\omega := [e_{\omega_1}, e_{\omega_2}, e_{\omega_3}]^T$, $\boldsymbol{\omega} := [\omega_x, \omega_y, \omega_\psi]^T$, and
$\boldsymbol{S}(\omega_\psi) = \begin{bmatrix} 0 & -\omega_\psi & 0 \\ \omega_\psi & 0 & 0 \\ 0 & 0 & 0 \end{bmatrix}$.

Since the error system (16) possesses the canonical form of linear integral chain, the trajectory-tracking controller can be easily designed by

$$\boldsymbol{\tau} = \boldsymbol{C}(\boldsymbol{\nu})\boldsymbol{\nu} + \boldsymbol{D}(\boldsymbol{\nu}) + \boldsymbol{M}\boldsymbol{R}^T(\psi)(\ddot{\boldsymbol{\eta}}_d - \boldsymbol{S}(\omega_\psi)\boldsymbol{\omega} - \boldsymbol{K}_p\boldsymbol{e}_\eta - \boldsymbol{K}_d\boldsymbol{e}_\omega) \tag{17}$$

where $\boldsymbol{K}_p = \text{diag}(k_{p1}, k_{p2}, k_{p3}) > 0$ and $\boldsymbol{K}_d = \text{diag}(k_{d1}, k_{d2}, k_{d3}) > 0$.

Theorem 1. *Under the Assumption 1, the proposed controller (17) can make the trajectory-tracking system (16) asymptotically stable.*

Proof. Substituting (17) into (16) yields the closed-loop system

$$\dot{\boldsymbol{e}} = \boldsymbol{K}\boldsymbol{e} \tag{18}$$

where $\boldsymbol{e} = [\boldsymbol{e}_\eta^T, \boldsymbol{e}_\omega^T]^T$, and $\boldsymbol{K} = \begin{bmatrix} \boldsymbol{0}_{3\times3} & \boldsymbol{I}_{3\times3} \\ -\boldsymbol{K}_p & -\boldsymbol{K}_d \end{bmatrix}$.

Note that it can be readily verify that $\boldsymbol{K}$ is a Hurwitz matrix. As a consequence, there exists an unique positive definite matrix $\boldsymbol{P} \in \mathbb{R}^{3\times3}$ for any positive definite matrix $\boldsymbol{Q} \in \mathbb{R}^{3\times3}$, such that

$$\boldsymbol{K}^T\boldsymbol{P} + \boldsymbol{P}\boldsymbol{K} = -\boldsymbol{Q} \tag{19}$$

always holds.

Consider the Lyapunov candidate as follows

$$V = e^T P e \tag{20}$$

and differentiating V along (18) and (19) yields

$$\dot{V} = -e^T Q e$$

$$\leq -\frac{\lambda_{min}(Q)}{\lambda_{max}(P)} V \tag{21}$$

where $\lambda_{min}(Q) > 0$ is the minimum eigenvalue of Q, and $\lambda_{max}(P) > 0$ represents the maximum eigenvalue of P.

From (21), we can immediately have $\dot{V} < 0$, which implies that V is asymptotically stable. Together with (20), we can eventually conclude that $\lim_{t \to \infty} e_\eta(t) = 0_3$ and $\lim_{t \to \infty} e_\omega(t) = 0_3$. This completes the proof.

4   Simulation Studies

To validate the effectiveness of both the proposed TG and trajectory-tracking controller in this section, the famous benchmark prototype CyberShip II [9] is deployed to conduct simulations, whereby its model parameters are intensively given in Table 1.

Table 1. Main model parameters of the CyberShip II [9].

Parameters	Values	Parameters	Values	Parameters	Values
m	23.8000	I_z	1.7600	x_g	0.0460
X_u	-0.7225	$X_{\dot{u}}$	-2.0000	Y_v	-0.8612
Y_r	0.1079	$Y_{\dot{v}}$	-10.0000	$Y_{\dot{r}}$	-0.0000
N_v	0.1052	N_r	-1.9000	$N_{\dot{v}}$	-0.0000
$N_{\dot{r}}$	-1.0000	$X_{|u|u}$	-1.3274	$Y_{|v|v}$	-36.2823
$Y_{|v|r}$	-0.8450	$Y_{|r|v}$	-8.0500	$Y_{|r|r}$	-3.4500
$N_{|v|v}$	5.0437	$N_{|v|r}$	0.0800	$N_{|r|v}$	0.1300
$N_{|r|r}$	-0.7500	X_{uuu}	-5.8664		

To setup simulations, a sequence of WPs are randomly predefined as shown in Table 2. In practice, they can be predesignated by users in light of the electronic chart, so as to generate the desired trajectory. To this end, the adjustable parameter is set by $k = 0.5$ to obtain a medium curvature, and the reference speed is simply selected as

$$u_r(t) = \begin{cases} 0.5 & t \in [0, 40] \\ 1 & t \in (40, 70] \\ 1.5 & t \in (70, 100] \\ 2 & t \in (100, 120] \end{cases} \tag{22}$$

Table 2. A sequence of WPs used in simulations.

WPs	Values	WPs	Values	WPs	Values
P_{d_1}	$[-28,-3]^T$	P_{d_2}	$[-19,0]^T$	P_{d_3}	$[-8,5]^T$
P_{d_4}	$[0,-3]^T$	P_{d_5}	$[6,0]^T$	P_{d_6}	$[8,10]^T$
P_{d_7}	$[5,30]^T$	P_{d_8}	$[-10,33]^T$	P_{d_9}	$[-20,30]^T$
$P_{d_{10}}$	$[-28,25]^T$	$P_{d_{11}}$	$[-28,15]^T$	$P_{d_{12}}$	$[-20,5]^T$

In order to smooth this piecewise signal, the initial output of the second-order filter is chosen as $u_d(0) = 0$, its damping ratio and natural frequency $\iota = 0.5$ and $\varsigma = 0.5$, respectively.

4.1　Performance on the TG

Simulation results are shown in Fig. 3. By virtue of the proposed TG, as shown in Fig. 3(a), the generated trajectory passes through user-predesignated WPs in sequence, and corresponding tangent angle along the trajectory is set as the USV course angle. It should be highlighted that, as shown in Fig. 3(b), the trajectory is continuous in time, which is favorable for the USV to be tracked. Here, ψ_d is uniformly projected into $(-\pi, \pi]$ by the normalized operation. More importantly, as shown in Figs. 3(c) and 3(d), the desired velocity and acceleration are both continuous, which will not lead to switching control inputs when tracked by the USV. Actually, continuous signals η_d, $\dot{\eta}_d$ and $\ddot{\eta}_d$ benefit from the seventh-order polynominal and second-order low-pass filter, which are exclusively incorporated into the proposed TG. Clearly, if we intend to generate the desired trajectory and its derivatives as same as Fig. 3, it is not easy to decide setup parameters when using the trigonometric function or virtual ship method. In this context, the proposed TG is more intuitive and practical.

4.2　Performance on the Trajectory-Tracking Controller

To track the generated trajectory by the USV, the PD-like trajectory-tracking controller is synthesized in this paper. In simulations, initial states of the USV are set as $\eta(0) = [-30, 2, -0.4]^T$ and $\nu(0) = [0, 0, 0]^T$. Furthermore, control gains are simply given by $K_p = \text{diag}(0.1, 0.1, 0.1)$ and $K_d = \text{diag}(0.5, 0.5, 0.5)$.

Simulation results are shown in Fig. 4. Thanks to the smooth trajectory generated by the proposed TG, all control inputs of the USV are continuous as shown in Fig. 4(a), although the reference velocity is piecewise. Clearly, continuous signals are easier to be implemented by practical actuators. In this sense, the

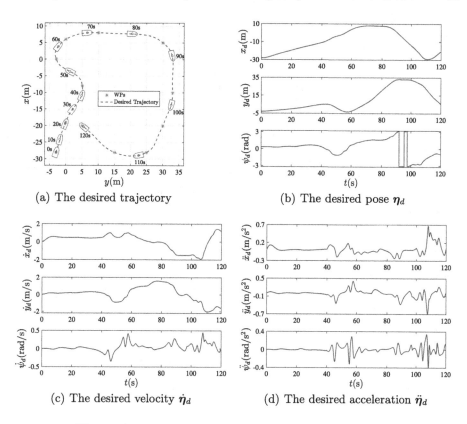

(a) The desired trajectory

(b) The desired pose $\boldsymbol{\eta}_d$

(c) The desired velocity $\dot{\boldsymbol{\eta}}_d$

(d) The desired acceleration $\ddot{\boldsymbol{\eta}}_d$

Fig. 3. The reference signals generated by the proposed TG.

consideration of continuity and differentiability when devising the TG is vital for applications. Moreover, driven by the continuous controller, both trajectory- and velocity-tracking errors asymptotically converge to zero as shown in Figs. 4(b) and 4(c), respectively. Note that these results are consistent with the Theorem 1 and corresponding stability analyses. Eventually, as shown in Fig. 4(d), the desired trajectory is exactly tracked by the USV in the absence of unmodeled dynamics and external disturbances.

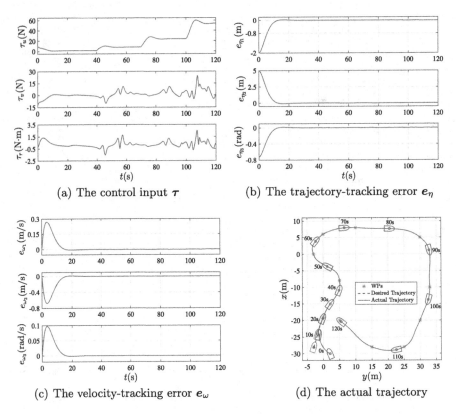

(a) The control input $\boldsymbol{\tau}$

(b) The trajectory-tracking error $\boldsymbol{e}_\eta$

(c) The velocity-tracking error $\boldsymbol{e}_\omega$

(d) The actual trajectory

Fig. 4. The performance of the proposed trajectory-tracking controller.

5   Conclusions

In this paper, a novel TG has been proposed to generate the desired trajectory for the USV in light of successive WPs and reference speed, rather than the trigonometric function or virtual ship method. To be specific, the seventh-order polynominal has been exclusively deployed such that the resultant parameterized path satisfies spatial constraints, and is sufficiently differentiable. Also, the second-order low-pass filter has been exploited to smooth the reference speed, guaranteeing that the generated trajectory and its derivatives are continuous in time. By designing the path speed to meet temporal constraints, the parameterized path has been naturally translated into the time-varying trajectory, which is more practical for users to assign the trajectory-tracking task in advance. Based on the USV model information, the trajectory-tracking controller has been synthesized by virtue of Lyapunov theorem. Eventually, comprehensive simulations conducted on the CyberShip II have verified the effectiveness of both the proposed TG and trajectory-tracking controller. In future work, unmodeled dynamics and external disturbances will be taken into account in the trajectory-tracking control of the USV.

References

1. Fossen, T.I.: Handbook of Marine Craft Hydrodynamics and Motion Control. Wiley, Hoboken (2011)
2. Gao, Y., Wang, N., Zhang, W.: Disturbance observer based finite-time trajectory tracking control of unmanned surface vehicles with unknown dead-zones. In: Youth Academic Annual Conference on Chinese Association Automation, pp. 263–268. IEEE, Hefei, China, May 2017
3. He, H., Wang, N.: Monocular visual servo of unmanned surface vehicles with view-field constraints. In: Chinese Control Decision Conference, pp. 973–978. IEEE, Kunming, China, May 2021
4. Huang, H., Gong, M., Zhuang, Y., Sharma, S., Xu, D.: A new guidance law for trajectory tracking of an underactuated unmanned surface vehicle with parameter perturbations. Ocean Eng. **175**(1), 217–222 (2019)
5. Li, L., Dong, K., Guo, G.: Trajectory tracking control of underactuated surface vessel with full state constraints. Asian J. Control **23**(4), 1762–1771 (2021)
6. Qin, H., Li, C., Sun, Y., Li, X., Du, Y., Deng, Z.: Finite-time trajectory tracking control of unmanned surface vessel with error constraints and input saturations. J. Franklin Inst. **357**(16), 11472–11495 (2020)
7. Qin, H., Li, C., Sun, Y.: Adaptive neural network-based fault-tolerant trajectory-tracking control of unmanned surface vessels with input saturation and error constraints. IET Intel. Transport Syst. **14**(5), 356–363 (2020)
8. Qu, Y., Xiao, B., Fu, Z., Yuan, D.: Trajectory exponential tracking control of unmanned surface ships with external disturbance and system uncertainties. ISA Trans. **78**, 47–55 (2018)
9. Skjetne, R., Fossen, T.I., Kokotović, P.V.: Adaptive maneuvering, with experiments, for a model ship in a marine control laboratory. Automatica **41**(2), 289–298 (2005)
10. Song, S., Park, J.H., Zhang, B., Song, X.: Event-triggered adaptive practical fixed-time trajectory tracking control for unmanned surface vehicle. IEEE Trans. Circuits Syst. II: Express Briefs **68**(1), 436–440 (2021)
11. Stateczny, A., Burdziakowski, P., Najdecka, K., Domagalska-Stateczna, B.: Accuracy of trajectory tracking based on nonlinear guidance logic for hydrographic unmanned surface vessels. Sensors **20**(3), 1–16 (2020)
12. Wang, N., Gao, Y., Zhao, H., Ahn, C.K.: Reinforcement learning-based optimal tracking control of an unknown unmanned surface vehicle. IEEE Trans. Neural Netw. Learn. Syst. **32**(7), 3034–3045 (2021)
13. Wang, N., Ahn, C.K.: Coordinated trajectory tracking control of a marine aerial-surface heterogeneous system. IEEE/ASME Trans. Mechatron. **26**(6), 3198–3210 (2021)
14. Wang, N., Er, M.J., Sun, J.C., Liu, Y.C.: Adaptive robust online constructive fuzzy control of a complex surface vehicle system. IEEE Trans. Cybern. **46**(7), 1511–1523 (2016)
15. Wang, N., Gao, Y., Zhang, X.: Data-driven performance-prescribed reinforcement learning control of an unmanned surface vehicle. IEEE Trans. Neural Netw. Learn. Syst. **32**(12), 5456–5467 (2021)
16. Wang, N., He, H.: Adaptive homography-based visual servo for micro unmanned surface vehicles. Int. J. Adv. Manuf. Technol. **105**(12), 4875–4882 (2019)
17. Wang, N., He, H.: Dynamics-level finite-time fuzzy monocular visual servo of an unmanned surface vehicle. IEEE Trans. Ind. Electron. **67**(11), 9648–9658 (2020)

18. Wang, N., He, H.: Extreme learning-based monocular visual servo of an unmanned surface vessel. IEEE Trans. Ind. Inform. **17**(8), 5152–5163 (2021)
19. Wang, N., Karimi, H.R., Li, H.Y., Su, S.F.: Accurate trajectory tracking of disturbed surface vehicles: a finite-time control approach. IEEE/ASME Trans. Mechatron. **24**(3), 1064–1074 (2019)
20. Wang, N., Su, S.F., Pan, X.X., Yu, X., Xie, G.M.: Yaw-guided trajectory tracking control of an asymmetric underactuated surface vehicle. IEEE Trans. Ind. Inform. **15**(6), 3502–3513 (2019)
21. Wang, N., Zhang, Y., Ahn, C.K., Xu, Q.: Autonomous pilot of unmanned surface vehicles: bridging path planning and tracking. IEEE Trans. Veh. Technol. **71**(3), 2358–2374 (2022)
22. Wang, R., Xue, H., Li, Z., Li, H.W.N., Zhao, H.: Fixed-time trajectory tracking control of an unmanned surface vehicle. In: International Conference on Systems, Science and Engineering, pp. 1–6. Kagawa, Japan, September 2020
23. Xu, D., Liu, Z., Zhou, X., Yang, L., Huang, L.: Trajectory tracking of underactuated unmanned surface vessels: non-singular terminal sliding control with nonlinear disturbance observer. Appl. Sci. **12**(6), 1–17 (2022)
24. Yao, Q.: Fixed-time trajectory tracking control for unmanned surface vessels in the presence of model uncertainties and external disturbances. Int. J. Control **95**(5), 1133–1143 (2022)
25. Zheng, Z., Huang, Y., Xie, L., Zhu, B.: Adaptive trajectory tracking control of a fully actuated surface vessel with asymmetrically constrained input and output. IEEE Trans. Control Syst. Technol. **26**(5), 1851–1859 (2017)

Adaptive Channel Attention-Based Deformable Generative Adversarial Network for Underwater Image Enhancement

Tingkai Chen[1]🆔, Ning Wang[2]([✉])🆔, Xiangjun Kong[1], and Yanzheng Chen[2]

[1] School of Marine Electrical Engineering, Dalian Maritime University,
Dalian 116026, China
[2] School of Marine Engineering, Dalian Maritime University, Dalian 116026, China
`n.wang@ieee.org`

Abstract. In this paper, to effectively strengthen quality of underwater image enhancement from both channel and spatial viewpoints, an adaptive channel attention-based deformable generative adversarial networks (ACADGAN) framework is established. Main contributions are as follows. 1) By virtue of multi-branch convolution architecture with dilated convolution mechanism, the adaptive channel attention (ACA) is devised, such that channel weight can be adaptively recalibrated, and thereby significantly contributing to preserving content features from channel viewpoint. 2) By augmenting offset position of sampling point with respect to convolution kernel, the deformable convolution network (DCN) is created, such that detailed information of underwater image can be dramatically retained from spatial aspect. 3) The ACADGAN scheme is eventually proposed by integrating ACA and DCN modules with a deep generative adversarial network. Comprehensive experiments demonstrate the remarkable effectiveness and superiority of the developed ACADGAN scheme.

Keywords: Underwater image enhancement · Generative adversarial network · Adaptive channel attention · Deformable convolution network

1 Introduction

With the rapid development of intelligence [40,43], intelligent remotely operated vehicle possessing underwater image enhancement (UIE) capability is highly desired for visually pleasing quality in terms of marine archaeology [32], ocean exploration [48], benthonic organism detection [8], *etc.* It should be mentioned

This work is supported by the National Natural Science Foundation of China (Grant 52271306), Innovative Research Foundation of Ship General Performance (Grant 31422120), and the Cultivation Program for the Excellent Doctoral Dissertation of Dalian Maritime University (Grant 2022YBPY004).

H. R. Karimi and N. Wang (Eds.): S-Cube 2022, LNICST 487, pp. 17–32, 2023.
https://doi.org/10.1007/978-3-031-34899-0_2

that selective wavelength-dependent attenuation can inevitably lead to bluish and/or greenish tones owing to light absorption and scattering effects. To some extent, the water body would present different degradation characteristics, such as low contrast, blurring detail, color distortion, *etc.* In this context, the UIE possessing strong generalization in multi-domain underwater environment is still an active field, which can dramatically promote the development of autonomous intelligent systems [41,42].

To address aforementioned underwater image degradation challenges, numerous state-of-the-art approaches have been innovatively proposed, which can be primarily divided into three families covering model-free enhancement, physical model-based restoration and data driven-based image-to-image conversion. Actually, the model-free enhancement can be effectively achieved by directly adjusting pixel without explicit model, whereby the enhancement can be realized in both space and frequency domains [15,22,23,37]. To be specific, the contrast limited adaptive histogram equalization (CLAHE) [54] and white balance [13] techniques have been developed by solving color distortion and low contrast issues in single color space. Besides, a two-step method has been proposed to conduct color correction and enhancement tasks in [16]. Moreover, by virtue of employing both bilateral and trilateral filtering techniques in each channel pertaining to CIELAB space, the multi-scale Retinex [51] framework has been devised to deal with image degradation. Deploying completely different concepts, the Fusion [4] scheme has been elaborately established via white balance and local histogram equalization strategies, whereby four representative weight maps with respect to laplacian contrast, local contrast, saliency and exposedness are utilized to conduct pixel-level fusion, and thereby contributing to presenting corresponding pixel with higher weight [3,38].

Compared to foregoing model-free enhancement works, the underwater image models [1,21,34] are sufficiently considered by model-based restoration approaches. In essence, the restoration is inversion solution to obtain potential underwater image. Concretely, to furthest increase visual quality, the dark channel prior (DCP)-based scheme has been proposed to estimate transmission map (TM) and background light [19,20,25]. Furthermore, the TM can be efficiently smoothed and optimized with the aid of median filter technique in [49]. Besides, in [9,10], the artificial light can be accurately estimated by determining intensity difference between background and foreground while the water depth can be estimated by computing residual energy ratio, respectively, such that the visual visibility can be tremendously reformed. It should be noted that, in [12], by comprehensively considering transformation difference between in-air and underwater scenes, the underwater DCP (UDCP) framework has been designed. In sequence, the phenomenon that the pixel value in blue channel is occasionally lower than that in red channel within complicated underwater environment has been intensively investigated, a dual channels-based scheme [31] is employed to estimate TM, such that the halo effect can be dramatically alleviated. Nevertheless, the foregoing existing physical model-based methods usually follow that the attenuation coefficients are only related to water body and keep consistent among different channels, which can undoubtedly cause visual untruthfulness and unstable restoration, simultaneously.

Recently, with the high-speed prosperity of computational resource, the convolutional neural network (CNN)-based image-to-image conversion becomes available and feasible on large-scale synthetic and/or real datasets [24,39,44, 45,47]. Specifically, by training on simulated underwater scene constructed via combining air image and depth pairings, a two-stage WaterGAN [28] scheme has been devised, such that the color cast removal can be readily achieved. Similarly, by virtue of both revised underwater image formation model and scene parameters, the UWCNN [26] approach has been developed on the basis of synthetic underwater images. To eliminate the limitation of using paired underwater images, the Water CycleGAN [27] method has been proposed with the aid of cycle-consistency loss in a weakly supervised learning manner [53]. It should be noted that the training process of above-mentioned generative adversarial network (GAN) is extremely unstable. In the context, to dramatically increase training stability, the Wasserstein GAN [5] has been created by adequately computing distance between data and model distribution. Besides, the EBGAN [52], LSGANs [33] and conditional GAN [35] deploy the energy function, least-square loss function and restriction mechanism to address unstable training, respectively. However, accommodating multi-scale and geometric transformation for UIE task does not receive sufficient attention according to input information in an adaptive manner from both channel and spatial aspects.

To be specific, the receptive field of same convolutional processing layer usually shares same size, which could cause that multi-scale object information can hardly be efficiently captured at the same time from channel aspect [2,17,29]. In addition, preserving integrated information of underwater object with irregular transformation and unknown geometric scale would become impractical or infeasible due to inherently limited modeling mechanism in encoder structure from spatial side [11,46].

To circumvent foregoing weakness, an adaptive channel attention-based deformable generative adversarial network (ACADGAN) scheme has been devised for UIE in this paper. Significant highlights are summarized as follows:

- To effectively preserve image contents from channel perspective, the adaptive channel attention (ACA) is exclusively developed to adaptively recalibrate channel weight by virtue of multi-branch architecture using 3×3 and 5×5 convolutional kernels, simultaneously.
- To capture integrated information for object with irregular transformation and/or unknown geometric scale, the deformable convolution network (DCN) module is innovatively created, whereby offset position and modulation weight can be adaptively accommodated from the spatial aspect.
- Furthermore, combining ACA and DCN modules can contribute to entire ACADGAN scheme from both channel and spatial viewpoints, and thereby contributing to improving UIE quality.

The rest of paper is organized as follows. The problem formulation is presented in Sect. 2. Section 3 provides the developed ACADGAN scheme.

Experiment studies and comparisons are given in Sect. 4. Eventually, the conclusion is summarized in Sect. 5.

2   Problem Formulation

The classical underwater image formulation of Jaffe-McGlamery model [21] can be given by

$$U_\lambda = I_\lambda(x)e^{-\beta_\lambda d(x)} + B_\lambda(1 - e^{-\beta_\lambda d(x)}) \tag{1}$$

where U is output image, $\lambda \in \{r, g, b\}$ denotes red, green and blue channels, respectively, I represents original input image, d is distance between camera and object, β denotes underwater scattering coefficient associated with water body, vertical depth and turbidity [6].

Notably, instead of employing foregoing underwater image formation, complex nonlinear mapping between degraded and enhanced images can be adaptively learned without explicit modeling, which can be formulated by

$$I = \mathcal{F}(U) \tag{2}$$

where $\mathcal{F}$ is an end-to-end multi-layer CNN with adversarial mechanism in an encoder-decoder pattern.

3   ACADGAN Scheme

In this section, the devised ACADGAN scheme is systematically presented, and is composed of three modules, i.e., ACA, DCN and GAN.

3.1   Adaptive Channel Attention

The ACA module is devised by recalibrating channel weight. Note that enhancing feature via employing convolutional kernel with different sizes from the channel aspect can dramatically improve visual quality. Accordingly, as shown in Fig. 1, the convolutional operation of utilizing 3×3 and 5×5 kernel can be given by

$$u_k^\star = X \otimes F_k^\star = \sum_{i=1}^{c} x^i \otimes f_k^{i,\star} \tag{3}$$

where $\star \in \{3, 5\}$ is 3×3 and 5×5 convolutional filters, respectively, $x^i \in \mathbb{R}^{w \times h}$, $X = [x^1, x^2, \cdots, x^c] \in \mathbb{R}^{c \times w \times h}$ denotes input feature, $f_k^{i,\star} \in \mathbb{R}^{\star \times \star}$, $F_k^\star = [f_k^1, f_k^2, \cdots, f_k^c] \in \mathbb{R}^{c \times \star \times \star}$ refers to kernel weight of the k-th filter.

Subsequently, the fusion operation is formulated by

$$U = \tilde{U} + \hat{U} \tag{4}$$

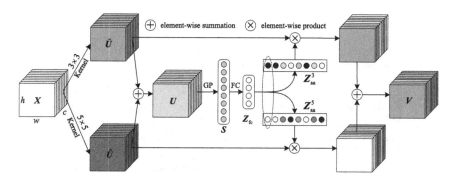

Fig. 1. Adaptive channel attention.

where $\widetilde{U}$ and $\widehat{U}$ represent convolutional output derived from previous layer by deploying 3×3 and 5×5 kernels, respectively, $U \in \mathbb{R}^{c \times w \times h}$ is fusion output by element-wise summation operation.

Afterwards, the global average pooling is implemented to obtain representative response for each feature map, and can be derived by

$$s^i = \frac{1}{w \times h} \sum_{m=1}^{w} \sum_{n=1}^{h} \boldsymbol{u}^i(m,n), i = 1, 2, \cdots, c \qquad (5)$$

where $S = [s^1, s^2, \cdots, s^c] \in \mathbb{R}^{c \times 1}$, $U = [\boldsymbol{u}^1, \boldsymbol{u}^2, \cdots, \boldsymbol{u}^c] \in \mathbb{R}^{c \times w \times h}$, w and h are width and height of feature map, respectively.

Besides, the single-hidden layer feedforward network is exploited to increase nonlinear fitting capability, and can be described by

$$\boldsymbol{Z}_{\text{fc}} = \text{R}(\boldsymbol{w}_{\text{fc}} \boldsymbol{S}) \qquad (6)$$

where $\boldsymbol{Z}_{\text{fc}} \in \mathbb{R}^{d \times 1}$ is output of fully connected layer, $\boldsymbol{w}_{\text{fc}} \in \mathbb{R}^{d \times c}$ refers to corresponding weight, $d = \max(c/r, L)$, r denotes reduction ratio of channel dimension, L presents minimal value of d, R is Leaky ReLU activation function.

Furthermore, the soft attention associated with channel is adopted to adaptively select proper spatial scale according to feedback loss, and can be determined by

$$\boldsymbol{Z}_{\text{sa}}^3 = \frac{e^{\boldsymbol{w}_{\text{sa}}^3 \boldsymbol{Z}_{\text{fc}}}}{e^{\boldsymbol{w}_{\text{sa}}^3 \boldsymbol{Z}_{\text{fc}}} + e^{\boldsymbol{w}_{\text{sa}}^5 \boldsymbol{Z}_{\text{fc}}}}$$

$$\boldsymbol{Z}_{\text{sa}}^5 = \frac{e^{\boldsymbol{w}_{\text{sa}}^5 \boldsymbol{Z}_{\text{fc}}}}{e^{\boldsymbol{w}_{\text{sa}}^3 \boldsymbol{Z}_{\text{fc}}} + e^{\boldsymbol{w}_{\text{sa}}^5 \boldsymbol{Z}_{\text{fc}}}} \qquad (7)$$

where $\boldsymbol{w}_{\text{sa}}^3 \in \mathbb{R}^{c \times d}$ and $\boldsymbol{w}_{\text{sa}}^5 \in \mathbb{R}^{c \times d}$ are weights of soft attention, $\boldsymbol{Z}_{\text{sa}}^3 \in \mathbb{R}^{c \times 1}$ and $\boldsymbol{Z}_{\text{sa}}^5 \in \mathbb{R}^{c \times 1}$ are outputs of soft attention for 3×3 and 5×5 convolutional branches, respectively.

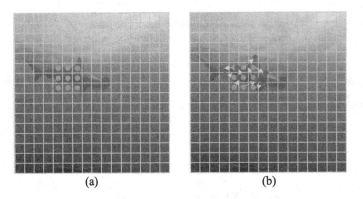

(a)   (b)

Fig. 2. Deformable convolution network. (a) Standard sampling positions (green points). (b) Deformed sampling positions (red points). (Color figure online)

Eventually, the recalibrated feature map V is defined by

$$V = Z_{sa}^3 \cdot \widetilde{U} + Z_{sa}^5 \cdot \widehat{U} \tag{8}$$

where $V \in \mathbb{R}^{c \times w \times h}$ represents final feature map by fusing two attention maps.

Remark 1. Fusing multiple convolutional outputs from different branches using 3×3 and 5×5 kernels, appropriate receptive field pertaining to involved object with different scales can be adaptively selected in encoder stage.

Remark 2. In order to furthest decrease the number of parameters and keep consistent receptive field characteristic, simultaneously, by using 3×3 convolutional kernel with dilation philosophy, the foregoing 5×5 convolution is effectively achieved.

3.2   Deformable Convolution Network

The DCN module is achieved by adaptively adjusting fixed sampling position of convolution kernel, which is conductive to establishing integrated feature descriptor for object with unknown transformation and/or large geometric dimension from the spatial viewpoint. As shown in Fig. 2, the sampling positions of standard convolutional kernel can be represented by

$$P = \{(u, v) \mid u, v \in \{-k, -(k-1), \cdots, k\}\} \tag{9}$$

where $k = \lfloor \frac{w}{2} \rfloor_{odd}$, and w refers to width of current convolutional kernel.

Accordingly, the deformed sampling position can be given by

$$\widetilde{p}_m = p_0 + p_m + \Delta p_m \tag{10}$$

where p_0 denotes the center point of convolutional kernel, $p_m = (x_m, y_m)$ is the m-th standard sampling position, $m = 1, 2, \cdots, n$, $n = |P|$, Δp_m represents offset

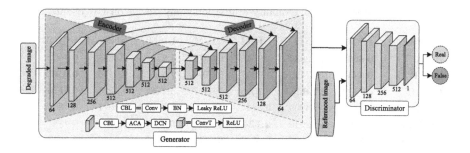

Fig. 3. The entire ACADGAN framework.

of the m-th element within convolutional kernel, $\widetilde{p}_m = (\widetilde{x}_m, \widetilde{y}_m)$ is deformed sampling position.

Note that the deformed sampling position should satisfy

$$0 \leqslant \widetilde{x}_m \leqslant w$$
$$0 \leqslant \widetilde{y}_m \leqslant h \tag{11}$$

Accordingly, the bilinear interpolation strategy is used to compute feature value of non-integer position from X direction, and can be derived by

$$F(\widetilde{x}_m, y_j) = \frac{\widetilde{x}_m - x_i}{x_{i+1} - x_i} F(x_{i+1}, y_j) + \frac{x_{i+1} - \widetilde{x}_m}{x_{i+1} - x_i} F(x_i, y_j) \tag{12}$$

where $p_{\mathrm{tl}} = (x_i, y_j)$, $p_{\mathrm{tr}} = (x_{i+1}, y_j)$, $p_{\mathrm{bl}} = (x_i, y_{j+1})$, $p_{\mathrm{br}} = (x_{i+1}, y_{j+1})$ are top-left, top-right, bottom-left and bottom-right integer coordinate positions which are closest to the deformed sampling position, respectively.

Similarly, the feature value $F(\widetilde{x}_m, y_{j+1})$ can be described by

$$F(\widetilde{x}_m, y_{j+1}) = \frac{\widetilde{x}_m - x_i}{x_{i+1} - x_i} F(x_{i+1}, y_{j+1}) + \frac{x_{i+1} - \widetilde{x}_m}{x_{i+1} - x_i} F(x_i, y_{j+1}) \tag{13}$$

Furthermore, the feature value $F(\widetilde{x}_m, \widetilde{y}_m)$ is given by

$$F(\widetilde{x}_m, \widetilde{y}_m) = \frac{\widetilde{y}_m - y_j}{y_{j+1} - y_j} F(\widetilde{x}_m, y_{j+1}) + \frac{y_{j+1} - \widetilde{y}_m}{y_{j+1} - y_j} F(\widetilde{x}_m, y_j) \tag{14}$$

where $F(\widetilde{x}_m, \widetilde{y}_m)$ is the feature value in deformed position $(\widetilde{x}_m, \widetilde{y}_m)$.

Ultimately, the deformable output can be formulated as follows:

$$O(x_0, y_0) = \sum_{m=1}^{n} w_m^{\mathrm{F}} F(\widetilde{x}_m, \widetilde{y}_m) \sigma(w_m) \tag{15}$$

where $O(x_0, y_0)$ is eventual output after performing deformation convolution operation corresponding to position (x_0, y_0), w_m^{F} denotes the m-th element weight within convolutional kernel, $\sigma(w_m)$ refers to modulation operation utilized to emphasize significance of the m-th offset position and w_m is constrained within the range $(0,1)$.

Table 1. The objective image quality evaluation comparisons on UIEB dataset.

Scheme	SSIM	PSNR	UIQM	UICM	UISM	UIConM	UCIQE
IBLA	0.6505	15.2930	1.9546	<u>6.6576</u>	4.4284	0.1285	<u>0.4902</u>
UDCP	0.4433	10.7593	1.6257	5.6709	4.4114	0.0456	**0.4913**
CLAHE	0.7119	**17.6431**	2.7026	5.0877	5.4467	0.2261	0.4170
UCM	<u>0.7344</u>	16.3005	2.5844	**7.2730**	5.5500	0.2071	0.4861
FUnIE-GAN	0.6593	15.2940	**2.7248**	5.0241	**6.1299**	0.2162	0.4351
UWCNN	0.7112	15.5927	2.2504	3.8042	4.5116	<u>0.2267</u>	0.3847
ACADGAN	**0.8097**	<u>16.3171</u>	<u>2.7191</u>	4.4317	<u>5.9843</u>	**0.2711**	0.4007

Table 2. The objective image quality evaluation comparisons on URPC dataset.

Scheme	UIQM	UICM	UISM	UIConM	UCIQE
IBLA	2.3393	<u>3.6788</u>	4.2001	0.2783	0.375
UDCP	1.7634	**4.4328**	4.0194	0.1263	0.3995
CLAHE	2.5963	3.1805	4.8888	0.2808	0.3456
UCM	2.5847	3.5418	4.8931	0.2908	<u>0.4054</u>
FUnIE-GAN	<u>2.6713</u>	2.2178	**5.1713**	0.3025	0.3525
UWCNN	2.2726	1.5492	3.4277	**0.3403**	0.3022
ACADGAN	**2.7301**	2.8468	<u>5.1205</u>	<u>0.3347</u>	**0.4517**

3.3 Generative Adversarial Network

As shown in Fig. 3, the designed GAN is divided into generator and discriminator, whereby ACA and DCN modules are organically integrated into the encoder framework with respect to generator. Besides, the WGAN-GP loss, $L1$ loss and image gradient difference loss are combined to implement adversarial training [14].

Remark 3. By combining ACA and DCN modules within encoder structure of generator in the sequential manner, the proposed ACADGAN scheme with residual mechanism can be eventually developed by integrating discriminator, and thereby contributing to dramatically avoiding vanishing gradient and promoting to generate high-quality underwater image, simultaneously.

4   Experimental Studies and Comparisons

In order to sufficiently investigate the effectiveness and superiority of the proposed ACADGAN scheme, the physical model-based restoration approaches, model-free enhancement methods and image-to-image conversion techniques are

Table 3. The Feature Expression Comparisons on UIEB Dataset.

Scheme	SIFT	Harris	Canny
IBLA	1381.4444	652.9444	0.0763
UDCP	1030.6778	501.4889	0.0588
CLAHE	<u>1908.6667</u>	**822.6444**	0.1022
UCM	1804.6000	<u>792.3000</u>	<u>0.1046</u>
FUnIE-GAN	1615.9444	631.0444	0.0656
UWCNN	803.7778	498.5333	0.0456
ACADGAN	**1991.4333**	522.0778	**0.1060**

Table 4. The Feature Expression Comparisons on URPC Dataset.

Scheme	SIFT	Harris	Canny
IBLA	1106.5333	241.4368	0.0317
UDCP	738.9759	250.4428	0.0258
CLAHE	1198.1516	<u>356.7569</u>	0.0528
UCM	**1409.0626**	330.9964	**0.0608**
FUnIE-GAN	555.9627	210.1793	0.0273
UWCNN	260.8893	94.3755	0.0106
ACADGAN	<u>1398.9302</u>	**358.7016**	<u>0.0575</u>

employed to implement comparisons under typical underwater challenging situations covering artificial light (first column), bluish light (second column), greenish light (third column), low light (fourth column) and violet light (fifth column). As shown in Fig. 4, from which we can clearly observe that the physical model-based image restoration approaches can hardly achieve satisfactory visual performance. To be specific, the UDCP approach can bring in more serious aggravation of color deviation effect in aforementioned scenarios. Obviously, the model-free-based underwater image enhancement approach, i.e., UCM, can tend to introduce reddish color cast, and thereby resulting in enhancement failure by directly adjusting pixel value. It should be noted that the FUnIe-GAN and UWCNN schemes can only obtain pretty limited enhancement effect. Meanwhile, the FUnIE-GAN method can cause apparent color deviation under violet-light situation. Intuitively, the devised ACADGAN framework can ultimately achieve the optimal visual enhancement quality by employing ACA and DCN modules in a sequential manner. Furthermore, the consistent conclusion can also be summarized from Fig. 5.

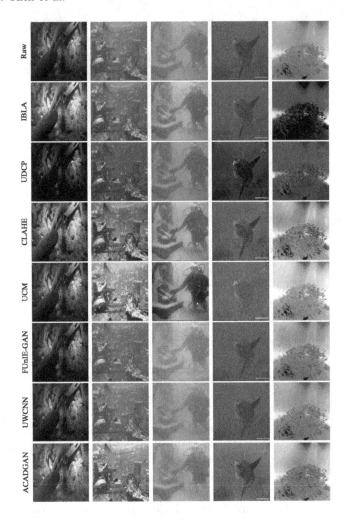

Fig. 4. The subjectively visual comparisons on UIEB dataset.

4.1 Quantitative Comparisons

To further sufficiently demonstrate superiority of the developed ACADGAN scheme, the peak signal to noise ratio (PSNR), structural similarity (SSIM), underwater color image quality evaluation (UCIQE) [50], underwater image quality measures (UIQM) related to underwater image colorfulness, sharpness, contrast (i.e., UICM, UISM and UIConM) [36] indices are comprehensively considered, and the comparison results are summarized in Table 1 and Table 2 derived from average value of 90 and 831 test images on UIEB and URPC datasets, respectively, from which we can readily obtain that the proposed ACADGAN scheme can achieve the optimal (highlighted in bold) or sub-optimal (highlighted in underscore) performances on most metrics. Concretely, on the one hand, the

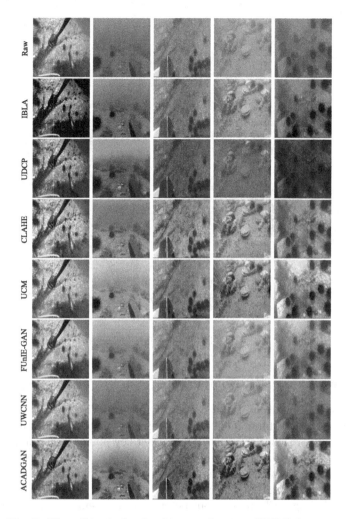

Fig. 5. The subjectively visual comparisons on URPC dataset.

image structure, texture and contrast are effectively preserved according to the optimal SSIM and UIConM metrics on UIEB dataset, simultaneously. More ambitiously, the proposed ACADGAN scheme can perfectly accomplish preservation in terms of the image content. Additionally, in terms of evaluation on URPC dataset, the developed ACADGAN scheme achieves the optimal UIQM score, which implies that the enhanced images are more consistent with human visual perception. More importantly, the proposed ACADGAN scheme can realize better balance in terms of chroma, saturation and contrast on the basis of the optimal UCIQE score.

Fig. 6. The keypoint matching comparisons.

4.2 Feature Expression Comparisons

In order to verify effectiveness and superiority of the devised ACADGAN scheme from the perspective of fundamental feature expression, the SIFT [30], Harris [18] and Canny [7] approaches are utilized to extract key point, corner and pixel-level edge ratio. Correspondingly, the key point matching result is shown in Fig. 6, from which we can clearly see that few key points can be correctly extracted and matched on raw underwater image due to the poor quality. Meanwhile, the key point matching performance can be enhanced by employing restoration or enhancement approaches. Furthermore, the proposed ACADGAN scheme can achieve the optimal keypoint matching performance, which implies that the proposed ACADGAN scheme can make degraded underwater image restore more fundamental features. It should be emphasized that the average performance on UIEB and URPC datasets are provided in Table 3 and Table 4, from which we can obviously observe that the proposed ACADGAN scheme can achieve optimal or sub-optimal performance in terms of extraction of SIFT keypoint, Harris corner and Canny edge, which indicates the proposed ACADGAN scheme can contribute to extraction of fundamental features.

5 Conclusion

In this paper, an ACADGAN framework has been exclusively devised for UIE task. To be specific, the ACA module has been created to preserve content feature from channel perspective. In addition, the DCN module has been developed to augment sampling capability pertaining to convolutional kernel. Integrating ACA and DCN modules can eventually contribute to the proposed ACADGAN scheme. Comprehensive experiments and comparisons have thoroughly demonstrated that the proposed ACADGAN scheme can remarkably outperform plenty of state-of-the-art UIE approaches.

References

1. Akkaynak, D., Treibitz, T.: A revised underwater image formation model. In: Proceedings of the IEEE Conference on Computer Vision and Pattern Recognition, Salt Lake City, UT, USA, pp. 6723–6732 (2018)
2. Alipour-Fard, T., Paoletti, M., Haut, J.M., Arefi, H., Plaza, J., Plaza, A.: Multi-branch selective kernel networks for hyperspectral image classification. IEEE Geosci. Remote Sens. Lett. **18**(6), 1089–1093 (2020)
3. Ancuti, C.O., Ancuti, C., Bekaert, P.: Effective single image dehazing by fusion. In: International Conference on Image Processing, Hong Kong, China, pp. 3541–3544 (2010)
4. Ancuti, C., Ancuti, C.O., Haber, T., Bekaert, P.: Enhancing underwater images and videos by fusion. In: Proceedings of the IEEE Conference on Computer Vision and Pattern Recognition, Providence, RI, USA, pp. 81–88 (2012)
5. Arjovsky, M., Chintala, S., Bottou, L.: Wasserstein generative adversarial networks. In: Proceedings of the International Conference on Machine Learning, Sydney, Australia, pp. 214–223 (2017)
6. Berman, D., Treibitz, T., Avidan, S.: Diving into haze-lines: color restoration of underwater images. In: Proceedings of the British Machine Vision Conference, London, UK, vol. 1, pp. 1–12 (2017)
7. Canny, J.: A computational approach to edge detection. IEEE Trans. Pattern Anal. Mach. Intell. **8**(6), 679–698 (1986)
8. Chen, T., Wang, N., Wang, R., Zhao, H., Zhang, G.: One-stage CNN detector-based benthonic organisms detection with limited training dataset. Neural Netw. **144**, 247–259 (2021)
9. Chiang, J.Y., Chen, Y.C.: Underwater image enhancement by wavelength compensation and dehazing. IEEE Trans. Image Process. **21**(4), 1756–1769 (2011)
10. Chiang, J.Y., Chen, Y.C., Chen, Y.F.: Underwater image enhancement: using wavelength compensation and image dehazing (WCID). In: International Conference on Advanced Concepts for Intelligent Vision Systems, Ghent, Belgium, pp. 372–383 (2011)
11. Dai, J., et al.: Deformable convolutional networks. In: Proceedings of the IEEE International Conference on Computer Vision, Venice, Italy, pp. 764–773 (2017)
12. Drews, P., Nascimento, E., Moraes, F., Botelho, S., Campos, M.: Transmission estimation in underwater single images. In: Proceedings of the IEEE International Conference on Computer Vision Workshops, Sydney, Australia, pp. 825–830 (2013)
13. Ebner, D.H.: Color constancy. Vis. Res. **51**(7), 674–700 (2011)

14. Fabbri, C., Islam, M.J., Sattar, J.: Enhancing underwater imagery using generative adversarial networks. In: International Conference on Robotics and Automation, Brisbane, QLD, Australia, pp. 7159–7165 (2018)
15. Feifei, S., Xuemeng, Z., Guoyu, W.: An approach for underwater image denoising via wavelet decomposition and high-pass filter. In: International Conference on Intelligent Computation Technology and Automation, Shenzhen, China, vol. 2, pp. 417–420 (2011)
16. Fu, X., Fan, Z., Ling, M., Huang, Y., Ding, X.: Two-step approach for single underwater image enhancement. In: International Symposium on Intelligent Signal Processing and Communication Systems, Xiamen, China, pp. 789–794 (2017)
17. Gao, W., Zhang, L., Huang, W., Min, F., He, J., Song, A.: Deep neural networks for sensor-based human activity recognition using selective kernel convolution. IEEE Trans. Instrum. Meas. **70**, 1–13 (2021)
18. Harris, C., Stephens, M., et al.: A combined corner and edge detector. In: Proceedings of the Alvey Vision Conference, vol. 15, pp. 10–5244. Citeseer (1988)
19. He, K., Sun, J., Tang, X.: Single image haze removal using dark channel prior. In: Proceedings of the IEEE Conference on Computer Vision Pattern Recognition, Miami Beach, FL, USA, pp. 1956–1963 (2009)
20. He, K., Sun, J., Tang, X.: Single image haze removal using dark channel prior. IEEE Trans. Pattern Anal. Mach. Intell. **33**(12), 2341–2353 (2010)
21. Jaffe, J.S.: Computer modeling and the design of optimal underwater imaging systems. IEEE J. Oceanic Eng. **15**(2), 101–111 (1990)
22. Jia, D., Ge, Y.: Underwater image de-noising algorithm based on nonsubsampled contourlet transform and total variation. In: International Conference on Computer Science and Information Processing, Xi'an, China, pp. 76–80 (2012)
23. Jian, S., Wen, W.: Study on underwater image denoising algorithm based on wavelet transform. In: International Conference on Control Engineering and Artificial Intelligence, Kuala Lumpur, Malaysia, vol. 806, p. 012006 (2017)
24. Jing, Y., Yang, Y., Feng, Z., Ye, J., Yu, Y., Song, M.: Neural style transfer: a review. IEEE Trans. Vis. Comput. Graph. **26**(11), 3365–3385 (2019)
25. Lee, S., Yun, S., Nam, J.H., Won, C.S., Jung, S.W.: A review on dark channel prior based image dehazing algorithms. EURASIP J. Image Video Process. **2016**(1), 4–26 (2016)
26. Li, C., Anwar, S., Porikli, F.: Underwater scene prior inspired deep underwater image and video enhancement. Pattern Recogn. **98**, 107038 (2020)
27. Li, C., Guo, J., Guo, C.: Emerging from water: underwater image color correction based on weakly supervised color transfer. IEEE Signal. Proc. Lett. **25**(3), 323–327 (2018)
28. Li, J., Skinner, K.A., Eustice, R.M., Johnson-Roberson, M.: WaterGAN: unsupervised generative network to enable real-time color correction of monocular underwater images. IEEE Robot. Autom. Lett. **3**(1), 387–394 (2017)
29. Li, X., Wang, W., Hu, X., Yang, J.: Selective kernel networks. In: Proceedings of the IEEE/CVF Conference on Computer Vision and Pattern Recognition, Long Beach, CA, USA, pp. 510–519 (2019)
30. Lowe, D.G.: Distinctive image features from scale-invariant keypoints. Int. J. Comput. Vis. **60**(2), 91–110 (2004)
31. Lu, H., Li, Y., Zhang, L., Serikawa, S.: Contrast enhancement for images in turbid water. J. Opt. Soc. Am. A-Opt. Image Sci. **32**(5), 886–893 (2015)
32. Ludvigsen, M., Sortland, B., Johnsen, G., Singh, H.: Applications of geo-referenced underwater photo mosaics in marine biology and archaeology. Oceanography **20**(4), 140–149 (2007)

33. Mao, X., Li, Q., Xie, H., Lau, R.Y., Wang, Z., Paul Smolley, S.: Least squares generative adversarial networks. In: Proceedings of the IEEE International Conference on Computer Vision, Venice, Italy, pp. 2794–2802 (2017)
34. McGlamery, B.: A computer model for underwater camera systems. In: Ocean Optics, Monterey, CA, USA, vol. 208, pp. 221–231 (1980)
35. Mirza, M., Osindero, S.: Conditional generative adversarial nets (2014). https://arxiv.org/abs/1411.1784
36. Panetta, K., Gao, C., Agaian, S.: Human-visual-system-inspired underwater image quality measures. IEEE J. Ocean. Eng. 41(3), 541–551 (2015)
37. Priyadharsini, R., Sharmila, T.S., Rajendran, V.: A wavelet transform based contrast enhancement method for underwater acoustic images. Multidimension. Syst. Signal Process. 29(4), 1845–1859 (2018)
38. Singh, R., Biswas, M.: Adaptive histogram equalization based fusion technique for hazy underwater image enhancement. In: IEEE International Conference on Computational Intelligence and Computing Research, Chennai, India, pp. 1–5 (2016)
39. Wang, N., Er, M.J.: Self-constructing adaptive robust fuzzy neural tracking control of surface vehicles with uncertainties and unknown disturbances. IEEE Trans. Control Syst. Technol. 23(3), 991–1002 (2014)
40. Wang, N., Er, M.J.: Direct adaptive fuzzy tracking control of marine vehicles with fully unknown parametric dynamics and uncertainties. IEEE Trans. Control Syst. Technol. 24(5), 1845–1852 (2016)
41. Wang, N., Er, M.J., Sun, J.C., Liu, Y.C.: Adaptive robust online constructive fuzzy control of a complex surface vehicle system. IEEE Trans. Cybern. 46(7), 1511–1523 (2015)
42. Wang, N., Karimi, H.R., Li, H., Su, S.F.: Accurate trajectory tracking of disturbed surface vehicles: a finite-time control approach. IEEE/ASME Trans. Mechatron. 24(3), 1064–1074 (2019)
43. Wang, N., Qian, C., Sun, J.C., Liu, Y.C.: Adaptive robust finite-time trajectory tracking control of fully actuated marine surface vehicles. IEEE Trans. Control Syst. Technol. 24(4), 1454–1462 (2015)
44. Wang, N., Wang, Y., Er, M.J.: Review on deep learning techniques for marine object recognition: architectures and algorithms. Control. Eng. Pract. 118, 104458 (2022)
45. Wang, W., Wu, X., Yuan, X., Gao, Z.: An experiment-based review of low-light image enhancement methods. IEEE Access 8, 87884–87917 (2020)
46. Wang, X., Chan, K.C., Yu, K., Dong, C., Change Loy, C.: EDVR: video restoration with enhanced deformable convolutional networks. In: Proceedings of the IEEE/CVF Conference on Computer Vision and Pattern Recognition Workshops, Long Beach, CA, USA, pp. 1954–1963 (2019)
47. Wang, Z., Chen, J., Hoi, S.C.: Deep learning for image super-resolution: a survey. IEEE Trans. Pattern Anal. Mach. Intell. 43(10), 3365–3387 (2020)
48. Whitcomb, L., Yoerger, D.R., Singh, H., Howland, J.: Advances in underwater robot vehicles for deep ocean exploration: navigation, control, and survey operations. In: Hollerbach, J.M., Koditschek, D.E. (eds.) Robotics Research, pp. 439–448. Springer, London (2000). https://doi.org/10.1007/978-1-4471-0765-1_53
49. Yang, H., Chen, P., Huang, C., Zhuang, Y., Shiau, Y.: Low complexity underwater image enhancement based on dark channel prior. In: International Conference on Innovations in Bio-inspired Computing and Applications, Shenzhen, China, pp. 17–20 (2011)
50. Yang, M., Sowmya, A.: An underwater color image quality evaluation metric. IEEE Trans. Image Process. 24(12), 6062–6071 (2015)

51. Zhang, S., Wang, T., Dong, J., Yu, H.: Underwater image enhancement via extended multi-scale Retinex. Neurocomputing **245**, 1–9 (2017)
52. Zhao, J., Mathieu, M., LeCun, Y.: Energy-based generative adversarial network (2016). https://arxiv.org/abs/1609.03126
53. Zhu, J.Y., Park, T., Isola, P., Efros, A.A.: Unpaired image-to-image translation using cycle-consistent adversarial networks. In: Proceedings of the IEEE International Conference on Computer Vision, Venice, Italy, pp. 2223–2232 (2017)
54. Zuiderveld, K.: Contrast limited adaptive histogram equalization. In: Graphics Gems, pp. 474–485 (1994). https://doi.org/10.1016/B978-0-12-336156-1.50061-6

Coordinate Attention and Transformer Neck-Based Marine Organism Detection

Xiangjun Kong[1], Ning Wang[2](✉), Tingkai Chen[1], and Yanzheng Chen[2]

[1] School of Marine Electrical Engineering, Dalian Maritime University, Dalian 116026, China
[2] School of Marine Engineering, Dalian Maritime University, Dalian 116026, China
`n.wang.dmu.cn@gmail.com`

Abstract. Marine organism detection is crucial for the intelligent construction of open-sea farm. Suffering from low-contrast, color-deviation and detail-blurry underwater environment, a coordinate attention and transformer neck-based benthonic organism detection (CATNBOD) scheme has been devised. Main contributions are as follows: 1) The coordinate attention (CA) module is designed in the feature extraction network to obtain meaningful features, such that the small-scale benthonic organisms can be accurately detected. 2) To efficiently address the challenge derived from intra- and inter-class occlusions of benthonic organism, the rotation window-based swin transformer (ST) module is devised in the neck structure. Combining with CA and ST modules contributes to the proposed CATNBOD scheme. The effectiveness and superiority have been sufficiently demonstrated on publicly available UDD dataset.

Keywords: Marine organism detection · Coordinate attention · Swin transformer · Model optimization

1 Introduction

With the gradual regional saturation of offshore mariculture capacity, water quality deteriorated and aquaculture quality decreased. In order to improve the quality of mariculture, aquaculture enterprises are gradually turning their eyes to the far sea. Open-sea farm refers to the planned and purposeful marine stocking of marine resources by using the natural marine ecological environment, such as sea cucumbers, sea urchins and scallops. Currently, marine ranching has entered the era of fine management, which requires information such as the health status, individual size and density of marine organisms.The above information needs to be collected manually, which is low efficiency, high cost and dangerous. In order to effectively avoid dangerous and heavy works, intelligent marine robots

This work is supported by the National Natural Science Foundation of China (Grant 52271306), Innovative Research Foundation of Ship General Performance (Grant 31422120), and the Cultivation Program for the Excellent Doctoral Dissertation of Dalian Maritime University (Grant 2022YBPY004).

H. R. Karimi and N. Wang (Eds.): S-Cube 2022, LNICST 487, pp. 33–48, 2023.
https://doi.org/10.1007/978-3-031-34899-0_3

with biological status monitoring system have been gradually put into use [1–3]. Note that the underwater object detection is the most critical technique in above-mentioned system [4,5]. Due to the scattering and absorption of light in the water, underwater image usually presents color distortion, degradation blur, and dim light [6], which makes high-precision detection and recognition become challenging. In addition, marine organisms resemble degraded underwater background and possess small-size characteristic, which makes that rich hierarchical features can hardly be efficiently extracted. In this context, benthonic organism detection still faces severe challenges.

1.1 Related Works

Many scholars have conducted extensive research on underwater target detection techniques, which can be divided into two categories: traditional machine learning and deep learning. By virtue of sliding window technique [7], the traditional target detection algorithm firstly selects the region of interest. Subsequently, feature extraction is performed for each region of interest by using feature extractors, such as HOG [8], SURF [9], SIFT [10], *etc.* Finally, the extracted features are classified to determine whether the window contains object or not by deploying SVM technique [11,12]. Specifically, Ravanbakhsh et al. [13] used contour features for automatic fish detection. Note that the foregoing extracted features are poorly scalable in complex underwater environments. However, the color and structure of marine organisms are similar to seafloor background, which dramatically limits the feature extraction of manual extractors.

Compared with traditional machine methods, deep learning-based target detection algorithms have more powerful feature extraction capabilities. Deep learning-based target detection algorithms can be divided into two categories: region-proposal and regression-based target detection algorithms [14]. The former is also known as two-stage target detection algorithm, such as R-CNN [15], Faster R-CNN [16], and Mask R-CNN [17], which firstly extracts the feature from proposed regions of interest. Subsequently, the classifier is used to perform regression task. Besides, regression-based target detection algorithms, such as SSD [18], YOLOv3 [19], RetinaNet [20], *etc*, work in an end-to-end manner. To be specific, [21] designed an improved feature pyramid-based cucumber detection network. [22] proposed an one-stage CNN detector-based benthonic organism detection scheme. [23]proposed a data augmentation-based marine organism detection and recognition algorithm. Inspired by the human visual system, attention mechanisms have been used for various target detection tasks [24–26]. [27] added the SE attention mechanism to the deep convolutional layer for the aim of improving the detection accuracy of small fish, crabs, shrimps, and starfish. [28]proposed a residual block possessing channel attention mechanism to extract multi-scale effective features for underwater creature detection. [29]explored a visual attention for marine organism detection.

Many scholars mainly focus on the small target of marine organisms and the lightweight of detection model, and propose solutions such as feature fusion, prior anchor frame and data enhancement. However, most of them ignore the multi-target aggregation caused by the unique social property of marine organisms.

1.2 Contributions

The above methods have shown significant improvements in integrating attention mechanisms in the backbone feature extraction network and in target recognition, but not to the extent of considering that marine organisms such as sea urchins and sea cucumbers have swarming properties and there are a large number of aggregation and occlusion situations, and in addition, marine benthonic organism targets occupy only a small part of the image, and most of the image is background information [30], and in deep convolutional neural networks, a large number of image background information convolution iterations will accumulate a large amount of redundant invalid information and swamp the target information, these phenomena exacerbate the difficulty of detection, thus failing to obtain satisfactory detection performance on marine targets. In this paper, to overcome the above challenges, we propose a new lightweight marine life detection model based on deep learning.

Our contributions are as follows:

- We integrate coordinate attention (CA) into the backbone network, which helps the network find regions of interest in images with large areas and improves the feature extraction capability of the model.
- We integrate swin transformer (ST) into YOLOv5 neck structure, which can precisely locate marine organisms in high-density scenes;
- Finally, by integrating CA, ST and YOLOv5, a CATNBOD scheme is established, which has been experimentally demonstrated that the improved network detection accuracy can reach 72.7% (mAP), which exceeds its baseline detection accuracy of 66.1% (mAP), significantly improving the accuracy and robustness of marine organism detection and outperforming other general target detection models. It provides a new solution for the marine organism detection.

2   CATNBOD Network Design

In this section, we detail the proposed CATNBOD network architecture design, including CNN-based backbone network, coordinate attention module, and swin transformer, as shown in Fig. 1.

2.1   Model Backbone Network

Considering the tight computational resources underwater, the accuracy and speed required for marine organism detection, this work uses YOLOv5, a one-stage detection model with fewer parameters and excellent detection performance,

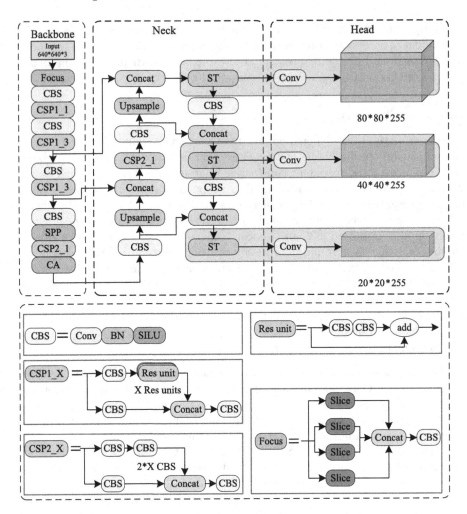

Fig. 1. Network structure for CATNBOD.

as the benchmark model. Depending on the length and width of the backbone network, it is divided into four versions, YOLOv5s, YOLOv5m, YOLOv5l and YOLOv5x. We use YOLOv5s, which has the smallest parameters and the fastest inference speed, to embed into the proposed CATNBOD marine organism detection model. The backbone consists of Focus, Conv BN SiLU (CBS), Cross Stage Part (CSP) and Spatial Pyramid Pool (SPP) modules. The detailed architecture of these modules is shown in Fig. 1. The Focus role is to slice the image before it enters the backbone to expand the output space by a factor of four, and the original three channels become twelve channels with no information loss, reducing the amount of operations. The CSP module, inspired by CSPNet [31], halves the number of channels by performing a separate convolution operation to allow the model to learn more distinguishing features. To achieve FeatherMap-level fusion of local and global features, the SPP module is in-serted at the end of the backbone network.

2.2 Coordinate Attention Fusion Module

The information of marine organisms in underwater images is easily obscured by redundant background information in convolutional iterations, which affects the accuracy of underwater biological target detection and recognition. Existing studies have shown that incorporating attention mechanisms into convolutional neural network models can lead to relatively significant performance improvements, but traditional attention mechanisms applied to lightweight networks significantly lag behind deep networks, and the resulting computational overhead is unaffordable for light-weight networks. The popular attention mechanisms include SE (Squeeze and Excitation) [32], BAM (Bottleneck Attention Module) and CBAM (Convolutional Block Attention Module) [33]. Among them, SE only considers internal channel information and ignores location information and spatial structure, which are important for vision tasks, and are crucial for generating spatially selective attention maps. BAM and CBAM introduce local location information by global pooling on channels, but can-not capture long-range dependencies on feature maps.

Coordinate Attention(CA) is a new efficient attention mechanism, the principle of which is shown in Fig. 2. We apply the CA module at the end of the backbone network because the feature mapping resolution at the end of the backbone network is low. Using CA on low-resolution feature maps can reduce the expensive computational overhead. The first step embeds the location information into the channel attention, allowing the lightweight network to obtain information about a larger area, reducing the number of parameters of the attention module while avoiding excessive computational overhead. In the coordinate information embedding process, a specific input $X = [x^1, x^2, \cdots, x^c] \in \mathbb{R}^{c \times w \times h}$ is given and each channel in the horizontal direction is encoded by a mean pooling layer of size $(H, 1)$ to obtain a perceptual feature map in the horizontal direction. As the XAvgPool part of the CA structure diagram, it is the result $z_c^h(h)$ obtained from the output of the $c - th$ channel of width h. The vertical perceptual feature map is obtained by encoding each channel in the vertical direction through an average pooling layer of size $(1, W)$. As the YAvgPool part in the CA structure diagram. $z_c^h(w)$ is the result obtained by matching the output of the $c - th$ channel of width w.

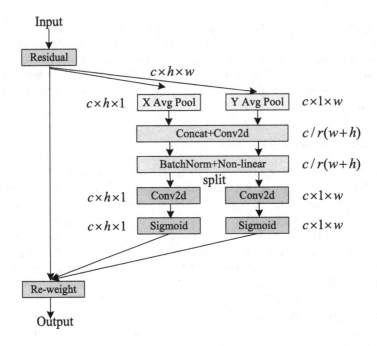

Fig. 2. Coordinate Attention structure schematic.

The resulting operation saves the position information. The principle equations are shown in Eqs. (1) and (2):

$$z_c^h(h) = \frac{1}{W} \sum_i x_c(h, i) \tag{1}$$

$$z_c^h(w) = \frac{1}{H} \sum_i x_c(j, i) \tag{2}$$

In the second step, the vertical and horizontal perceptual feature maps obtained by pooling are cascaded using Concat. Two feature maps z^h and z^w are obtained.

In the third step, on this basis, a convolutional transform function with a convolutional kernel size of 1 is used to transform the information operation to obtain the spatial information in two to encode the intermediate feature mapping law. The transformation formula is shown in Eq. (3):

$$f = \delta(F_1([z^h, z^w])) \tag{3}$$

where: $f \in \mathbb{R}^{c/r \times (H+W)}$ is the intermediate feature map of spatial information in the vertical and horizontal directions, δ is the activation function, F_1 is the convolutional transform function, $[z^h, z^w]$ operation is the two feature map splicing operation.

In the fourth step, two 1×1 convolutional transform functions F_h and F_w are used to transform the two tensors $\boldsymbol{f}^h$ and $\boldsymbol{f}^w$, respectively, into a tensor with the same number of channels as the output. The transformation equations are shown in Eqs. (4) and (5):

$$g^h = \sigma(F_h(\boldsymbol{f}^h)) \tag{4}$$

$$g^w = \sigma(F_w(\boldsymbol{f}^w)) \tag{5}$$

where σ is the sigmoid function, $f^h \in \mathbb{R}^{c/r \times H}$ and $f^w \in \mathbb{R}^{c/r \times W}$, and F^h and F^w are the convolutional transform functions.

In the fifth step, the outputs g^h and g^w are extended as the attention weight assignment values, which can help the network to focus its resources more on channel effective information and spatial effective information, respectively. Combining the above equation, the final extended output equation can be obtained as shown in Eq. (6):

$$y_c(i, j) = x_c(i, j) \times g_c^h(i) \times g_c^w(j) \tag{6}$$

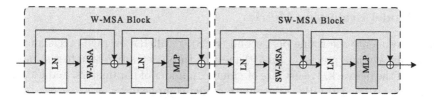

Fig. 3. The swin transformer architecture.

2.3   Swin Transformer Module

Due to the swarming property of marine organisms, this leads to occlusion between objects and thus requires high detector performance. Inspired by swin transformer [34] and TPH-YOLOv5 [35], we replace some convolution blocks and CSP bottleneck blocks in the original version of YOLOv5 with swin transformer, which is compared with the original bottleneck in CSPDarknet53 blocks in CSPDarknet53, we believe that swin transformer can capture global information and rich contextual information. We only apply the swin transformer block in the YOLOv5 neck part. The swin transformer module introduced in this paper consists of two consecutive structures, as shown in Fig. 3. W-MSA block and SW-MSA block are multi-head self attention modules with regular and shifted windowing configurations, respectively.

3   Experiments and Analysis

3.1   Experimental Environment and Data Set

The experimental environment is windows operating system, Intel Xeon Silver 4210 (CPU), 16 GB random access memory (RAM), GTX 2080Ti (GPU), and deep learning framework is Pytorch 1.6.5, software environment is CUDA 10.1, CUDNN 7.6.5, and python 3.8. The model is optimized using SGD (stochastic gradient descent) method was used for optimization. The specific settings of the network training hyperparameters are 40 for the training period, 10 for the batch size, 0.01 for the initial learning rate, 0.0005 for the weight decay, and 0.9 for the SGD momentum.

Optical images are mainly acquired by means of underwater robots carrying cameras when exploring fishery resources in marine pastures. Therefore, this paper uses the open source dataset UDD from Dalian University of Technology to verify the reliability of the algorithm in this paper. The dataset contains a total of 2227 images of three types of underwater biological targets, sea cucumber, seaurchin and scallop in multiple scenes, of which 1827 are used for training and 400 for testing.

3.2   Model Evaluation Metrics

The experiments use frame per second (FPS), recall(R), average precision (AP) and mean average precision (mAP) metrics to objectively evaluate the performance of the network. We use size of moudle, number of parameters, and Floating Point Operations (FLOPs) to evaluate model complexity.

The FPS metric is used to evaluate the detection speed of the network, and the larger the value, the faster the network detection speed.

The AP metric is used to evaluate the detection accuracy of a single category, which can be calculated as follows:

$$AP = \int_0^1 P(R)\mathrm{d}R \tag{7}$$

where P represents the precision rate, which refers to the probability that all detected targets are correctly detected, and R represents the recall rate, which refers to the probability that all true positive samples are correctly detected, and the calculation can be expressed as follows:

$$P = \frac{TP}{TP + FP} \tag{8}$$

$$R = \frac{TP}{TP + FN} \tag{9}$$

where TP represents the number of positive samples detected correctly, FP represents the number of samples detected as positive but actually negative, and FN represents the number of samples detected as negative but actually positive.

Using mAP to evaluate the combined detection accuracy of the model, the calculation can be expressed as follows:

$$mAP = \sum_{i=1}^{N} AP_i/N \tag{10}$$

where N represents the number of all categories and AP_i represents the average precision of category i. The model weight file size can visually reflect the complexity of the model, and the larger the weight file is, the more complex the model is.

The marine organism detection model is trained using the official pre-training weights to obtain new training weights. The model weight file size can visually reflect the complexity of the model, and a larger weight file indicates a more complex model.

The number of parameters is a common evaluation metric for network complexi-ty, and for the convolutional layer, the calculation of the number of parameters on the fully connected and batch normalized layers follows the following formula.

Denote the number of parameters for the convolutional layer as M^{conv}, which is calculated as follows:

$$M^{conv} = K_1 \times K_2 \times C_{in}^{conv} \times C_{out}^{conv} + C_{out}^{conv} \tag{11}$$

where K_1 and K_2 denote the size of the convolution kernel, C_{in}^{conv} and C_{out}^{conv} denote the number of input feature map channels and the number of output feature map channels of the convolution layer, respectively.

The number of parameters of the fully connected layer is M^{fc}, which is calculated as follows:

$$M^{fc} = C_{in}^{fc} \times C_{out}^{fc} + C_{out}^{fc} \tag{12}$$

where C_{in}^{fc} and C_{out}^{fc} denote the number of input features and output features of the fully connected layer, respectively.

Denote the number of parameters of the batch normalization layer as M^{bn}, which is calculated as follows:

$$M^{bn} = 2 \times C^{bn} \tag{13}$$

where C^{bn} denotes the number of channels in the batch normalization layer.

Denoting the total number of parameters in the model as M, which is calculated as follows:

$$M = \sum_{i=1}^{C} M_i^{conv} + \sum_{j=1}^{F} M_j^{fc} + \sum_{k=1}^{B} M_k^{bn} \tag{14}$$

where C, F, and B denote the number of layers in the model for the convolutional, fully connected, and batch normalized layers, respectively.

FLOPs is a common metric for evaluating the computation of the model and measuring the performance of CNNs, and the calculation of FLOPs on convolutional, fully connected and batch normalized layers follows the following formula.

The FLOPs of the convolutional layer are F^{conv} and are calculated as follows:

$$F^{conv} = B \times H_{out} \times W_{out} \times (2 \times C_{in}^{conv} \times K_1^{conv} \times K_2^{conv} + 1) \times C_{out}^{conv} \quad (15)$$

where B denotes the size of the batch size, H_{out} and W_{out} denote the height and width of the output feature map of the convolutional layer, C_{in}^{conv} and C_{out}^{conv} denote the number of input and output feature map channels of the convolutional layer, respectively, and K_1^{conv} and K_2^{conv} denote the size of the convolutional kernel.

The FLOPs of the fully connected layer are denoted as F^{fc} and are calculated as follows:

$$F^{fc} = B \times (2 \times C_{in}^{fc} + 1) \times C_{out}^{fc} \quad (16)$$

where C_{in}^{fc} and C_{out}^{fc} denote the number of input features and output features of the fully connected layer, respectively.

The FLOPs of the pooling layer are F^{pl}, which are calculated as follows:

$$F^{pl} = B \times (C^{pl} \times K_1 \times K_2 \times H_{out} \times W_{out}) \quad (17)$$

where C^{pl} denotes the number of channels of the pooling layer, K_1^{pl} and K_2^{pl} denote the size of the convolution kernel of the pooling layer, and H_{out} and W_{out} denote the height and width of the output feature map of the pooling layer, respectively.

The FLOPs of the batch normalization layer are denoted as F^{bn}, which are calculated as follows:

$$F^{bn} = B \times (2 \times C^{bn}) \quad (18)$$

where C^{bn} denotes the number of channels in the batch normalization layer, which is multiplied by 2, because the batch normalization is subject to multiplication and addition operations.

Denoting the total floating-point operations of the model as G, we have:

$$G = B \times \left(\sum_{i=1}^{C} F_i^{conv} + \sum_{j=1}^{F} F_j^{fc} + \sum_{l=1}^{P} F_l^{pl} + \sum_{k=1}^{N} F_k^{bn} \right) \quad (19)$$

where C, F, P, and N denote the number of layers of convolutional, fully connected, pooling, and batch normalization layers in the model, respectively.

3.3 Ablation Experiments

To evaluate the effectiveness of the improved algorithm in this paper, three aspects of detection accuracy, detection speed and model complexity were compared and analyzed with YOLOv5s algorithm, and the experimental results are shown in Table 1 and Table 2.

Table 1. Ablation studies within different modules.

Model	AP(%) seacucumber	AP(%) seaurchin	AP(%) scallop	mAP(%) @.5	mAP(%) @[.5, .95]	R	FPS/s
YOLOv5s	59.6	88.9	50.0	66.1	27.3	61.5	63
YOLOv5s+CA	56.7	90.1	60.5	69.1	28.4	64.7	59
YOLOv5s+ST	53.6	90.2	56.2	66.7	27.9	62.7	61
CATNBOD	57.9	90.5	69.7	72.7	30.0	70.7	58

Table 2. Comparison with YOLOv5s algorithm model complexity M/G denotes million/billion ($10^6/10^9$)respectively.

Model	Bacbone nework	Size/MB	Params/M	FLOPs/G
YOLOv5s	CSPDarknet53	14.1	7.1	16.3
YOLOv5s+CA	CSPDarknet53	15.5	8.0	17.5
YOLOv5s+ST	CSPDarknet53	14.2	7.3	16.7
CATNBOD	CSPDarknet53	16.0	8.2	17.7

As shown in Table 1 and Table 2, after YOLOv5s+CA introduces coordinate attention module, the model size, number of parameters, and floating point computation increase by 1.4 MB, 0.9 M, and 1.2 G, respectively, and the model inference speed decreases slightly, but the average detection accuracy increases by 3%. It shows that coordinate attention increases the model complexity and reduces the network inference speed, but this attention mechanism can capture the location information and channel relationship, suppress the non-essential feature information, make the network pay more attention to the target feature information, improve the quality of the feature map extracted by the network, and significantly improve the detection accuracy of the model.

It is worth noting that usually the shells of scallops are mostly grayish-brown in color similar to the background of sand and silt on the seabed. In the baseline model, the scallop detection rate of 50% is the lowest detection success rate among the three types of targets, but the addition of CA attention mechanism significantly improves the detection accuracy to 60.5%, indicating that the CA module plays a great role.

YOLOv5s+ST enhances the detection capability of dense small targets by introducing swin transformer module in the detection head, with 1.2%improvement in seaurchin and recall rate and 0.7% improvement in average detection accuracy. The model size, number of parameters, and floating point computation only increase by 0.1MB, 0.1M, and 0.4G, achieving detection performance improvement with little impact on model complexity.

CATNBOD integrated coordinate attention module and swin transformer module, compared with baseline, the detection accuracy of seaurchin improved by 1.6%, scallop detection accuracy improved by 19.7%, sea cucumber detection accuracy decreased slightly, and the average detection accuracy improved by 6.6%. The scallop targets account for only 1.9% of the total number of targets, and are usually small in size, fuzzy in feature information and similar to the background, so the detection accuracy is low. This paper shows that the combination of different improvement strategies can significantly improve the feature extraction ability of the network, which can alleviate the limitation of the lack of data samples to some extent, and improve the detection ability of small and fuzzy targets.

Table 3. Comparison with other state-of-the-art detectors.

Model	Backbone	AP(%) seacucumber	AP(%) seaurchin	AP(%) scallop	mAP(%) @.5	mAP(%) @[.5, .95]
Faster R-CNN	ResNet50	66.8	76.2	51.0	64.7	26.8
YOLOv3	DarkNet53	62.9	89.6	49.4	67.3	28.7
YOLOv5	CSPDarknet53	59.6	88.9	50.0	66.1	27.3
CATNBOD	CSPDarknet53	57.9	90.5	69.7	72.7	30.0

To demonstrate the superiority of our proposed CATNBOD scheme, a comprehensive comparison with typical two-stage and one-stage detection methods including Faster R-CNN, YOLOv3, and YOLOv5 is performed. To ensure a fair comparison, the above schemes are thoroughly pre-trained on the COCO dataset, followed by fine-tuned training on the UDD dataset. Therefore, comparing the results listed in Table 3, from which we can observe that the proposed CATNBOD scheme gives the best results in the detection of sea urchins and scallops. While the Faster R-CNN scheme using Region Proposal Network has the best detection accuracy for sea cucumbers. the YOLOv3 algorithm also achieves good results for detecting sea cucumbers, but performs poorly for scallops. In the absence of CA and ST techniques, YOLOv5 cannot achieve the same detection accuracy as the proposed scheme. Our proposed algorithm achieves the best results in both mAP@.5 and mAP@[.5, .95]. In addition, the proposed algorithm can obtain better real-time performance by using the lightweight CSPDarknet53 backbone network.

3.4   Image Detection Effect Analysis

In order to fully demonstrate the superiority of the proposed CATNBOD scheme in terms of practical validation, we selected four more representative marine benthonic organism scenes from the validation set for comparison experiments, and Fig. 4 shows the sample detection results by adding different method modules.

It can be clearly seen from columns (a), (c) and (d) that more marine organisms can be detected accurately after adding CA module, which proves the necessity of adding CA attention to marine life detection scenes. After adding the ST

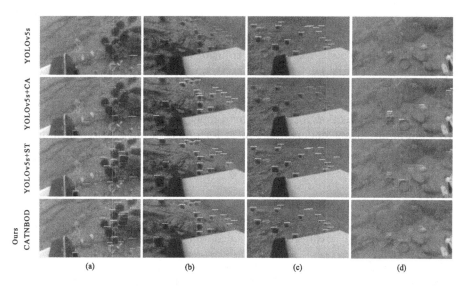

Fig. 4. Comparison of real-world detection results.

module, it can be seen from the complex and dense scenes in columns (a) and (d) that YOLOv5s+ST helps detect small targets of sea cucumbers and scallops in the rock crevices and improves the detection performance of marine organisms. However, when the environment is too complex, the YOLOv5s+CA and YOLOv5s+ST models still suffer from false detection and missed detection problems. (d) Columns of water plants were incorrectly identified as sea cucumbers, rocks were identified as scallops, and multiple scallops were not detected.

From the comparison Fig. 4 in column (a), it can be seen that YOLOv5s missed one sea cucumber, one seaurchin and multiple scallops between the stone gaps, and our proposed CATNBOD achieved accurate and complete identification of all sea cucumbers and sea urchins. From the comparison graphs in columns (b) and (c), it can be seen that our algorithm is able to identify more minute sea cucumber targets. From column (d), it can be seen that our algorithm can identify more scallop targets and only one false detection. In conclusion, the analysis of the detection results shows that the detection and recognition effect of the improved model in this paper is much better than the original YOLOv5s detection effect, and the false detection rate and the missed detection rate of the target organisms are reduced.

4   Conclusions

For the unique group living properties of marine organisms to produce target aggregation, obscuration phenomenon, thus leading to the problem of missed detection, wrong detection, as well as small target information and the background of the seabed similar to the problem of difficult to extract features. A CATNBOD framework is proposed for marine organism detection. Specifically, the coordinate attention mechanism is introduced in the backbone network to capture location information and channel relationships to improve the feature extraction capability of the network; the swin transformer neck-based is constructed to improve the detection capability of the network for small targets; we conduct comprehensive experiments to illustrate the effectiveness of the proposed algorithm.

In our future research, we will continue to improve the performance of marine organism target detection in turbid environment, and integrate the improved algorithm in intelligent underwater robots for practical marine organism detection tasks.

References

1. Wang, N., Wang, Y., Er, M.J.: Review on deep learning techniques for marine object recognition: architectures and algorithms. Control. Eng. Pract. **118**(3), 104458 (2022)
2. Wang, N., Qian, C., Sun, J., Liu, Y.: Adaptive robust finite-time trajectory tracking control of fully actuated marine surface vehicles. IEEE Trans. Cybern. **24**(4), 1454–1462 (2016)
3. Wang, N., Er, M.J.: Direct adaptive fuzzy tracking control of marine vehicles with fully unknown parametric dynamics and uncertainties. IEEE Trans. Control Syst. Technol. **24**(5), 1845–1852 (2016)
4. Yeh, C., et al.: Lightweight deep neural network for joint learning of underwater object detection and color conversion. IEEE Trans. Neural Netw. Learn. Syst. **99**, 1–15 (2021)
5. Wang, Y., et al.: Real-time underwater onboard vision sensing system for robotic gripping. IEEE Trans. Instrum. Meas. **70**, 1–11 (2020)
6. Han, M., Lyu, Z., Qiu, T., Xu, M.: A review on intelligence dehazing and color restoration for underwater images. IEEE Trans. Syst. Man Cybern. Syst. **50**(5), 1820–1832 (2020)
7. Forsyth, D.: Object detection with discriminatively trained part-based models. Computer **47**(02), 6–7 (2016)
8. Dalal, N., Triggs, B.: Histograms of oriented gradients for human detection. In: 2005 IEEE Computer Society Conference on Computer Vision and Pattern Recognition, pp. 886–893, San Diego, CA, USA (2005)
9. Bay, H., Tuytelaars, T., Van Gool, L.: SURF: speeded up robust features. Lect. Notes Comput. Sci. **3951**, 404–417 (2006)
10. Lowe, D.G.: Distinctive image features from scale-invariant keypoints. Int. J. Comput. Vis. **60**(2), 91–110 (2004)
11. Cherkassky, V., Ma, Y.: Practical selection of SVM parameters and noise estimation for SVM regression. Neural Netw. **17**(1), 113–126 (2004)
12. Wang, N., Er, M.J.: Self-constructing adaptive robust fuzzy neural tracking control of surface vehicles with uncertainties and unknown disturbances. IEEE Trans. Control Syst. Technol. **23**(3), 991–1002 (2014)
13. Villon, S.; Chaumont, M.; Subsol, G.; Villéger, S.; Claverie, T.; Mouillot, D.: Coral reef fish detection and recognition in underwatervideos by supervised machine learning: Comparison between Deep Learning and HOG+ SVM methods. In Proceedings of the International Conference on Advanced Concepts for Intelligent Vision Systems, Lecce, Italy, pp. 160–171 (2016)

14. Serban, A., Poll, E., Visser, J.: Adversarial examples on object recognition: a comprehensive survey. ACM Comput. Surv. **53**(3), 1–38 (2020)
15. Girshick, R.: Fast R-CNN. In: Proceedings of the IEEE International Conference on Computer Vision, pp. 1440–1448 (2015)
16. Ren, S., He, K., Girshick, R., Sun, J.: Faster R-CNN: towards real-time object detection with region proposal networks. IEEE Trans. Pattern Anal. Mach. Intell. **39**(6), 1137–1149 (2015)
17. He, K., Gkioxari, G., Dollár, P.: Mask R-CNN. In: Proceedings of the IEEE International Conference on Computer Vision, pp. 2961–2969 (2017)
18. Liu, W., et al.: SSD: single shot multibox detector. In: Leibe, B., Matas, J., Sebe, N., Welling, M. (eds.) ECCV 2016. LNCS, vol. 9905, pp. 21–37. Springer, Cham (2016). https://doi.org/10.1007/978-3-319-46448-0_2
19. Redmon, J., Farhadi, A.: Yolov3: An incremental improvement. arXiv 2018. arXiv:1804.02767
20. Lin, T., Goyal, P., Girshick, R., He, K., Dollar, P.: Focal loss for dense object detection. In: Proceedings of the IEEE International Conference on Computer Vision, pp. 2980–2988 (2017)
21. Peng, F., Miao, Z., Li, F., Li, Z.: S-FPN: a shortcut feature pyramid network for sea cucumber detection in underwater images. Expert Syst. Appl. **182**, 115306 (2021)
22. Chen, T., Wang, N., Wang, R., Zhao, H., Zhang, G.: One-stage CNN detector based benthonic organisms detection with limited training dataset. Neural Netw. **144**, 247–259 (2021)
23. Huang, H., Zhou, H., Yang, X.: Faster R-CNN for marine organisms detection and recognition using data augmentation. Neurocomputing **337**, 372–384 (2019)
24. Wang, N., Karimi, H.R., Li, H., Su, S.-F.: Accurate trajectory tracking of disturbed surface vehicles: a finite-time control approach. IEEE/ASME Trans. Mechatron. **24**(3), 1064–1074 (2019)
25. Wang, N., Er, M.J., Sun, J., Liu, Y.: Adaptive robust online constructive fuzzy control of a complex surface vehicle system. IEEE Trans. Cybern. **46**(7), 1511–1523 (2016)
26. Carion, N., Massa, F., Synnaeve, G., Usunier, N., Kirillov, A., Zagoruyko, S.: End-to-End object detection with transformers. In: Vedaldi, A., Bischof, H., Brox, T., Frahm, J.-M. (eds.) ECCV 2020. LNCS, vol. 12346, pp. 213–229. Springer, Cham (2020). https://doi.org/10.1007/978-3-030-58452-8_13
27. Wei, X., Yu, L., Tian, S., Feng, P., Ning, X.: Underwater target detection with an attention mechanism and improved scale. Multimed. Tools Appl. **80**(25), 33747–33761 (2021). https://doi.org/10.1007/s11042-021-11230-2
28. Li, A., Yu, L., Tian, S.: Underwater biological detection based on YOLOv4 combined with channel attention. J. Mar. Sci. Eng. **10**(4), 469 (2022)
29. Shi, Z., et al.: Detecting marine organisms via joint attention-relation learning for marine video surveillance. IEEE J. Ocean. Eng. **47**(4), 959–974 (2022)
30. Xu, F., Wang, H., Peng, J., Fu, X.: Scale-aware feature pyramid architecture for marine object detection. Neural Comput. Appl. **33**(8), 3637–3653 (2021)
31. Wang, C., Liao, H., Wu, Y., Chen, P., Hsieh, J., Yeh, I.: CSPNet: A new backbone that can enhance learning capability of CNN. In: roceedings of the IEEE/CVF Conference on Computer Vision and Pattern Recognition Workshops, pp. 390–391 (2020)
32. Hu, J., Shen, L., Sun, G.: Squeeze-and-excitation networks. In: Proceedings of the IEEE Conference on Computer Vision and Pattern Recognition, pp. 7132–7141 (2018)

33. Woo, S., Park, J., Lee, J., Kweom, I.: CBAM: convolutional block attention module. In: Proceedings of the European Conference on Computer Vision, pp. 3–19 (2018)

34. Liu, Z., et al.: Swin transformer: Hierarchical vision transformer using shifted windows. In: Proceedings of the IEEE/CVF International Conference on Computer Vision, pp. 10012–10022 (2021)

35. Zhu, X., Lyu, S., Wang, X., Zhao, Q.: TPH-YOLOv5: improved YOLOv5 based on transformer prediction head for object detection on drone-captured scenarios. In: Proceedings of the IEEE/CVF International Conference on Computer Vision, pp. 2778–2788 (2021)

Marine Vessel Detection in Sea Fog Environment Based on SSD

Yuanyuan Wang[1]🄳, Ning Wang[2(✉)]🄳, Luyuan Tang[1], and Wei Wu[1]

[1] School of Marine Electrical Engineering, Dalian Maritime University,
Dalian 116026, China
[2] School of Marine Engineering, Dalian Maritime University, Dalian 116026, China
n.wang@ieee.org

Abstract. Aiming at solving the problem of low marine vessel detection accuracy in the sea fog environment, a deep learning-based anti-fog marine vessel detection method is proposed in this paper by combining defogging preprocessing with marine vessel detection model. Firstly, gated context aggregation network (GCANet) network is used to process the marine vessel image. Then, the processed image is sent to a modified SSD network, wherein anchors are tuned by statistical characteristics of the shape of marine vessel to detect the position of the marine vessel. Furthermore, to alleviate the loss of feature information due to defogging processing, channel attention mechanism based on the squeeze and excitation module (SE) is added to base convolutional layer of SSD. The comprehensive experiments and comparison results show that the proposed G-SEMSSD network is more suitable for marine vessel detection under sea fog environment.

Keywords: Deep learning · Marine vessel detection · Fog image object detection

1 Introduction

Marine safety including shipwreck, naval battle and marine accidents, *etc.*, is still a serious matter [1]. As the autonomous marine platform, underwater robotics [2,3] and unmanned surface vehicles (USVs) that can conduct long-term and large-scale marine operations have gain more attention in the fields of intelligent control [4], collision avoidance [5] and trajectory tracking [6,7]. With increasingly rapid development of computer vision and deep learning, more intelligent USVs [8] are desired to achieve high-effect marine object detection, recognition and tracking.

By far, marine vessel detection methods are roughly summarized into two kinds, i.e., traditional methods based on prior information and modern methods

This work is supported by the National Natural Science Foundation of China (Grant 52271306) and Innovative Research Foundation of Ship General Performance (Grant 31422120).

H. R. Karimi and N. Wang (Eds.): S-Cube 2022, LNICST 487, pp. 49–62, 2023.
https://doi.org/10.1007/978-3-031-34899-0_4

based on deep learning. The former strongly requires manual features such as contour, radiation, shape and moment invariants, *etc.*, thereby leading to time-consuming and empirical interventions. State-of-the-art (SOTA) deep learning-based object detectors mainly consist of two-stage and one-stage approaches. The two-stage methods generate a series of candidate boxes as samples which are classified by virtue of the convolution neural networks (CNN) [9–11]. For instance, R-CNN [12,13], SPP-net [14], Fast R-CNN [15] and Faster R-CNN [16], *etc.* The latter techniques, also named end-to-end algorithms, which mean that input an image to the network and then the probabilities and locations information of targets in the image are directly obtained. Therefore, compared to two-stage approaches, one-stage approaches are faster. The typical methods include YOLO [17] and its variants (YOLOs), i.e., YOLOv2 [18], YOLOv3 [19], YOLOv4 [20], YOLOv5, RetinaNet [21], SSD [22] and EfficientDet D0-D6 [23]. Particularly, SSD scheme features the advantages of anchors and regression from both Fast R-CNN and YOLOs, and thereby it not only reaches real-time detection but does not sacrifice accuracy.

USVs navigate in complex and unknown marine environments [24–26], such as wind turbine, ocean wave and currents, sea fog and rain, which inevitably leads to degradation of acquired image. However, deep learning methods largely depends on high quality data, for which deep learning-based marine vessel detection methods as described above are facing great challenges. At present, there is no systematic and efficient methods of marine vessel recognition to defend against the extreme weathers. Naturally, increasing related works based on CNN for dehazing algorithms have been produced, since great progresses have been made in some tasks owing to implementations of CNN. By far, the mainstreams of image defog algorithms can be roughly summarized into three categories, i.e., image enhancement, image restoration, and deep learning-based defog methods. Image enhancement algorithms aim to restore a clear image without fog by removing image noise and improving image contrast, such as histogram equalization (HE), adaptive histgram equalization (AHE), contrast limited adaptive histgram equalization (CLAHE) [27], Retinex [28] and filtering algorithms, *etc.* The second usually depends on atmospheric scattering model. For example, dark channel prior (DCP) [29], color attenuation prior (CAP) [30]. It should be noted that the second tends to outperform the former. Deep learning-based imaging defogging is to input foggy image to CNN and directly output the defoggy image. For example, DehazeNet [31], all-in-one network (AOD-Net) [32], densely connected pyramid dehazing network (DCPDN) [33], gated fusion network (GFN) [34] and gated context aggregation network (GCANet) [35]. The end-to-end networks for image dehazing are easily to be embedded into other CNN models mentioned above. Sequentially, some comprehensive results and comparisons among various defogging algorithms mentioned above are conducted in paper [36], which concluded that Faster R-CNN trained on the image processed by defogging algorithms increases detection accuracy by a range of 0.2% to 2.0%, except for DehazeNet. In conclusion, not all of defoggy algorithms are absolutely benefit to object detection, but most.

In this paper, SOTA defogging algorithm GCANet is firstly utilized to process images, and then the clean images are used to fine-tune SSD model to satisfy the specific detection task. GCANet is a defogging network based on CNN and it not only can remove the fog in a single image but has little effect on clear images. Furthermore, we have modified and optimized the SSD network: 1) designing more reasonable aspect ratio (AR) by the statistical characteristics of marine vessel; 2) inserting channel attention mechanism based on SE block to the base convolutional layer of SSD, to alleviate the loss of key features due to defogging processing. In this context, fusing GCANet, AR and SE techniques, the G-SEMSSD detection method is eventually established to defend against sea fog environment. Main contributions of this paper are summarized as follows:

* Adding an image preprocessing module named GCANet to the SSD scheme, both detection precision and recall have been significantly enhanced.
* Formulating new default boxes of marine vessel with statistical characteristics of MVDD13 dataset, the detection accuracy is further improved.
* Inserting the channel attention mechanism SE block into the base convolutional layer, the loss of key features caused by defogging processing is dramatically decreased.

The remainder of this paper is organized as follows. Section 2 briefly introduces related works on marine vessel model, including image processing module, SSD model and optimization. In Sect. 3, the comprehensive experimental results and comparisons are given and analyzed. Conclusions are laid in Sect. 4.

2   Marine Vessel Detection Model

There are many abbreviations are utilized in the paper, for convenience, the commonly used words are summarized in Table 1.

Table 1. The full names and responding abberviations included in paper.

Abbreviation	Full Name
AR	aspect ratio
SE	squeeze and excitation module
GCANet	gated context aggregation network
SSD	single shot multibox detector
MVDD13	marine vessel detection dataset including 13 categories
AP	IoU = 0.5 and for each category
mAP@.5	IoU = 0.5 and averaged across 13 categories
mAP@.75	IoU = 0.75 and averaged across 13 categories
mAP@[.5 : .95]	averaged across 10 IoU thresholds and 13 categories

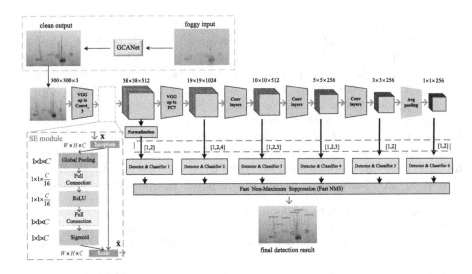

Fig. 1. The flow chart of defogging preprocessing and detection.

As shown in Fig. 1, the flow chart of marine vessel detection in foggy environment is divided into two steps: GCANet is firstly used to defog the marine vessel image. Then, the processed image is input to the modified SSD network to detect the position of marine vessel.

2.1 Image Processing Module

GCANet was proposed by Chen et al. [35]. It applies the smooth dilated convolution to extract image features, and the residual between clean and foggy image features are calculated to remove fog, instead of reling on prior information.

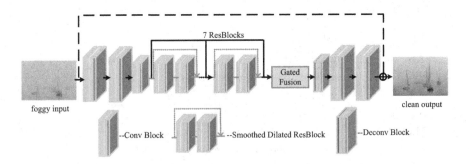

Fig. 2. Structure of GCANet.

The structure of GCANet and the defogging processing are shown in Fig. 2. Firstly, three convolutional layers are used to encode the foggy image, and only the last one downsamples the feature maps by 1/2 once. Then seven smoothed dilated resblocks are used to aggregate image features. These features from different level are fused into a gate fusion subnetwork, which is used to calculate the residual between the foggy and the fog-free image. During the defogging processing, the residuals are adaptively adjusted by different concentrations of fog in the input image. In decoder part, one deconvolutional layer with stride 1/2 is used to upsample the feature maps to the original resolution, then the following two convolutional layers convert the feature maps back to the image space to get the final target fog residue.

Fig. 3. Comparison of defogging effect.

During the runtime, the GCANet will predict the residue between the target clean image and the hazy input image in an end-to-end way. Specifically, Fig. 3 shows the effective of GCANet, whereby the first raw is original foggy images and the below is defoggy images.

2.2   SSD Model and Optimization

By far, Faster R-CNN, YOLOs and SSD are SOTA deep learning models, which have been widely applied in object detection field. According to our previous work, SSD with a 300×300 input size significantly outperforms SOTA object detector counterparts as stated in [22], especially in terms of speed.

Default Box. The SSD framework is vividly shown in Fig. 1. VGG16 is selected as its base network, of which fc6 and fc7 are converted to two convolutional layers and the following three scale-different feature layers predict the offsets to default boxes of different scales, aspect ratios and their associated confidences.

For each bounding box, the relationships between its width (w), height (h), scale (s) and aspect ratio (α_r) are expressed as following:

$$w \cdot h = s, \quad \frac{w}{h} = \alpha_r \tag{1}$$

According to bounding box of each target annotated in dataset, α_r can be computed. In SSD scheme [22], aspect ratios are designed as $\alpha_r \in \left\{ 1, 2, 3, \frac{1}{2}, \frac{1}{3} \right\}$, and then the width and height for each default box can be computed as following:

$$w = s\sqrt{\alpha_r}, \qquad h = \frac{s}{\sqrt{\alpha_r}} \tag{2}$$

Suppose that m feature maps are utilized for prediction. For each feature map $k \in [1, m]$, the scale of default boxes is computed as:

$$\begin{cases} s_k = s_{min} + \dfrac{s_{max} - s_{min}}{m - 1}(k - 1), \ \alpha_r \in \left\{ 2, 3, \dfrac{1}{2}, \dfrac{1}{3} \right\}, \\ s_k, and\sqrt{s_k s_{k+1}}, \qquad\qquad\qquad \alpha_r = 1 \end{cases} \tag{3}$$

where $s_{min} = 0.2$ and $s_{max} = 0.9$, meaning the lowest layer has a scale of 0.2 and the highest layer has a scale of 0.9, and all layers in between are regularly spaced.

The center of each default boxes is $\left(\dfrac{i + 0.5}{|f_k|}, \dfrac{j + 0.5}{|f_k|} \right)$, where $|f_k|$ is the size of the k-th square feature map, $i, j \in [0, |f_k|)$.

Channel Attention Module-SE Block. Due to low contrast and brightness of the foggy image captured in complex and changeable marine environment, the edges of targets in image are often blurred and the texture features are not obvious. As shown in Fig. 1, SE module is inserted to the base convolutional layer (conv4-3) and learns the importance of each feature channel through the attention mechanism. Previous works have shown that using feature maps from the lower layers can strengthen feature extraction, since more details of objects are contained in lower layers. The computation processing is summaried in **Algorithm 1**. In this context, the ability of the network to aggregate effective features or feature extraction will be greatly improved.

3   Experiential Results and Analysis

In order to demonstrate the effectiveness and superiority of the proposed G-SEMSSD model, we set groups of comparisonal experiments. More details of experimental procedure are described in the following subsections.

3.1   Experimental Setups

All experiments are conducted on a Linux PC platform with an Intel Core i7-8700K CPU, and a single NVIDIA TITAN Xp GPU (12GB). In addition, both training and testing environments are built in Ubuntu 18.04 operation system running CUDA 10.0 and Python 3.7. The stochastic gradient descent with the initial learning rate $2 \cdot 10^{-3}$ and ending learning rate 10^{-4} is employed. In addition, 50 and 150 epochs are set in freezing and full training stages.

Algorithm 1: Channel attention mechanism SE

Input: feature map $\mathbf{X} \in \mathbb{R}^{\acute{W} \times \acute{H} \times \acute{C}}$, where width, height and channel: $\acute{W}$, $\acute{H}$ and $\acute{C}$

1. /*__Inception__*/   convolutional transformation: $f(\mathbf{X}) = \mathbf{U} \in \mathbb{R}^{W \times H \times C}$

2. /*__Global pooling__*/   calcute mean of feature map: $z = \dfrac{1}{H \times W} \sum_{i=1}^{W} \sum_{j=1}^{H} u(i,j)$

3. /*__Full connection__*/ $fcl1 = \mathbf{W}_1 \mathbf{z}, \mathbf{W}_1 \in \mathbb{R}^{\frac{C}{r} \times C}$, where $r = 16$

4. /*__ReLU__*/ $R = max(0, fcl)$

5. /*__Full connection__*/ $fcl2 = \mathbf{W}_2 \mathbf{R}, \mathbf{W}_2 \in \mathbb{R}^{C \times \frac{C}{r}}$, where $r = 16$

6. /*__sigmoid__*/ $s = \dfrac{1}{e^{fcl2}}$

7. /*__Scale__*/

Output: $\tilde{\mathbf{X}} = s \cdot u$

3.2 Experimental Dataset

In our previous work, we have established a marine vessel dataset and named MVDD13. By virtue of LabelImg tool, objects are annotated by 13 categories, i.e., *cargo, passenger, cruise, bulker, tanker, sailingboat, tug, fishing, drill, fire-fighting, containership, warship* and *submarine*, and their number distribution in MVDD13 and corresponding pinyin abbreviation are shown in Table 2.

In all experiments, 25,541, 2,838 and 7,095 images are used for training, validation and testing sets. The techniques including transfer learning and fine-tuning are implemented on pretrained SSD on PASCAL VOC0712.

3.3 Evaluation Metrics

In the following experiments, the evaluation metrics are used to measure the performance of marine vessel detection models.

Intersection over Union (IoU). The IoU is defined by

$$\text{IoU} = \frac{area(B_p \bigcap B_{gt})}{area(B_p \bigcup B_{gt})} \tag{4}$$

where B_p and B_{gt} are predicted and ground-truth bounding boxes, respectively.

Average Precision (AP). Given an IoU threshold, the Recall and Precision can be determined accordingly. For each ship type, a Precision-Recall (P-R) curve can be governed under an IoU threshold. In this context, the AP defines the area surrounded by the P-R curve $P(R)$ as follows:

$$\text{AP} = \int_0^1 P(R)dR \tag{5}$$

where P and R are Precision and Recall, respectively.

Table 2. Number of objects of each marine vessel category.

Category	Short of Name	Objects	Percentage
cargo	zhc	7,640	0.1871
passenger	kc	5,685	0.1392
cruise	lyl	5,307	0.1299
bulker	shc	5,270	0.1290
tanker	yl	4,589	0.1124
sailingboat	fc	3,830	0.0938
tug	tc	2,733	0.0669
fishing	yc	1,427	0.0349
drill	qzc	1,336	0.0327
firefighting	sjc	1,278	0.0313
containership	jzxc	1,074	0.0263
warship	zc	420	0.0103
submarine	qt	250	0.0061

Mean Average Precision (mAP). Intuitively, the mAP measures the average value of AP over all C categories to be detected, and evaluates the overall performance of a detector by the following equation:

$$\text{mAP} = \sum_{i=1}^{C} \text{AP}_i \Big/ C \qquad (6)$$

where AP_i is the AP of i-th category and C is the number of categories.

3.4   Statistical Characteristics-Based Anchors

In SSD scheme [22], aspect ratios are designed as $\alpha_r \in \left\{1, 2, 3, \frac{1}{2}, \frac{1}{3}\right\}$. It should be noted that the size and shape of prior boxes are closely related with the data, i.e., the ratios of width and height of targets need to be accurately calculated.

We can see from Fig. 4(a) and Fig. 4(b) that the distribution characteristics of aspect ratios is high in the middle and low on both sides. Similar to the normal distribution that the mean $\mu = 2.33$ and variance $\sigma^2 = 1.77$, about 68.2% of targets are in the ratio interval $[\mu - \sigma, \mu + \sigma]$, i.e., interval $[1, 4]$. In other words, most of marine vessel in MVDD13 dataset features long and narrow side. In different feature map layers of SSD scheme, the aspect ratios can be set as different values. By conducting experiments on MVDD13 dataset, the aspect ratios of each feature map layer has been reasonably set, and the specific details in the revised MSSD scheme are clearly shown in Fig. 1 and Table 3.

To thoroughly illustrate that the superiority and effectiveness of the proposed MSSD scheme, the typical SSD framework is utilized to make fair comparison,

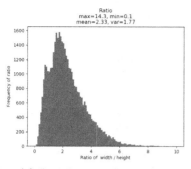

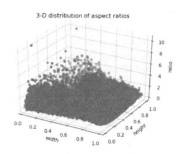

(a) Distribution of aspect ratios   (b) 3D distribution of aspect ratios

Fig. 4. Distributions of aspect ratio in MVDD13 dataset.

Table 3. Comparison of detection results.

Backbone	Model	mAP@.5 (%)	Feature-map layer					
			1	2	3	4	5	6
VGG16	SSD	88.47	$[1,2]$	$[1,2,3]$	$[1,2,3]$	$[1,2,3]$	$[1,2]$	$[1,2]$
	MSSD	**92.17**	$[1,2]$	$[1,2,4]$	$[1,2,3]$	$[1,2,3]$	$[1,2]$	$[1,2]$

and experimental result is summarized in Table 3, whereby the VGG16 is used as backbone, from which we can clearly see that the developed MSSD scheme is 3.7% higher than SSD framework in mAP@.5. It is reasonable to conclude that the use of proper default boxes from the statistical characteristics of data can enhance detection performance of SSD to some extent. This sufficiently illustrated that fine-tunning aspect ratios is truely good to detection for SSD model.

3.5 Ablation Studies and Analysis

To thoroughly illustrate that the superiority and effectiveness of the proposed model in more details, we carried out seven controlled experiments to examine how each component affects performance. The developed models are as follows:

(1) The original SSD module trained on defoggy image by GCANet (i.e., G-SSD),
(2) The default boxes of SSD are designed according to MVDD13 dataset(i.e., MSSD),
(3) The SE module is inserted into SSD convolutional layer (i.e., SESSD),
(4) The SE module is inserted into M-SSD convolutional layer (i.e., SE-MSSD),
(5) The MSSD module trained on defoggy image by GCANet (i.e., G-MSSD),
(6) The SESSD module trained on defoggy image by GCANet (i.e., G-SESSD),
(7) The SE-MSSD module trained on defoggy image by GCANet (i.e., G-SEMSSD).

Different models generated by various design choices on SSD together with corresponding comparisons of performance in terms of mAP@.5, are shown in Table 4.

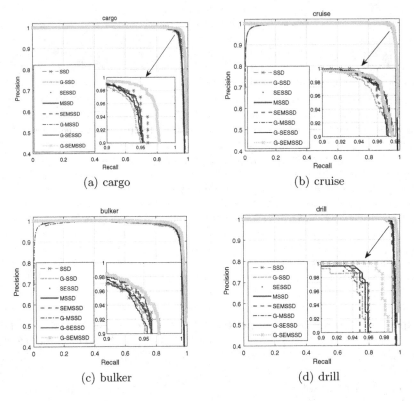

Fig. 5. Detection results of (a) cargo (b) cruise (c) bulker and (d) drill.

In order to sufficiently demonstrate the superiority of GCANet, the training set processed by GCANet is leveraged to train models including SSD, MSSD, SESSD and SE-MSSD, i.e., G-SSD, G-MSSD, G-SESSD and G-SEMSSD. We can see that models trained on training set with GCANet are mostly better than those without GCANet, apart from G-SESSD. The reason might be that there is a conflict in the preservation of image features between GCANet and SE. In fact, as depicted in previous work [37], there is no exact theory to prove that the image after dehazing preprocessing must benefit the detection task.

Compared to original SSD, G-SSD, MSSD and SESSD models surprisingly promote by 1.00%, 3.70% and 3.96% mAP, respectively. It is reasonable to conclude that the three techniques can individually enhance detection performance of SSD to some extent. Specifically, MSSD is significantly more accurate due to the use of proper default boxes from the statistical characteristics of data. Furthermore, G-MSSD improves 3.1% mAP over G-SSD. This sufficiently

Table 4. Detection results of different models for each category.

Model	Technique			mAP @.5 (%)	Marine vessel category												
	G-CANet	AR	SE		zhc	kc	lyl	shc	yl	fc	tc	yc	qzc	sjc	jzxc	zc	qt
SSD				88.47	96.22	90.18	97.09	96.56	94.54	87.85	83.71	75.55	96.39	89.35	83.46	69.45	89.82
G-SSD	✓			89.47	96.83	90.87	97.58	96.33	96.58	89.96	84.23	76.25	96.19	90.14	82.85	78.52	86.75
MSSD		✓		92.17	97.06	92.92	98.20	96.91	**97.40**	90.22	86.67	80.73	97.24	94.04	87.90	85.22	93.73
SESSD			✓	92.43	96.92	92.74	98.16	97.23	97.30	89.71	87.48	81.16	97.14	93.71	88.56	87.17	94.36
SE-MSSD		✓	✓	92.14	97.22	93.00	98.06	96.92	97.26	89.22	86.06	80.36	96.45	95.02	88.29	86.38	93.58
G-SESSD	✓		✓	91.79	97.14	93.18	98.17	96.43	97.16	89.84	86.54	78.47	96.99	94.42	87.97	83.73	93.20
G-MSSD	✓	✓		92.57	97.00	92.97	98.20	96.93	97.33	90.35	87.07	80.49	96.90	95.44	88.37	87.49	94.82
G-SEMSSD	✓	✓	✓	**94.32**	**98.46**	**94.40**	**98.22**	**98.19**	97.19	**94.27**	**89.07**	**86.17**	**98.43**	**97.38**	**90.10**	**88.81**	**95.51**

* Numbers in bold indicate the best results of each category.

illustrated that tunning aspect ratios is truely good to detection, except for similar effects between SESSD and SE-MSSD.

As shown in Table 4, G-SESSD has a significant superiority over G-SSD. Promising results are shown in G-SEMSSD model which gains a dramatic performance 94.32% mAP. To further validate the superiority of SE bolock, the comparisons between SESSD (92.43) and SSD (88.47), SE-MSSD (92.14) and MSSD (92.17), and G-SEMSSD (94.32) and G-MSSD (92.57) are designed. Ignoring the basically same results between SE-MSSD and MSSD, we can clearly see that SSD models with SE block perform really well. In this context, it implies that inserting SE block can effectively enhance the detection performance.

For each category, the effect of different models can be vividly shown in Fig. 5 and 6, wherein the P-R curves with comparisons are based on IOU with threshold 0.5. It should be emphasized that, in some range of precision (here, precision is greater than 0.4), the higher recall the better performance. In this context, for the curves distributed densely in the upper right corners, we enlarge them. We can clearly observe that by using GCANet, AR and SE strategies, the G-SEMSSD model achieves remarkably superior trade-off between precision and recall for all categories. Especially in *caro, drill, sailingboat* and *fishing*, the G-SEMSSD is far superior compared to other models. It should be noticed that these ship types own salient shape feature, i.e., width (height) is greatly more than height (width), fitting better to the new designed default boxes. In addition, we find that *cruise* performs best and robust for each model, since it not only features better aspect ratio, but is less affected by fog.

In summary, the proposed G-SEMSSD model performs remarkable superiority in detection accuracy, and it can be applied in sea fog environment.

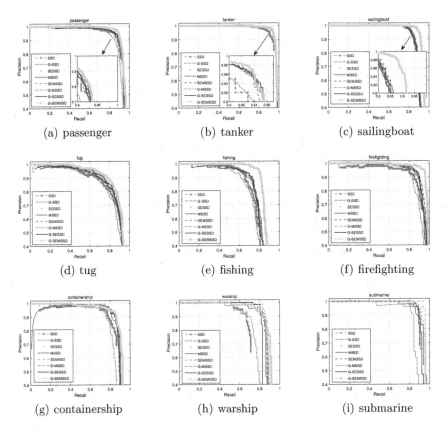

Fig. 6. Detection results of (a) passenger (b) tanker (c) sailingboat (d) tug (e) fishing (f) firefighting and (g) containership (h) warship (i) submarine.

4   Conclusion

In this paper, we propose a marine vessel detection method G-SEMSSD to defend against sea fog environment. By using GCANet defogging preprocessing method, a high accuracy of recognition can be achieved not only in sunny day but in foggy environment. Moreover, the new default boxes elaborately designed by statistical characteristics of data are benefit for detection task. Furthermore, inserting SE module has been devised to significantly strengthen extraction of key features in complex marine environments. Eventually, the G-SEMSSD detection method is established. Comprehensive experiments and comparisons have demonstrated that the model can achieve more accurate detection performance for marine vessel detection in sea fog environment.

References

1. Wang, N., Wang, Y., Er, M.J.: Review on deep learning techniques for marine object recognition: architectures and algorithms. Control. Eng. Pract. **118**(3), 104458 (2022)
2. Huang, H., Zhou, H., Yang, X., Zhang, L., Qi, L., Zang, A.: Faster R-CNN for marine organisms detection and recognition using data augmentation. Neurocomputing **337**, 372–384 (2019)
3. Chen, T., Wang, N., Wang, R., Zhao, H., Zhang, G.: One-stage CNN detector-based benthonic organisms detection with limited training dataset. Neural Netw. **144**, 247–259 (2021)
4. Wang, N., Gao, Y., Yang, C., Zhang, X.: Reinforcement learning-based finite-time tracking control of an unknown unmanned surface vehicle with input constraints. Neurocomputing **484**, 26–37 (2022)
5. Huang, Y., Chen, L., Chen, P., Negenborn, R.R., Van Gelder, P.H.A.J.M.: Ship collision avoidance methods: state-of-the-art. Saf. Sci. **121**, 451–473 (2020)
6. Wang, N., Qian, C., Sun, J., Liu, Y.: Adaptive robust finite-time trajectory tracking control of fully actuated marine surface vehicles. IEEE Trans. Control Syst. Technol. **24**(4), 1454–1462 (2016)
7. Wang, N., Er, M.J.: Direct adaptive fuzzy tracking control of marine vehicles with fully unknown parametric dynamics and uncertainties. IEEE Trans. Control Syst. Technol. **24**(5), 1845–1852 (2016)
8. Wang, N., Karimi, H.R., Li, H., Su, S.-F.: Accurate trajectory tracking of disturbed surface vehicles: a finite-time control approach. IEEE/ASME Trans. Mechatron. **24**(3), 1064–1074 (2019)
9. Lecun, Y., Bottou, L., Bengio, Y., Haffner, P.: Gradient-based learning applied to document recognition. Proc. IEEE **86**(11), 2278–2324 (1998)
10. Krizhevsky, A., Sutskever, I., Hinton, G. E.: Imagenet classification with deep convolutional neural networks. In: Advances in Neural Information Processing Systems, vol. 25 (2012)
11. Russakovsky, O., et al.: Imagenet large scale visual recognition challenge. Int. J. Comput. Vision **115**(3), 211–252 (2015)
12. Girshick, R., Donahue, J., Darrell, T., Malik, J.: Region-based convolutional networks for accurate object detection and segmentation. IEEE Trans. Pattern Anal. Mach. Intell. **38**(1), 142–158 (2016)
13. van de Sande, K.E.A., Uijlings, J.R.R., Gevers, T., Smeulders, A.W.M.: Segmentation as selective search for object recognition. In: IEEE International Conference on Computer Vision, pp. 1879–1886 (2011)
14. He, K., Zhang, X., Ren, S., Sun, J.: Spatial pyramid pooling in deep convolutional networks for visual recognition. IEEE Trans. Pattern Anal. Mach. Intell. **37**(9), 1904–1916 (2015)
15. Girshick, R.: Fast R-CNN. In: IEEE International Conference on Computer Vision, pp. 1440–1448 (2015)
16. Ren, S., He, K., Girshick, R., Sun, J.: Faster R-CNN: towards real-time object detection with region proposal networks. IEEE Trans. Pattern Anal. Mach. Intell. **39**(6), 1137–1149 (2017)
17. Redmon, J., Divvala, S., Girshick, R., Farhadi, A.: You only look once: unified, real-time object detection. In: IEEE Conference on Computer Vision and Pattern Recognition, pp. 779–788 (2016)

18. Redmon, J., Farhadi, A.: Yolo9000: better, faster, stronger. In: IEEE Conference on Computer Vision and Pattern Recognition, pp. 6517–6525 (2017)

19. Redmon, J., Farhadi, A.: Yolov3: an incremental improvement, arXiv preprint arXiv:1804.02767 (2018)

20. Bochkovskiy, A., Wang, C, Liao, H.: Yolov4: optimal speed and accuracy of object detection. arXiv preprint, arXiv:2004.10934 (2020)

21. Lin, T., Goyal, P., Girshick, R., He, K., Dollar, P.: Focal loss for dense object detection. IEEE Trans. Pattern Anal. Mach. Intell. **99**, 2999–3007 (2017)

22. Liu, W., et al.: SSD: single shot MultiBox detector. In: Leibe, B., Matas, J., Sebe, N., Welling, M. (eds.) ECCV 2016. LNCS, vol. 9905, pp. 21–37. Springer, Cham (2016). https://doi.org/10.1007/978-3-319-46448-0_2

23. Tan, M., Pang, R., Le, Q.V.: EfficientDet: scalable and efficient object detection. In: IEEE/CVF Conference on Computer Vision and Pattern Recognition, pp. 10778–10787 (2020)

24. Wang, N., Er, M.J., Sun, J., Liu, Y.: Adaptive robust online constructive fuzzy control of a complex surface vehicle system. IEEE Trans. Cybern. **46**(7), 1511–1523 (2016)

25. Wang, X., Zhang, L., Heath, W.P.: Wind turbine blades fault detection using system identification-based transmissibility analysis. Insight-Non-Destructive Test. Condition Monit. **64**(3), 164–169 (2022)

26. Wang, N., Er, M.J.: Self-constructing adaptive robust fuzzy neural tracking control of surface vehicles with uncertainties and unknown disturbances. IEEE Trans. Control Syst. Technol. **23**(3), 991–1002 (2015)

27. Zuiderveld, K.: Contrast limited adaptive histogram equalization. In: Graphics Gems, pp. 474–485 (1994)

28. Rahman, Z., Jobson, D., Woodell, G.: Retinex processing for automatic image enhancement. J. Electron. Imaging **13**(1), 100–110 (2004)

29. He, K., Sun, J., Tang, X.: Single image haze removal using dark channel prior. IEEE Trans. Pattern Anal. Mach. Intell. **33**(12), 2341–2353 (2010)

30. Zhu, Q., Mai, J., Shao, L.: A fast single image haze removal algorithm using color attenuation prior. IEEE Trans. Image Process. **24**(11), 3522–3533 (2015)

31. Cai, B., Xu, X., Jia, K., Qing, C., Tao, D.: Dehazenet: an end-to-end system for single image haze removal. IEEE Trans. Image Process. **25**(11), 5187–5198 (2016)

32. Li, B., Peng, X., Wang, Z., Xu, J., Feng, D.: An all-in-one network for dehazing and beyond. arXiv preprint arXiv:1707.06543 (2017)

33. Zhang, H., Patel, V.M.: Densely connected pyramid dehazing network. In: Proceedings of the IEEE Conference on Computer Vision and Pattern Recognition, pp. 3194–3203 (2018)

34. Ren, W., et al.: Gated fusion network for single image dehazing. In: Proceedings of the IEEE Conference on Computer Vision and Pattern Recognition, pp. 3253–3261 (2018)

35. Chen, D., et al.: Gated context aggregation network for image dehazing and deraining. In: 2019 IEEE Winter Conference on Applications of Computer Vision, pp. 1375–1383 (2019)

36. Li, C., Guo, C., Guo, J., Han, P., Fu, H., Cong, R.: PDR-Net: perception-inspired single image dehazing network with refinement. IEEE Trans. Multimedia **22**(3), 704–716 (2020)

37. Chen, X., Lu, Y., Wu, Z., Yu, J., Wen, L.: Reveal of domain effect: How visual restoration contributes to object detection in aquatic scenes. arXiv preprint arXiv:2003.01913 (2020)

Sailboat Path Following Control Based on LOS with Sideslip Angle Observation and Finite-Time Backstepping

Kangjian Shao[1], Yujin Wu[1], Ning Wang[2(✉)], and Hongde Qin[1]

[1] Harbin Engineering University, Harbin 150001, China
[2] Dalian Maritime University, Dalian 116026, China
n.wang@ieee.org

Abstract. Suffering from complex sideslip angles, path following control of sailboat becomes significantly challenging. In this article, double finite-time observers-based line-of-sight guidance and finite-time control (DFLOS-FC) scheme is presented for path following of sailboat. Double finite-time sideslip observers (DFSO) are employed to observe the time-varying sideslip angle caused by external disturbances, which improves the accuracy of line-of-sight guidance. To avoid differential explosion problem caused by virtual control law, we designed a finite-time filter. The finite-time disturbance observer (FDO) is designed to accurately observe unknown external disturbances, which enables the controller to have excellent tracking accuracy and precise disturbance rejection. Considering the rotation limit of actuator rudder angle, we limit the rudder angle. The finite-time stability of the integrated guidance and control system is strictly guaranteed by Lyapunov method. Finally, the effectiveness of this method is verified by simulation and comparison with the traditional backstepping method.

Keywords: Sideslip Angle Observation · Line-of-sight Guidance · Finite-time Control · Sailboat · Path following

1 Introduction

As underactuated marine vehicles (USV) play an outstanding role in port protection, mine countermeasures, reconnaissance and surveillance tasks [1], they have attracted wide attention in recent years. When performing a mission, most of the USV's energy is used for propulsion, which reduces the USV's endurance, while the sailboat relies on wind, which reduces energy consumption and is suitable for large-scale and long-term missions. Therefore, the study of unmanned sailboat is of great significance for marine exploration and environmental monitoring.

Autonomous navigation is the core technology of unmanned sailboats, and how to make good decisions and control is a problem to realize autonomous navigation. In [2], Wang proposed an autonomous navigation scheme for the first time for USV that integrates waypoint generation, path smoothing and policy guidance, which perfectly

© ICST Institute for Computer Sciences, Social Informatics and Telecommunications Engineering 2023
Published by Springer Nature Switzerland AG 2023. All Rights Reserved
H. R. Karimi and N. Wang (Eds.): S-Cube 2022, LNICST 487, pp. 63–78, 2023.
https://doi.org/10.1007/978-3-031-34899-0_5

combined decision-making and control. In terms of control, path following is the key technology to achieve autonomous navigation, so it is necessary to study path following control of sailboat. The path following of the sailboat includes guidance and control goals. Guidance is the specific method to guide the sailboat to reach a certain point or reference route; control refers to the execution strategy of implementing the guidance.

The technology of line-of-sight (LOS) guidance is widely used in USV. In [3], LOS was applied to the way-point tracking control. In [4], Li designed integral LOS (ILOS) for underactuated vessels, which successfully implemented point-to-point navigation. In actual navigation, the sideslip angle is complex and time-varying, which affects the accuracy of LOS guidance. In [5], Wan designed a reduced-order state observer, which can estimate the time-varying sideslip angle online, thus improving the accuracy of LOS guidance. In [6], Su proposed an improved adaptive integral LOS (AILOS), which constructed three adaptive variables to replace the unmeasurable current and sideslip angle, and adjusted the adaptive variables online according to the tracking error, thus reducing the error. In [7], the complex sideslip angle is estimated by an improved extended state observe based LOS (ELOS). The precise observation of sideslip angle is of great significance to the path tracking of sailboat, but there are still few related studies.

Due to the uncertainty and complexity of the actual ocean environment, it is difficult to establish an accurate mathematical model for sailboat [8]. For computational convenience, the model is usually simplified. In previous studies, most scholars ignored the rolling motion [9–11], but the sailboat needs to consider the roll response due to the existence of the sail. In [12], Xiao proposed the four-degree-of-freedom mathematical model of keel-sailboat, took roll moment into consideration. However, external disturbances are not considered in [12]. To ensure the accuracy of the simulation, the uncertainty of external disturbances need to be considered [13, 14]. In [15], finite-time differentiator (FTD) was designed for disturbance estimation, and good observation results have been achieved. In [16], Wang designed a single-hidden layer feedforward network based adaptive compensating identifier (SACI), which can compensate for the overall uncertainty. Neural networks and fuzzy logic systems are also commonly used to approximate unknown models and external disturbances [17–20], but neural networks will increase the amount of computation, and fuzzy logic systems are difficult to build. In [21], Rong devised an adaptive nonlinear disturbance observer (NDO) to observe the uncertainty of external disturbances and model, and obtained the accurate observation results. Path following is a key technology in the field of control. Nowadays, the technology about path following is becoming more and more mature. In [22], a coordinated trajectory-tracking control (CTTC) scheme was designed for path following of marine aerial-surface heterogeneous (MASH) system, and high tracking accuracy was obtained. In [16], Wang proposed a finite-time unknown observer-based interactive trajectory tracking control (FUO-ITTC) scheme, which has remarkable performance in terms of transient and steady-state tracking accuracy. In [23], accurate trajectory tracking problem of a surface vehicle disturbed by complex marine environments is solved by creating a finite-time control (FTC) scheme, and both disturbance observation and trajectory tracking errors can exactly reach to zero in a finite time. But finite-time stability of heading control system is also not taken into account by the existing methods.

Driven by the above observations, the double finite-time observers-based LOS guidance and finite-time control (DFLOS-FC) scheme is proposed, and the contributions of this article are summarized as follows:

(1) The DFSO devised in this paper can observe time-varying sideslip angle, which can be applied to more complex working conditions.
(2) In order to prevent the large amount of computation caused by the direct derivation of the virtual control law, a finite-time filter is introduced in this paper.
(3) The finite-time disturbance observer (FDO) is introduced to compensate for external disturbances, so that the controller has high control accuracy.

This paper is arranged as follows: In Sect. 2, the problem formulation and some preliminaries are put forward. We design double finite-time sideslip angle observers for sideslip observation in Sect. 3. Section 4 presents the design and stability analysis of the sailboat controller. In Sect. 5, the simulation is carried out. Conclusions are drawn in Sect. 6.

2 Preliminaries and Problem Formulations

2.1 Preliminaries

Lemma 1: ([23]) For system

$$\dot{x} = f(x) \tag{1}$$

Suppose there exist a continuously differentiable function $V(x)$, which satisfies

$$\dot{V}(x) \leq -aV(x) - bV^\rho(x) + c \tag{2}$$

where $a > 0, b > 0, 0 < \rho < 1, 0 < c < \infty$.

Then the trajectory of system $\dot{x} = f(x)$ can achieve finite time stability. In addition, the finite setting time T_f satisfies

$$T_f = \max\left\{ t_0 + \frac{1}{a\theta_0(1-l)} \ln \frac{\theta_0 a V^{1-\rho}(t_0) + b}{b}, t_0 + \frac{1}{a(1-l)} \ln \frac{aV^{1-\rho}(t_0) + \theta_0 b}{\theta_0 b} \right\} \tag{3}$$

Lemma 2: ([24]) The following system:

$$
\begin{aligned}
\dot{\sigma}_0 &= -\lambda_0 L^{1/(n+1)} |\sigma_0|^{n/(n+1)} sign(\sigma_0) + \sigma_1 \\
\dot{\sigma}_1 &= -\lambda_1 L^{1/n} |\sigma_1 - \dot{\sigma}_0|^{(n-1)/n} sign(\sigma_1 - \dot{\sigma}_0) + \sigma_2 \\
&\vdots \\
\dot{\sigma}_{n-1} &= -\lambda_{n-1} L^{1/2} |\sigma_{n-1} - \dot{\sigma}_{n-2}|^{1/2} sign(\sigma_{n-1} - \dot{\sigma}_{n-2}) + \sigma_n \\
\dot{\sigma}_n &\in -\lambda_n L sign(\sigma_{n-1} - \dot{\sigma}_{n-2}) + [-L, L]
\end{aligned}
\tag{4}
$$

is finite-time stable, where $L > 0, \lambda_i > 0, i = 0, 1, 2, ..., n$.

2.2 Problem Formulations

As shown in Fig. 1, taking a 4-DOF sailboat as an example, its motion can be described by body-referenced frame and inertial-referenced frame. The 4-DOF sailboat kinematic and kinetic model can be expressed as follows [12]:

$$
\begin{cases}
\dot{x} = u\cos(\psi) - v\cos(\phi)\sin(\psi) \\
\dot{y} = u\sin(\psi) + v\cos(\phi)\cos(\psi) \\
\dot{\phi} = p \\
\dot{\psi} = r\cos(\phi)
\end{cases}
\tag{5}
$$

$$
\begin{cases}
m_u\dot{u} = F_{Su} + F_{Ru} - F_{Ku} + m_v vr - F_{Du} + d_{wu} \\
m_v\dot{v} = F_{Sv} + F_{Rv} - F_{Kv} + m_u ur - F_{Dv} + d_{wv} \\
m_p\dot{p} = M_{Sp} + M_{Rp} - M_{Kp} - c|p|p - a\phi^2 - b\phi - M_{Dp} + d_{wp} \\
m_r\dot{r} = M_{Sr} + M_{Rr} - M_{Kr} - (X_{\dot{u}} - Y_{\dot{v}})uv - M_{Dr} - d|r|r\cos(\phi) + d_{wr}
\end{cases}
\tag{6}
$$

where $m_u = m - X_{\dot{u}}$, $m_v = m - Y_{\dot{v}}$, $m_p = I_{xx} - K_{\dot{p}}$, $m_r = I_{zz} - N_{\dot{r}}$, and the forces and torques generated by the rudder, sail, keel and hull of the sailboat are denoted as F_{ij} and M_{ij} ($i = R, S, K, D, j = u, v, p, r$). $d_{wi}(i = u, v, p, r)$ are external disturbances. (x, y) and (ϕ, ψ) represent the position and direction of the sailing boat respectively. (u, v) denotes linear velocity and (p, r) denotes angular velocity.

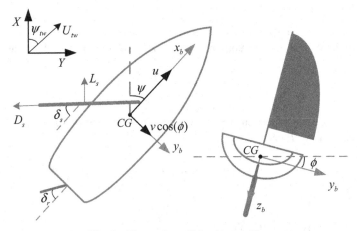

Fig. 1. Illustration of kinetic variables

The attack angle of sail is

$$
\alpha_s = \alpha_{aw} - \delta_s
\tag{7}
$$

where α_w is apparent wind angle, δ_s is sail angle.

The lift and drag forces of the sail can be written as

$$\begin{cases} L_s = \dfrac{1}{2}\rho_a A_s V_{as}^2 C_{Ls}(\alpha_s) \\[2mm] D_s = \dfrac{1}{2}\rho_a A_s V_{as}^2 C_{Ds}(\alpha_s) \end{cases} \tag{8}$$

where ρ_a is air density, V_{as} is apparent wind speed, A_s denotes the area of the sail, the coefficients of lift and drag are denoted as $C_{Ls}(\alpha_s)$, $C_{Ds}(\alpha_s)$.

Assuming that there is no effect of current, we get $\alpha_s = -\delta_r$. The steering moment generated by the rudder can be written as

$$M_{Rr} = -\frac{1}{2}\rho_w A_r V_{ar}^2 |x_r| C_{Lr}(-\delta_r) \tag{9}$$

where ρ_w denotes seawater density, A_r denotes the area of the rudder, x_r denotes the value of the rudder's center of gravity on the x-axis in the body-referenced frame. V_{ar} denotes the apparent speed of the rudder and $C_{Lr}(-\delta_r)$ denotes the lift coefficient of the rudder. And one can get more details on the model in [12].

According to the manual sailing experience, the value range of the apparent wind angle of tacking is $0° \sim \pm30°$ and the value range of the apparent wind angle of windward sailing is $\pm30° \sim \pm160°$. The sail angle is set to $0°$, the sail angle is set by linear interpolation and the rotation limit of the sail angle is set as $\pm90°$. The apparent wind angle of gybing is $\pm160° \sim \pm180°$, then the sail angle is set to $\pm90°$.

3 Sideslip Angle Observation and Line-Of-Sight Guidance

In this section, double finite-time sideslip observers are designed for sideslip angle observation.

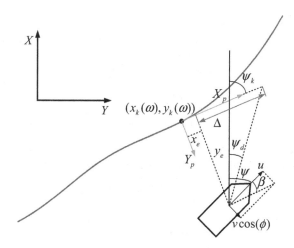

Fig. 2. Framework of LOS guidance

As shown in Fig. 2, ω is the path parameter variable, which determines the shape of the path. $(x_k(\omega), y_k(\omega))$ is a point on the prescribed path, the tangent angle of any point on the path can be denoted as $\psi_k = ac\tan(y_k'/x_k')$, and (x, y) is the current position of the sailboat. Then the position error can be described as

$$\begin{bmatrix} x_e \\ y_e \end{bmatrix} = \begin{bmatrix} \cos(\psi_k) & \sin(\psi_k) \\ -\sin(\psi_k) & \cos(\psi_k) \end{bmatrix} \cdot \begin{bmatrix} x - x_k(\omega) \\ y - y_k(\omega) \end{bmatrix} \tag{10}$$

The time derivative of (10) is

$$\begin{cases} \dot{x}_e = (\dot{x} - \dot{x}_k)\cos(\psi_k) + (\dot{y} - \dot{y}_k)\sin(\psi_k) + \dot{\psi}_k y_e \\ \dot{y}_e = -(\dot{x} - \dot{x}_k)\sin(\psi_k) + (\dot{y} - \dot{y}_k)\cos(\psi_k) + \dot{\psi}_k y_e \end{cases} \tag{11}$$

Substituting (9) into (11), we have:

$$\begin{cases} \dot{x}_e = U\cos(\psi - \psi_k + \beta) + \dot{\psi}_k y_e - u_p \\ \dot{y}_e = U\sin(\psi - \psi_k + \beta) - \dot{\psi}_k x_e \end{cases} \tag{12}$$

where the resultant speed of the sailboat is denoted as $U = \sqrt{u^2 + (v\cos(\phi))^2}$, $\beta = arc\tan(v\cos(\phi)/u)$ is sideslip angle of sailboat, and $u_p = \dot{\omega}\sqrt{x_k'^2 + y_k'^2}$ denotes the speed of the virtual target point.

The speed u_p can be selected as

$$u_p = U\cos\left(\psi - \psi_k + \hat{\beta}\right) + k_x x_e$$

$$\dot{\omega} = \frac{U\cos\left(\psi - \psi_r + \hat{\beta}\right) + k_x x_e}{\sqrt{x_r'^2 + y_r'^2}} \tag{13}$$

where k_x is a positive tuning parameter.

Double finite-time sideslip angle observer is designed as

$$\begin{cases} \dot{\hat{x}}_e = -\lambda_1 \mathrm{sig}^{4/5}(\tilde{x}_e) + \hat{h}_1 + \dot{\psi}_k y_e - u_p \\ \dot{\hat{h}}_1 = -\lambda_2 \mathrm{sig}^{3/5}(\tilde{x}_e) + \vartheta_1 \mathrm{sign}(\tilde{x}_e) \end{cases} \tag{14}$$

$$\begin{cases} \dot{\hat{y}}_e = -\lambda_3 \mathrm{sig}^{4/5}(\tilde{y}_e) + \hat{h}_2 - \dot{\psi}_k x_e \\ \dot{\hat{h}}_2 = -\lambda_4 \mathrm{sig}^{3/5}(\tilde{y}_e) + \vartheta_2 \mathrm{sign}(\tilde{y}_e) \end{cases} \tag{15}$$

where $h_1 = U\cos(\psi - \psi_k + \beta)$, $h_2 = U\sin(\psi - \psi_k + \beta)$, $\lambda_i (i = 1, 2, 3, 4)$ and $\vartheta_j (j = 1, 2)$ are tuning parameters, $\hat{x}_e, \hat{h}_1, \hat{y}_e$ and $\hat{h}_2$ are the estimates of x_e, h_1, y_e and h_2. Let $\tilde{x}_e = \hat{x}_e - x_e, \tilde{h}_1 = \hat{h}_1 - h_1, \tilde{y}_e = \hat{y}_e - y_e, \tilde{h}_2 = \hat{h}_2 - h_2$, the time derivative of $\tilde{x}_e, \tilde{h}_1, \tilde{y}_e, \tilde{h}_2$ are

$$\begin{cases} \dot{\tilde{x}}_e = -\lambda_1 \mathrm{sig}^{4/5}(\tilde{x}_e) + \tilde{h}_1 \\ \dot{\tilde{h}}_1 = -\lambda_2 \mathrm{sig}^{3/5}(\tilde{x}_e) \end{cases} \tag{16}$$

$$\begin{cases} \dot{\tilde{y}}_e = -\lambda_3 \mathrm{sig}^{4/5}(\tilde{y}_e) + \tilde{h}_2 \\ \dot{\tilde{h}}_2 = -\lambda_4 \mathrm{sig}^{3/5}(\tilde{y}_e) \end{cases} \qquad (17)$$

According to [25], there is a finite time $0 < T_\beta < \infty$ that makes $\hat{x}_e \equiv x_e$, $\hat{h}_1 \equiv h_1$, $\hat{y}_e \equiv y_e$, $\hat{h}_2 \equiv h_2$. The estimated sideslip angle is

$$\hat{\beta} = \arcsin\left(\frac{\hat{h}_2 \cos(\psi - \psi_k) - \hat{h}_1 \sin(\psi - \psi_k)}{U}\right) \qquad (18)$$

Then the error of sideslip angle is expressed as

$$\tilde{\beta} = \arcsin\left(\frac{\tilde{h}_2 \cos(\psi - \psi_k) - \tilde{h}_1 \sin(\psi - \psi_k)}{U}\right) \qquad (19)$$

Therefore, the observed error of sideslip angle converges to zero in finite time. The LOS method tracking angle is expressed as

$$\psi_d = \psi_k - \arctan\left(\frac{y_e}{\Delta}\right) - \hat{\beta} \qquad (20)$$

where Δ denotes a look-ahead distance.

Substituting (13) and (20) into (12), we have

$$\begin{cases} \dot{x}_e = -k_x x_e + \dot{\psi}_k y_e \\ \dot{y}_e = -\dfrac{U y_e}{\sqrt{y_e^2 + \Delta^2}} \cos(\tilde{\beta} + \tilde{\psi}) - \dfrac{U \Delta}{\sqrt{y_e^2 + \Delta^2}} \sin(\tilde{\beta} + \tilde{\psi}) - \dot{\psi}_k x_e \end{cases} \qquad (21)$$

Choose the Lyapunov function $V_1 = \frac{1}{2}x_e^2 + \frac{1}{2}y_e^2$, and the derivative of V_1 gives:

$$\begin{aligned}
\dot{V}_1 &= x_e \dot{x}_e + y_e \dot{y}_e \\
&= -k_x x_e^2 + \dot{\psi}_k y_e x_e - \frac{U y_e^2}{\sqrt{y_e^2 + \Delta^2}} \cos(\tilde{\beta} + \tilde{\psi}) \\
&\quad - \frac{U \Delta y_e}{\sqrt{y_e^2 + \Delta^2}} \sin(\tilde{\beta} + \tilde{\psi}) - \dot{\psi}_k x_e y_e \\
&\leq -k_x x_e^2 + 2U_{\max}(|y_e| + \Delta) \\
&= -k_x x_e^2 - k_x y_e^2 + 2U_{\max}(|y_e| + \Delta) + k_x y_e^2 \\
&= -k_x V_1 + 2U_{\max}(|y_e| + \Delta) + k_x y_e^2 \qquad (22)
\end{aligned}$$

where $U_{\max}$ is the maximum of U, consider the sets $\Omega_s = \{(x_e, y_e)|x_e^2 + y_e^2 \leq \sigma_s\}$, where σ_s is a positive constant. (18) can be expressed by $\dot{V}_1 = -k_x V_1 + \Delta_e$, and $\Delta_e = 2U_{\max}(|y_e| + \Delta) + k_x y_e^2$.

4 Heading Control

4.1 Finite-Time Controller Design

The 4-DOF model of the sailboat is simplified to:

$$\dot{\psi} = r\cos(\phi)$$
$$m_r\dot{r} = M_{Sr} + F_r\delta_r - M_{Kr} - (X_{\dot{u}} - Y_{\dot{v}})uv - M_{Dr} - d|r|r\cos(\phi) + dwr \tag{23}$$

Simplification of rudder lift coefficient in this paper refer to [16].
The tracking error is defined as:

$$z_1 = \psi - \psi_d \tag{24}$$

Choosing the following appropriate virtual control laws:

$$\alpha_r = \frac{1}{\cos(\phi)}(-k_1 z_1 + \dot{\psi}_d - \beta_1 sig^{\gamma}(z_1)) \tag{25}$$

where k_0 is tuning parameter.

To avoid the "explosion of complexity", we replace $\dot{\theta}$ with $\dot{\alpha}_r$, and the finite-time filter is devised as

$$\begin{cases} \dot{\theta} = l \\ l = -\zeta_1|\theta - \alpha_r|^{\frac{1}{2}}sign(\theta - \alpha_r) + \sigma_1 \\ \dot{\sigma}_1 = -\zeta_2 sign(\sigma_1 - l) \end{cases} \tag{26}$$

Lemma 3: ([26]) In the absence of input noise ($a_r = a_{r0}$), the filter is stable in finite time by choosing appropriate parameters ζ_1 and ζ_2, and meet:

$$\sigma_1 = \alpha_{r0}, l = \dot{\alpha}_{r0} \tag{27}$$

Lemma 4: ([26]) Considering that the input noise satisfies $|\alpha_r - \alpha_{r0}| \leq \kappa$, the following inequality can be realized in finite time:

$$|\sigma_1 - \alpha_{r0}| \leq \varpi_1\kappa$$
$$|l - \dot{\alpha}_{r0}| \leq \varpi_2\kappa^{\frac{1}{2}} \tag{28}$$

where ϖ_1, ϖ_2 are positive constants.

Define tracking error of α_r:

$$y_r = \theta - \alpha_r \tag{29}$$

Define error variable z_2 as follows

$$z_2 = r - \theta \tag{30}$$

The finite-time disturbance observer is devised as follows:

$$
\begin{aligned}
m_r \dot{\hat{r}} &= A_1 + M_{Sr} + M_{Rr} - M_{Kr} - (X_{\dot{u}} - Y_{\dot{v}})uv - M_{Dr} - d|r|r\cos(\phi) \\
A_1 &= -\lambda_5 L_d^{1/2} sig^{1/2}(m_r\hat{r} - m_r r) + \hat{d}_{wr} \\
\dot{\hat{d}}_{wr} &= -\lambda_6 L_d \, \text{sgn}(\hat{d}_{wr} - A_1)
\end{aligned}
\tag{31}
$$

where λ_5, λ_6, L are positive constants.

Define error:

$$
m_r \tilde{r} = m_r \hat{r} - m_r r
\tag{32}
$$

$$
\tilde{d}_{wr} = \hat{d}_{wr} - d_{wr}
\tag{33}
$$

Derivation of the above error gives:

$$
\begin{aligned}
m_r \dot{\tilde{r}} &= -\lambda_5 L_d^{1/2} sig^{1/2}(m_r\hat{r} - m_r r) + \hat{d}_{wr} + M_{Sr} + M_{Rr} - M_{Kr} \\
&\quad - (X_{\dot{u}} - Y_{\dot{v}})uv - M_{Dr} - d|r|r\cos(\phi) - m_r \dot{r} \\
&= -\lambda_5 L_d^{1/2} sig^{1/2}(m_r\tilde{r}) + \tilde{d}_{wr}
\end{aligned}
\tag{34}
$$

$$
\dot{\tilde{d}}_{wr} = -\lambda_6 L_d \, sign(\hat{d}_{wr} - A_1) - \dot{d}_{wr}
\tag{35}
$$

According to the lemma 2, the error of disturbance observation converges to zero in a finite time.

The control law is chosen as

$$
\begin{aligned}
\alpha_M &= -M_{Sr} + M_{Kr} + (X_{\dot{u}} - Y_{\dot{v}})uv + M_{Dr} + d|r|r\cos(\phi) \\
&\quad + (-k_2 z_2 - k_3 sig^\gamma(z_2) + \dot{\theta})m_r - \hat{d}_{wr}
\end{aligned}
\tag{36}
$$

$$
\delta_r' = \arcsin\left(\frac{2\alpha_M}{-1.2\rho A_R v_{ar}^2 |x_r|}\right)
\tag{37}
$$

Considering the rotation limit of the actuator rudder angle, limit the rudder angle:

$$
\delta_r =
\begin{cases}
\delta_r', & |\delta_r'| < \frac{\pi}{6} \\
\frac{\pi}{6} sign(\delta_r'), & |\delta_r'| \geq \frac{\pi}{6}
\end{cases}
\tag{38}
$$

4.2 Stability Analysis

Select the following Lyapunov function:

$$
V = \frac{1}{2}z_1^2 + \frac{1}{2}z_2^2
\tag{39}
$$

Taking the derivation of the Lyapunov function, we get:

$$
\dot{V} = z_1(\dot{\psi} - \dot{\psi}_d) + z_2(\dot{z}_2 - \dot{\theta})
$$

$$= z_1[(z_2 + y_r + \alpha)\cos(\phi) - \dot{\psi}_d] + z_2(\dot{z}_2 - \dot{\theta})$$

$$= z_1 z_2 \cos(\phi) + z_1 y_r \cos(\phi) - k_1 z_1^2 - \beta_1(z_1^2)^{\frac{\gamma+1}{2}} - k_2 z_2^2 - k_3(z_1^2)^{\frac{\gamma+1}{2}} \tag{40}$$

It is known that the heel angle of the sailboat is bounded and will not exceed plus or minus $\frac{\pi}{2}$, so $0 < \cos(\phi) \le 1$, the formula (36) can be simplified to:

$$\dot{V} \le z_1 z_2 + z_1 y_r - k_1 z_1^2 - \beta_1(z_1^2)^{\frac{\gamma+1}{2}} - k_2 z_2^2 - k_3(z_1^2)^{\frac{\gamma+1}{2}} \tag{41}$$

According to Young's inequality

$$z_1 z_2 \le \frac{1}{2}z_1^2 + \frac{1}{2}z_2^2 \tag{42}$$

$$z_1 y_r \le \frac{1}{2}z_1^2 + \frac{1}{2}y_r^2 \tag{43}$$

By Lemma 3 and Lemma 4,y_r is a bounded value, so it has $|y_r| \le d_1$.We have

$$\dot{V}_1 \le \frac{1}{2}z_1^2 + \frac{1}{2}z_2^2 + \frac{1}{2}z_1^2 + \frac{1}{2}y_r^2 - k_1 z_1^2 - \beta_1(z_1^2)^{\frac{\gamma+1}{2}} - k_2 z_2^2 - k_3(z_1^2)^{\frac{\gamma+1}{2}}$$

$$\le -(k_1 - 1)z_1^2 - \beta_1(z_1^2)^{\frac{\gamma+1}{2}} - (k_2 - \frac{1}{2})z_2^2 - k_3(z_1^2)^{\frac{\gamma+1}{2}} + \frac{1}{2}d_1^2 \tag{44}$$

From formula (40), the following inequality can be obtained:

$$\dot{V} \le -aV - bV^{\frac{\gamma+1}{2}} + c \tag{45}$$

where $a = \min\{k_1 - 1, k_2 - \frac{1}{2}\}$, $b = \min\{\beta_1 2^{\frac{\gamma+1}{2}}, k_3 2^{\frac{\gamma+1}{2}}\}$, $c = \frac{1}{2}d_1^2$, according to the lemma 1, it can be known that the heading tracking system is stable in a limited time.

As shown in Fig. 3, DFLOS-AFC scheme and manual experience controls sail are combined for path following of sailboat.

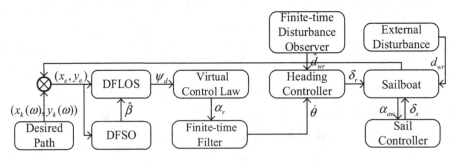

Fig. 3. Framework of sailboat control

5   Simulation Studies

To verify the feasibility of DFLOS-FC scheme, simulation study is conducted with 12 m class sailboat in [10]. The unknown external disturbances are assumed as follows

$$
\begin{cases}
d_{wu} = 500[0.2\cos(0.1t) + 0.4\sin(0.5t + \frac{\pi}{6}) + 0.8\sin(t + \frac{\pi}{3})] \\
d_{wv} = 600[0.2\sin(0.1t) + 0.4\cos(0.5t + \frac{\pi}{6}) + 0.8\sin(t + \frac{\pi}{3})] \\
d_{wp} = 100[0.2\sin(0.1t) + 0.8\sin(0.5t + \frac{\pi}{6}) + 0.4\cos(t + \frac{\pi}{3})] \\
d_{wr} = 200[0.2\sin(0.1t) + 0.4\sin(0.5t + \frac{\pi}{6}) + 0.8\sin(t + \frac{\pi}{3})]
\end{cases}
\tag{46}
$$

The wind speed and the wind angle are set to 5m/s and $\psi_{tw} = 0°$ respectively, and the parametric reference path is devised as

$$
\begin{cases}
x_k(\omega) = 70\sin(0.01\omega) + 0.7\omega \\
y_k(\omega) = 0.7\omega
\end{cases}
\tag{47}
$$

The design parameters of the DFLOS-FC scheme are chosen as follows: $k_x = 0.1$, $\lambda_1 = 4$, $\lambda_2 = 40$, $\lambda_3 = 4$, $\lambda_4 = 40$, $\vartheta_1 = 0.05$, $\vartheta_2 = 0.05$, $\Delta = 30$, $k_1 = 0.9$,

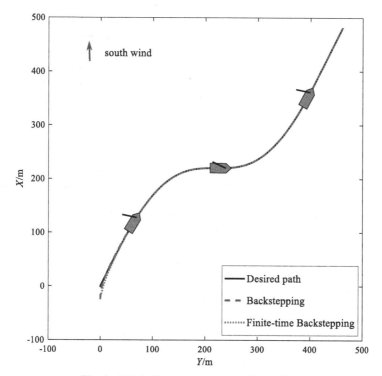

Fig. 4. Path following performance for sailboat

$\beta_1 = 0.01$, $\gamma = 0.6$, $\zeta_1 = 0.09$, $\zeta_2 = 0.001$, $\lambda_5 = 10$, $\lambda_6 = 10$, $L_d = 20$, $k_2 = 3$, $k_3 = 0.1$. Initial position of sailboat is $[-25 \text{ m}, 0 \text{ m}]$, and the remaining initial values are set to 0.

The simulation results of DFLOS-FC scheme are provided in Figs. 4, 5, 6, 7, 8, 9 and 10. In Fig. 4, the DFLOS-FC scheme achieves better performance in path following. As shown in Fig. 5, both along- and cross-track errors of DFLOS-FC can converge to zero in a shorter time. Compared with the traditional backstepping method, DFLOS-FC has better convergence effect and does not produce jitter. In Fig. 6, The convergence speed of DFLOS-FC is faster than that of traditional backstepping method. The estimated sideslip angle is shown in Fig. 7. Figure 8 shows that the designed finite time disturbance observer can accurately observe external disturbance. The variation of rudder angle and sail angle with time is shown in Fig. 9. As shown in Fig. 10, the maximum roll angle does not exceed 30°, which is in line with the sailing practice.

The presented results clearly indicate that the proposed DFLOS-FC schemes work well for path following of sailboat.

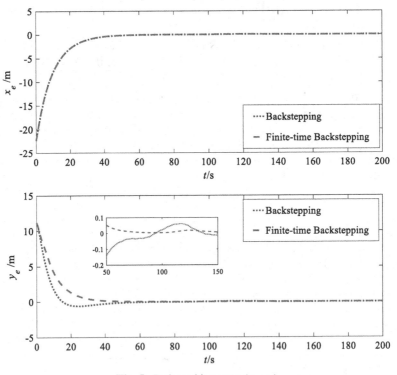

Fig. 5. Path tracking error (x_e, y_e)

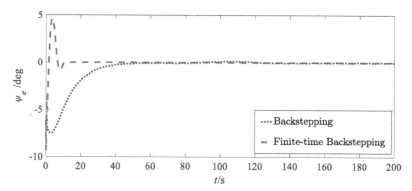

Fig. 6. Heading tracking error (ψ_e)

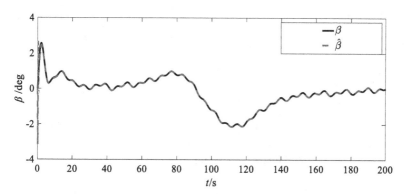

Fig. 7. Sideslip angle observation

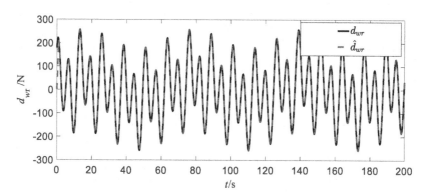

Fig. 8. External disturbance observation

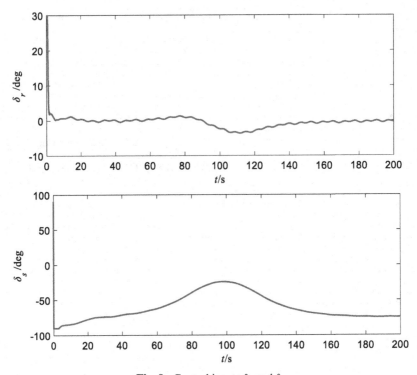

Fig. 9. Control inputs δ_r and δ_s

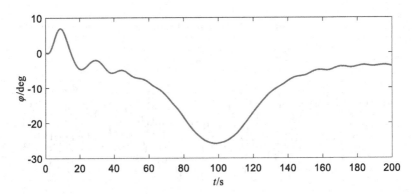

Fig. 10. Variation of sailboat roll angle

6   Conclusion

In this paper, considering the problem of accurate path following of sailboat under no upwind sailing, a LOS guidance framework based on double finite-time sideslip angle observers is proposed. The time-varying sideslip angle is accurately estimated by the DFSO, and the observation error can converge to the origin at short notice. The simulation results show that the designed DFLOS-FC has higher path tracking accuracy and smaller horizontal and vertical tracking errors. In the heading control system, the external disturbance is estimated by finite-time disturbance observer to reduce the computational complexity of the system. Eventually, Compared with the ordinary backstepping method, the designed DFLOS-FC converges faster and has a good convergence effect.

References

1. Manley, J.: Unmanned surface vehicles, 15 years of development. In: OCEANS 2008 Conference, Quebec City, Canada, pp. 1–3 (2008)
2. Wang, N., Zhang, Y.: Autonomous pilot of unmanned surface vehicles: Bridging path planning and tracking. IEEE Trans. Veh. Technol. **71**(3), 2358–2374 (2022)
3. Pettersen, K., Lefeber, A.: Way-point tracking control of ships. In: IEEE Conference on Decision and Control, Orlando, FL, USA, pp. 940–946. IEEE (2001)
4. Li, J., Lee, P., Jun, B., Lim, Y.: Point-to-point navigation of underactuated ships. Automatica **44**(12), 3201–3205 (2008)
5. Wan, L., Su, Y., Zhang, H.: An improved integral light-of-sight guidance law for path following of unmanned surface vehicles. Ocean Eng. **205**(3), 3–6 (2020)
6. Su, Y., Wan, L.: An improved adaptive integral line-of-sight guidance law for unmanned surface vehicles with uncertainties. Appl. Ocean Res. **108**(5), 3–7 (2020)
7. Liu, Z.: Improved ELOS based path following control for underactuated surface vessels with roll constraint. Ocean Eng. **245**(1), 2–8 (2022)
8. Wang, N., Gao, Y., Zhang, X.: Data-driven performance-prescribed reinforcement learning control of an unmanned surface vehicle. IEEE Trans. Neural Netw. Learn. Syst. **32**(12), 5456–5467 (2021)
9. Dos Santos, D., Goncalves, L.: A gain-scheduling control strategy and short-term path optimization with genetic algorithm for autonomous navigation of a sailboat robot. Int. J. Adv. Rob. Syst. **16**(1), 2–7 (2019)
10. Viel, C., Vautier, U., Wan, J., Jaulin, L.: Position keeping control of an autonomous sailboat. IFAC-PapersOnLine **51**(29), 14–19 (2018)
11. Wille, K., Hassani, V., Sprenger, F.: Modeling and course control of sailboats. IFAC PapersOnLine **49**(23), 532–539 (2016)
12. Xiao, L., Jouffroy, J.: Modeling and nonlinear heading control of sailing yachts. IEEE J. Oceanic Eng. **39**(2), 256–268 (2014)
13. Wang, N., Qian, C., Sun, J.C.: Adaptive robust finite-time trajectory tracking control of fully actuated marine surface vehicles. IEEE Trans. Control Syst. Technol. **24**(4), 1454–1462 (2016)
14. Wang, N., Karimi, H.R., Li, H.: Accurate trajectory tracking of disturbed surface vehicles: a finite-time control approach. IEEE/ASME Trans. Mechatron. **24**(3), 1064–1074 (2019)
15. Hou, Q., Ma, L.: Composite finite-time straight-line path-following control of an underactuated surface vessel. ScienceDirect **357**(16), 11496–11517 (2020)
16. Wang, N., He, H.: Extreme learning-based monocular visual servo of an unmanned surface vessel. IEEE Trans. Industr. Inf. **17**(8), 5152–5163 (2021)
17. Deng, Y., Zhang, X., Zhang, Q., Hu, Y.: Event-triggered composite adaptive fuzzy control of sailboat with heeling constraint. Ocean Eng. **211**(1), 2–5 (2020)
18. Wang, N., Er, M.J.: Self-Constructing adaptive robust fuzzy neural tracking control of surface vehicles with uncertainties and unknown disturbances. IEEE Trans. Control Syst. Technol. **23**(3), 991–1002 (2015)
19. Wang, N., Meng, J.E.: Direct adaptive fuzzy tracking control of marine vehicles with fully unknown parametric dynamics and uncertainties. IEEE Trans. Control Syst. Technol. **24**(5), 1845–2185 (2016)

20. Wang, N., Er, M.: Adaptive robust online constructive fuzzy control of a complex surface vehicle system. IEEE Trans. Cybern. **46**(7), 1511–1523 (2016)
21. Cui, R., Zhang, X., Cui, D.: Adaptive sliding-mode attitude control for autonomous underwater vehicles with input nonlinearities. Ocean Eng. **123**(1), 45–54 (2016)
22. Wang, N., Su, S.: Finite-time unknown observer based interactive trajectory tracking control of asymmetric underactuated surface vehicles. IEEE Trans. Control Syst. Technol. **29**(2), 794–803 (2021)
23. Yu, J., Shi, P., Zhao, L.: Finite-time command filtered backstepping control for a class of nonlinear systems. Automatica **92**, 173–180 (2018)
24. Shtessel, Y., Shkolnikov, I., Levant, A.: Smooth second-order sliding modes: missile guidance application. Automatica **43**(8), 1470–1476 (2007)
25. Basin, M., Yu, P., Shtessel, Y.: Finite- and fixed-time differentiators utilising HOSM techniques. IET Control Theory Appl. **11**(8), 1144–1152 (2016)
26. Zhao, L., Yu, J., Lin, C., Ma, Y.: Adaptive neural consensus tracking for nonlinear multiagent systems using finite-time command filtered backstepping. IEEE Trans. Syst. Man Cybern. Syst. **48**(11), 2003–2012 (2018)

Resilience Control Systems

An Improved Regression Partial Least Squares Method for Quality-Related Process Monitoring of Industrial Control Systems

Zhiqiang Zhang[1], Wenxiao Gao[2], Danlu Yu[3], and Aihua Zhang[1(⊠)]

[1] College of Physical Science and Technology, Bohai University, Jinzhou 121013, Liaoning, China
jsxinxi_zah@163.com
[2] Dalian Maritime University, Dalian 116026, Liaoning, China
[3] College of Control Science and Engineering, Bohai University, Jinzhou 121013, Liaoning, China

Abstract. Partial least squares (PLS) is a widely used and effective method in the field of fault detection. However, due to the fact that the standard PLS decomposes the process variable space into two subspaces which are not completely orthogonal, it is insufficient in quality-related fault detection. To solve this problem, principal component regression (PCR) is used to decompose the quality variables of PLS model and realize the reconstruction of the process variable space. In this way, the process variable space is decomposed into highly correlated and highly irrelevant parts of quality variables, and the two are monitored by designing statistics respectively. Furthermore, an adaptive threshold based on the idea of exponential weighted moving average (EWMA) is introduced to reduce the false positives and missed positives caused by the traditional fixed threshold, and this method is named as improved regression partial least squares (RPLS). Finally, linear and nonlinear numerical examples and Tennessee Eastman (TE) processes are used to verify the effectiveness of the proposed method which named improved regression partial least squares (IRPLS). Finally, linear and nonlinear numerical cases and Tennessee Eastman (TE) processes are used to verify the effectiveness of IRPLS. The results show that the proposed method can effectively improve the fault detection rate and algorithm follow-through performance, and reduce false positives.

Keywords: PLS · PCR · EWMA · IRPLS · TE

1 Introduction

With the integration and complexity of modern industrial system, security problems become more and more important. The fault detection method based on analytical model has made outstanding contributions to ensure the normal operation of the system and the safety of people's life and property in the past decades. At the same time, modern

H. R. Karimi and N. Wang (Eds.): S-Cube 2022, LNICST 487, pp. 81–106, 2023.
https://doi.org/10.1007/978-3-031-34899-0_6

industrial system is equipped with a large number of sensors, the collection of data and work log is more convenient and efficient. Data driven fault detection technology [1–5] can excavate and utilize the characteristics of these data to analyze and monitor the running state of the system, has received extensive attention. On the other hand, identifying whether process faults are related to product quality can improve product quality and extend the operating life of equipment by reducing unnecessary downtime and maintenance. PLS [6, 7] is a typical representative of multivariate statistical analysis, which is easy to operate and can efficiently process massive industrial data. It is a widely spread data-driven quality related fault detection technology.

The PLS seeks the maximum correlation between process variables and quality variables by sorting the maximum covariance between input and output matrices, and decompose the process variable space into subspaces related to quality and unrelated to quality, so as to achieve the monitoring purpose of quality-related faults. This also leads to the existence of quality-unrelated parts in the quality-related principal component space (PCS), which affects the accuracy of detection. At the same time, it is possible to leave the mass related part in the residual space (CS), which has a large variance and cannot be detected by SPE statistics [8]. According to the results, what PLS provides is not fully applicable to the actual industrial system. In order to solve such problems, Zhou et al. [9] proposed a post-processing method based on PLS for the first time. This method named total projection to latent structures (TPLS) further decomposes PCS and CS into four Spaces, which more clearly describes the relationship between each space and quality. By further orthogonal decomposition of coefficient matrices between input and output, Yin et al. [10] decompose the process variable space into quality-related and quality- unrelated parts, which are named MPLS. It has been verified that the strategy of this method is simpler and equally effective. Peng [11] and Zhang et al. [12] extend the previous work to apply to nonlinear systems. This kind of method develops rapidly in theory [13] and has been applied in many practical projects [14].

Although these methods have made outstanding contributions to the field of fault detection, there are still many problems worth studying. For example, the ability of some algorithms [15] to detect small faults needs to be improved. In addition, data-driven fault detection techniques often set thresholds [16] based on the method of fixed control limits. To some extent, this method of balancing the relationship between false alarm rate and missed alarm rate will also result in some false alarm and missed alarm. In this paper, a new quality-related fault detection method is proposed to improve the defects of the standard PLS method proposed in the previous paper. The quality variables are decomposed by PCR [17] technology and the relationship between the score matrix and the input matrix is established. By this means, the process variable space is reconstructed to monitor the quality-related and quality-unrelated parts respectively. Furthermore, an idea based on EWMA [18, 19] is introduced to set adaptive threshold, which can ensure the accuracy and integrity of the model by reducing the influence of noise damage data. In this way, the dynamic value with a certain range can be obtained to balance the deviation in the operation of the system more reasonably, which helps to make meaningful decisions. Finally, classical cases are used to verify the effectiveness of the proposed algorithm. The experimental results indicate that the proposed algorithm outperforms the compared algorithms in several aspects such as fault detection rate

(FDR), fault alarm rate (FAR), accuracy for minor faults and tracking performance for specific faults. In summary, the main contributions are outlined as follows.

1) A new spatial decomposition method is proposed, which theoretically solves the problem of incomplete feature space decomposition of the traditional PLS.
2) In order to circumvent the influence of previous samples, this paper introduces more flexible adaptive thresholds in both feature subspaces, which enhances the algorithm's ability to detect some specific faults and is more in line with practical engineering situations.
3) Experiments have been carried out in linear and non-linear numerical cases as well as in the classical TE process and the results show the superior detection results and the high potential of the proposed method for engineering applications.

The structure of this paper is as follows. The Sect. 2 introduces the related work and its disadvantages; The Sect. 3 gives the detailed content of the proposed algorithm. In the Sect. 4, two numerical cases and TE processes are introduced to verify the effectiveness of the algorithm. Finally, in Sect. 5, the work of this paper is summarized and prospected.

2 The Preparatory Work

A. Traditional Partial Least Squares (PLS)

Data are collected through the actual industrial system to form the input data set $U \in R^{N \times m}$ and output data set $Y \in R^{N \times s}$, where N, m and s respectively represent the number of samples, process variables and quality.

By using NIPLS, (U, Y) can be projected into a low-dimensional latent variable space $T = [t_1, t_2, ..., t_A]$, A represents the number of latent variables, usually obtained by cross-validation, etc. After standardization and normalization, U and Y can be decomposed into the following forms by PLS:

$$U = TP^T + E = \hat{U} + \tilde{U}$$
$$Y = TQ^T + F = \hat{Y} + \tilde{Y}$$

(1)

where T is called the score matrix, $P \in R^{m \times A}$ and $Q \in R^{s \times A}$ denote the load matrix of U and Y respectively, E and F represent the residuals of U and Y, respectively.

In this model, there is the following relationship:

$$PR^T = R^T P = I_{A \times A}$$

(2)

$$T = UR$$

(3)

Then the relationship between U and Y can be revealed by the coefficient matrix Δ:

$$Y = TQ^T = URQ^T = U\Delta$$

(4)

PLS decomposes a new online sample u into the following

$$u = \hat{u} + e$$

(5)

$$\hat{u} = PR^T u \tag{6}$$

$$e = (I - PR^T)u \tag{7}$$

$$t_{ns} = R^T u \tag{8}$$

where t_{ns} represents the score vector for the new sample.

T^2, SPE statistics and their corresponding thresholds are widely used in this category of process monitoring algorithm. The calculation method is as follows

$$T^2 = t_{ns}^T \Lambda^{-1} t_{ns} \sim J_{th,T^2}(\frac{A(N^2 - 1)}{N(N - A)} F_\alpha(A, N - A)) \tag{9}$$

$$SPE = \|e\|^2 \sim J_{th,SPE}(g\chi_{\alpha,\tilde{h}}^2) \tag{10}$$

where $\Lambda = \frac{1}{N-1}T^T T$, $F_\alpha(A, N - A)$ denotes the F distribution follow the significance level α, and its degree of freedom is set as A and $N - A$. $g\chi_{\alpha,\tilde{h}}^2$ denotes the χ^2 distribution, which obeys $\tilde{h} = 2\bar{u}^2/S_\delta$ freedom of degree, $g = S/2\bar{u}$. $\bar{u}$ and S_δ are the sample mean and variance of SPE.

During this process, when T exceeds the threshold, a quality-related fault is considered to occur. When only the SPE statistic exceeds its threshold, a quality-unrelated fault is considered to occur.

The purpose of PLS is to decompose processsssss variables into two completely orthogonal parts: quality-related and quality-unrelated.However, as can be seen from Formulas (6 and 7), it is obvious that $\hat{u}$ and e are not orthogonal to each other, which leads to the existence of parts irrelevant to KPIs in $\hat{u}$ and changes highly correlated to quality variables in e. Therefore, PLS model is not fully applicable to quality -related fault detection.

B. Improved principal component regression (IPCR)

PCA is a widely used method in the field of fault detection because of its ability to project high-dimensional data into low-dimensional latent variable space. But it is not suitable for practical industrial process because it is unable to identify whether the fault is related to quality. To solve this problem, a series of modified algorithms based on PCA are proposed. This part briefly introduces one of the improved algorithms called IPCR [15].

Execute the basic steps of PCA on U

1. Eigenvalues p and eigenvectors c are obtained by performing eigenvalue decomposition on $\frac{U^T U}{N-1}$, and they are collected to form matrices $P = [p_1 ... p_m]$ and $C = diag\{c_1, c_2, ..., c_m\}$ respectively.
2. The eigenvectors in P corresponding to the first A maximum eigenvalues of C are extracted to establish the load matrix $P = [p_1, ..., p_A]$.
3. Then $T = UP$

4. U is decomposed as follows

$$U = \hat{U} + \tilde{U} = TP^T + \tilde{U}$$

where T is the score matrix and $\tilde{U}$ represents the residual.

Considering that PCA is unable to identify whether the fault is related to quality, partial least squares regression is used to establish the relationship between T and Y. And in this way, the method, called IPCR, is used to detect quality-related failures.

$$Q^T = (T^T T)^{-1} T^T Y \tag{11}$$

$$\hat{Y} = TQ^T = UPQ^T = U\Upsilon \tag{12}$$

At this point, the relationship between U and Y is established, and Υ is the coefficient matrix.

PCR algorithm has a similar problem to PLS: it contains parts unrelated to quality in the principal component space, and changes related to quality exist in the residual space. In order to solve this problem, SVD is applied to further decompose the matrix $\Upsilon\Upsilon^T$.

$$\Upsilon\Upsilon^T = \begin{bmatrix} \Psi_\Upsilon & \tilde{\Psi}_\Upsilon \end{bmatrix} \begin{bmatrix} \Lambda_\Upsilon & 0 \\ 0 & 0 \end{bmatrix} \begin{bmatrix} \Psi_\Upsilon^T \\ \tilde{\Psi}_\Upsilon \end{bmatrix} \tag{13}$$

$$\Theta_\Upsilon = \Psi_\Upsilon \Psi_\Upsilon^T \in \mathbb{R}^{m \times m} \tag{14}$$

$$\Theta_\Upsilon^\perp = \tilde{\Psi}_T \tilde{\Psi}_\Upsilon^T \in \mathbb{R}^{m \times m} \tag{15}$$

where $\Psi_\Upsilon \in \mathbb{R}^{m \times s}$, $\tilde{\Psi}_\Upsilon \in \mathbb{R}^{m \times (m-s)}$ and $\Lambda_\Upsilon \in \mathbb{R}^{s \times s}$, Θ_Υ and $\Theta_\Upsilon^\perp$ are projection matrices that are orthogonal to each other. U is projected onto these two matrices and is represented as:

$$\hat{U} = U\Theta_\Upsilon = T_R \Psi_\Upsilon^T \in S_{\hat{U}} \equiv span\{\Upsilon\} \tag{16}$$

$$\tilde{U} = U\Theta_\Upsilon^\perp = T_U \tilde{\Psi}_\Upsilon^T \in S_{\tilde{U}} \equiv span\{\Upsilon\}^\perp \tag{17}$$

where $T_R = U\Psi \in \mathbb{R}^{N \times s}$ and $T_U = U\tilde{\Psi} \in \mathbb{R}^{N \times (m-s)}$ represent the score matrix of quality-related part $\hat{U}$ and quality-unrelated part $\tilde{U}$ respectively.

During the online detection process, an online sample u is available. According to the description above, the statistics are as follows:

$$t_R = \Psi^T x \in \mathbb{R}^{N \times m} \tag{18}$$

$$t_U = \tilde{\Psi}^T x \in \mathbb{R}^{m \times (s-m)} \tag{19}$$

$$x_r^T x_r = x^T \Psi_\Upsilon \Psi_\Upsilon^T \Psi_\Upsilon \Psi_\Upsilon^T x = t_r^T t_r \tag{20}$$

$$x_u^T x_u = x^T \tilde{\Psi}_\Upsilon \tilde{\Psi}_\Upsilon^T \tilde{\Psi}_\Upsilon \tilde{\Psi}_\Upsilon^T x = t_u^T t_u \tag{21}$$

Therefore, the T^2 statistic for the quality-related part and the quality-unrelated part:

$$T_R^2 = t_R^T (\frac{T_R^T T_R}{N-1})^{-1} t_R \tag{22}$$

$$T_U^2 = t_U^T (\frac{T_U^T T_U}{N-1})^{-1} t_U \tag{23}$$

According to the significance level α, the thresholds are as follows:

$$J_{th, T_R^2} = \frac{m(N^2-1)}{N(N-m)} F_\alpha(m, N-m) \tag{24}$$

$$J_{th, T_U^2} = \frac{(s-m)(N^2-1)}{N(N-m)} F_\alpha(s-m, N-s+m) \tag{25}$$

According to fault detection logic:

$T_R^2 > J_{th, T_R^2} \Rightarrow$ A quality-related fault has occurred

$T_U^2 > J_{th, T_U^2} \Rightarrow$ A quality -unrelated fault has occurred

3 The Proposed Method

A. Regression Partial Least Squares (RPLS)

To solve the problem of PLS oblique decomposition of process space, a new fault detection method named Regression partial least squares (RPLS) was proposed in this part.

Traditional PLS algorithm decomposed the process variable space U into the following form.

$$\begin{aligned} U &= TP^T + E = \hat{U} + \tilde{U} \\ Y &= TQ^T + F = \hat{Y} + \tilde{Y} \\ T &= UR \end{aligned} \tag{26}$$

T is reproject to $T_y T_y$

$$T_y = \hat{Y} Q_y = TQ^T Q_y = TM \tag{27}$$

where M is the projection matrix of T. Then, least square regression is carried out between T_y and $\hat{U}$ to get Ψ_y.

$$\Psi_y^T = (T_{yrpls}^T T_{yrpls})^{-1} T_{yrpls}^T \hat{U} \tag{28}$$

Reference formula (29)

$$U_y = T_{yrpls} \Psi_y^T = T_{yrpls} (T_{yrpls}^T T_{yrpls})^{-1} T_{yrpls}^T TP^T \tag{29}$$

$$U_u = U - U_y \tag{30}$$

where U_y and U_u are the parts that are highly correlated and independent of Y, respectively. The process variable space U is reconstructed during the above procedure.

The T^2 statistic is used to monitor both parts. PCA is performed on KPI-unrelated part U_u to obtain its score matrix T_u and the loading matrix P_u.

Lemma 1. After the decomposition of RPLS, U_u is completely unrelated to $\hat{Y}$.

Proof
According to formula (31):

$$U_u = U - U_y = (I - T_{yrpls}(T_{yrpls}^T T_{yrpls})^{-1} T_{yrpls})U \tag{31}$$

Then

$$T_{yrpls}^T U_u = (T_{yrpls}^T - T_{yrpls}^T T_{yrpls}(T_{yrpls}^T T_{yrpls})^{-1} T_{yrpls})U = 0 \tag{32}$$

T_{yrpls} is the score matrix obtained by PCA decomposition of $\hat{Y}$, so

$$\hat{Y} = T_{yrpls}Q_y^T = 0 \tag{33}$$

$$\hat{Y}U_u = T_{yrpls}Q_y^T U_u = 0 \tag{34}$$

It can be inferred that U_u is not related to $\hat{Y}$, the proof is complete.

For online processes, a new online sample u_{new} is available. Its score t_{new} can be given by

$$t_{new} = u_{new}^T P \tag{35}$$

Therefore, the score of the online sample can be calculated by the following formula

$$t_{ynew} = t_{new}^T Q^T Q_y = u_{new}^T PM \tag{36}$$

Thus, the score of quality-unrelated part can be expressed as formula (37)

$$t_{unew}^T = u_{unew}^T P = (u_{new}^T - t_{ynew}^T \Psi_y^T)P_u = (u_{new}^T - u_{new}^T PM \Psi_y^T)P_u \tag{37}$$

Considering the large variances of the two parts, quality-related and quality-unrelated T^2 statistic was selected for monitoring:

$$T_y^2 = t_{ynew}^T \left(\frac{T_y^T T_y}{N-1}\right)^{-1} t_{ynew} \tag{38}$$

$$T_u^2 = t_{unew}^T \left(\frac{T_u^T T_u}{N-1}\right)^{-1} t_{unew} \tag{39}$$

B. An adaptive threshold based on Exponentially Weighted Moving Average

Generally speaking, the fault detection methods based on multivariate statistics adopt the method of fixed control limit to set the threshold α. The control limit is generally determined by the confidence level. This method balances the relationship between false alarm rate and false alarm to a certain extent. According to the algorithm model, the T^2 statistic $T^2 = [t_1, t_2..., t_i]$ is obtained. When the statistic exceeds the threshold, the fault is considered to occur, that is, $t_i > J_{th}$. However, this method leads to a certain degree of false positives and missing positives, and is not sensitive to some specific types of faults.

In order to solve this problem, the exponential weighted moving average (EWMA) method is applied to improve the threshold. The core idea of the improved method is a moving average weighted by exponential decline, and the weight of each value decreases exponentially with time. The closer the data is to the current moment, the greater the weight. Based on this idea, the adaptive threshold at time i is:

$$t_i = \frac{\sum_{j=1}^{h} \lambda^j t_{i-h+j}}{\sum_{j=1}^{h} \lambda^j} = \frac{\lambda t_{i-h+1} + \lambda^2 t_{i-h+2} + ... + \lambda^h t_i}{\sum_{j=1}^{h} \lambda^j} \tag{40}$$

However, as this is a reverse summation method, the detection time for the handoff between normal data and abnormal data will be prolonged due to its hysteresis. To solve this problem, a new method, such as Eq. (41), is proposed.

$$t_i = \frac{(J_{th} \sum_{j=1}^{h} \lambda^j - \sum_{j=1}^{h-1} \lambda^j t_{i-h+j})}{\lambda^h} \tag{41}$$

This method combines two parts. The first part is the change of the traditional fixed threshold upper limit under a certain confidence level. The second part also considers the deviation of the previous non alarm samples, which is more suitable for setting the appropriate adaptive threshold according to the real-time samples. However, due to the cumulative effect of previous error samples, the adaptive threshold may be lower than the conventional level, which affects the normal detection effect. Therefore, a certain lower limit [20] can be set by Eq. (42) to improve this problem.

$$J_{thirpls} = \max \left\{ \frac{(J_{th} \sum_{j=1}^{h} \lambda^j - \sum_{j=1}^{h-1} \lambda^j t_{i-h+j})}{\lambda^h}, \frac{J_{th}}{2} \right\} \tag{42}$$

In this article, a fault is considered to have occurred when a statistic exceeds a threshold. In the above formula, the selection of weighting factor should be able to ensure that the most recent statistics are close to the healthy sample. The closer the weighting factor is to 1, the more false alarm can be reduced. However, problems similar to Formula (41) will also occur, leading to a high detection time delay, which is not suitable for intermittent fault detection. If the weight factor is too high, it will lead to too much correlation with the recent data. Although the detection time can be reduced, the ability of the algorithm itself to eliminate the cumulative effect will be reduced, and the detection rate will be indirectly reduced. The window length h represents the number of samples to be considered for setting the adaptive threshold. First of all, sufficient numbers are needed to ensure the credibility of the adaptive threshold. On the other hand, an excessively large h will cause the weight factor of the sample farthest from the current moment to be too small and ignored compared with the weight of the sample at the recent moment, losing the significance of adding this part of the sample to the formula.

In this part, the adaptive threshold is applied to PLS and IPCR algorithm instead of the original fixed threshold. The thresholds of PLS in Eqs. 9 and 10 are replaced by the following:

$$J_{thpls} = \max \left\{ \frac{(J_{th,T^2} \sum_{j=1}^{h} \lambda^j - \sum_{j=1}^{h-1} \lambda^j t_{i-h+j})}{\lambda^h}, \frac{J_{th,T^2}}{2} \right\} \tag{43}$$

$$J_{thpls} = \max \left\{ \frac{(J_{th,SPE} \sum_{j=1}^{h} \lambda^j - \sum_{j=1}^{h-1} \lambda^j t_{i-h+j})}{\lambda^h}, \frac{J_{th,SPE}}{2} \right\} \tag{44}$$

The thresholds of PLS in Eqs. 24, 25 and 26 are replaced by the following:

$$J_{thipcr} = \max \left\{ \frac{(J_{th,T_R^2} \sum_{j=1}^{h} \lambda^j - \sum_{j=1}^{h-1} \lambda^j t_{i-h+j})}{\lambda^h}, \frac{J_{th,T_R^2}}{2} \right\} \tag{45}$$

$$J_{thipcr} = \max \left\{ \frac{(J_{th,T_U^2} \sum_{j=1}^{h} \lambda^j - \sum_{j=1}^{h-1} \lambda^j t_{i-h+j})}{\lambda^h}, \frac{J_{th,T_U^2}}{2} \right\} \tag{46}$$

In the TE [21] process, the feed temperature of reactant C is changed to simulate a quality-related fault condition to verify the effectiveness of the adaptive threshold.

Figure 1 and Fig. 2 show the fault detection results of PLS and IPCR using traditional fixed threshold and adaptive threshold respectively. The solid black line represents the traditional fixed threshold, while the solid red line represents the adaptive threshold. It is clear that the red line in Fig. 1 is lower than the black line in most cases in both the quality-related subspace and the quality-unrelated subspace, which means that the PLS

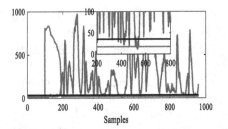
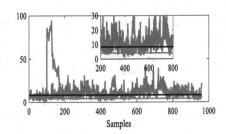

Fig. 1. Fault detection chart of modified PLS

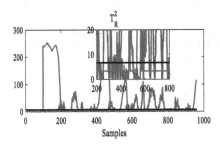
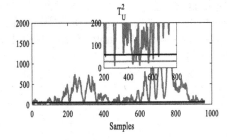

Fig. 2. Fault detection chart of modified IPCR

using the adaptive threshold can provide more alarm than the PLS using the traditional fixed threshold. In Fig. 2, IPCR using the adaptive threshold provides more alerts in the quality-unrelated subspace than the method using the fixed threshold. In the quality-related subspace, the statistics of the part where the red line is higher than the black line fail to exceed the threshold, indicating that this part of the fault has not been detected by IPCR and does not affect the validity of the verification of the adaptive threshold. Through this part of work, the validity of the adaptive threshold is verified.

C. IRPLS algorithm flow

The specific process based on IRPLS algorithm is as follows. Steps 1 to 6 are offline training, and steps 7 to 10 are online monitoring:

Offline Model Training:
Step 1: Normalize the input matrices X and output matrices Y.
Step 2: Establish PLS model by using input/output matrix.
Step 3: Perform PCA on the quality variables Y of the PLS model to get the score matrix T_{yrpls}.
Step 4: The load matrix Ψ_y is obtained by performing least square regression on X and T_{yrpls}.
Step 5: Calculate the quality-related U_y and quality-unrelated parts U_u according to Eqs. (29) and (30).
Step 6: Perform PCA on the quality- unrelated part U_u to get the corresponding score T_u and load matrix P_u.
On-line Monitoring:

Step 7: For an online sample u, score t_{ynew} and t_{unew} of quality-related and quality-unrelated parts were calculated by using Eqs. (34–36).

Step 8: Calculate the statistics T_y^2 and T_u^2 of the two subspaces according to the formulas (38–39).

Step 9: According to formula (42), the adaptive threshold is set in the following form

$$J_{thirpls} = max \left\{ \frac{(J_{th} \sum_{j=1}^{h} \lambda^j - \sum_{j=1}^{h-1} \lambda^j t_{i-h+j})}{\lambda^h}, \frac{J_{th,T_y^2}}{2} \right\} \tag{47}$$

$$J_{thirplsun} = max \left\{ \frac{(J_{th} \sum_{j=1}^{h} \lambda^j - \sum_{j=1}^{h-1} \lambda^j t_{i-h+j})}{\lambda^h}, \frac{J_{th,T_u^2}}{2} \right\} \tag{48}$$

Step 10: According to the fault detection logic to monitor the fault and determine whether the fault is related to quality.

$T_y^2 > J_{thirpls} \Rightarrow$ A quality-related fault was detected in quality-related subspace

$T_u^2 > J_{thirplsun} \Rightarrow$ A quality-unrelated fault detected in quality-unrelated subspace

$T_y^2 < J_{thirpls}$ and $T_u^2 < J_{thirplsun} \Rightarrow$ No fault detected

In order to clarify the algorithm steps, the process of IRPLS algorithm is presented here, as shown in Fig. 3.

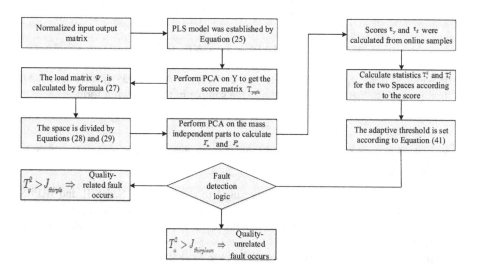

Fig. 3. Algorithm flow chart

4 Numerical Case Simulation

In this module, a linear numerical case and a nonlinear numerical case are used to simulate and compare the three algorithms of PLS, IPCR and IRPLS to reflect the effectiveness of the algorithm. FDR is introduced as a performance index to evaluate the algorithm.

$$FDR = \frac{N_r}{N_t} \qquad (49)$$

where N_t is the total number of samples, and N_r is the number of effective alarms.

An excellent algorithm that can be applied in industrial practice should be equipped with the following capabilities:

a) For quality-related faults: There are as many alerts as possible in the quality-related subspace and quality-unrelated subspace;
b) For quality-unrelated faults: There are as few or no alerts as possible in the quality-related subspace, and as many alerts as possible in the quality-unrelated subspace.

A. Linear numerical case

In order to verify the effectiveness of the method proposed in this paper, a widely circulated linear numerical case [9] is used here to simulate and verify PLS, IPCR and IRPLS. The case model description is shown in Eq. (50).

$$\begin{cases} u_l = Bz_l + e_l \\ y_l = \Xi u_l + v_l \end{cases} \qquad (50)$$

$$B = \begin{bmatrix} 1\,3\,4\,4\,0 \\ 3\,0\,1\,4\,1 \\ 1\,1\,3\,0\,0 \end{bmatrix}^T \quad e_l \in \mathbb{R}^5 \; u_l = [u_{l,1}\, u_{l,2}\, u_{l,3}\, u_{l,4}\, u_{l,5}]^T$$

$$\Xi = [2\,2\,1\,1\,0] \qquad u_l = N(0, 0.01^2)$$

in which $z_l \in \mathbb{R}^3$, $z_{l,i} \sim U([0, 1])(i = 1, 2, 3)$, $e_{l,j} \sim N(0, 0.05^2)(j = 1, 2, 3, 4, 5)$. In this case, the fault is introduced into the sample in the following form:

$$u_l = u_l^* + \Theta f$$

u_l is the failure-free value, Θ and f represent the direction and magnitude of fault, respectively.

In this part, 400 normal samples were used to model the PLS, IPCR and IRPLS algorithms, and another 400 samples were introduced to test the model performance. $\lambda = 1.06$, $h = 50$. The fault is introduced in the last 200 samples, and the fault scenario is as follows:

Failure Scenario 1: The fault direction is set to $\Theta = [0\,0\,0\,0\,1]$

$$y_l = \Xi(u_l^* + \Theta f) = \Xi u_l^* + \Xi\Theta f = \Xi u_l^*$$

It is clear that y is not affected by f, so this kind of failure scenario is quality-unrelated.

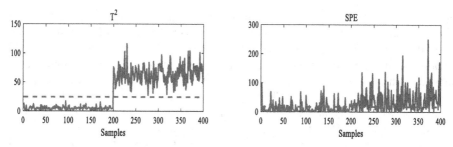

Fig. 4. PLS detection diagram for Failure Scenario 1 when f = 4

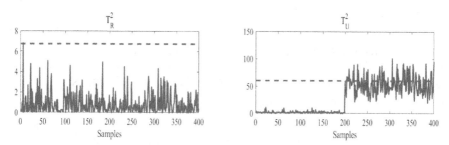

Fig. 5. IPCR detection diagram for Failure Scenario 1 when f = 4

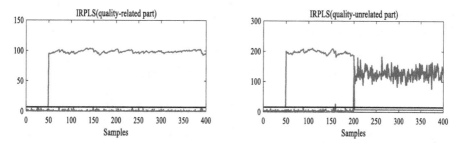

Fig. 6. IRPLS detection diagram for Failure Scenario 1 when f = 4

Figures 4, 5 and 6 are the detection diagrams of PLS, IPCR and IRPLS for fault scenario 1 when the fault intensity is 4, respectively. In Figs. 4, 5, PLS misjudged this quality-unrelated as a quality-related fault, while IPCR failed to detect such a fault scenario in quality-unrelated subspace. In Fig. 6, the solid black line represents RPLS algorithms using traditional thresholds, and the solid red lines represent IRPLS algorithms using adaptive thresholds. It can be seen that the red line in the quality-unrelated subspace is lower than the black line, indicating that for quality-unrelated faults, IRPLS algorithm can provide a higher fault detection rate than RPLS algorithm. So it is obvious that the adaptive threshold is valid in RPLS and IRPLS is more consistent with the fault detection logic than the other three algorithms.

Table 1 shows the FDRs of the three methods for the fault scenario 1 under different fault intensities. It can be seen that PLS has a good detection effect on quality-unrelated faults in the residual subspace, but it also generates a large number of alerts in the principal component space, which is not consistent with the actual situation. In general, when the fault magnitude is intense, both IPCR and IRPLS can give as few alarms as possible in the quality-related space and as many alarms in the quality-unrelated subspace, which is in line with the fault detection logic. However, it is worth noting that when the fault intensity is low, IPCR has a small number of false alarms in the quality-related subspace, and it also provides insufficient alarm rate in the quality-unrelated subspace. However, IRPLS does not have false positives in the quality-related subspace. When the fault level is at a low level, the alarm rate of IRPLS in the quality-unrelated subspace is more than 80%, and quickly reaches 100% with the increase of fault intensity. Therefore, the detection ability of IRPLS for linear quality-unrelated faults is higher than PLS and IPCR.

Table 1. FDRs of fault scenario 1 under different fault intensities

Fault magnitude	PLS		IPCR		IRPLS	
	T^2	SPE	T_R^2	T_U^2	T_y^2	T_u^2
2	0.285	0.45	0.005	0	0	0.88
4	1	0.89	0.01	0.265	0	0.99
6	1	1	0.005	0.97	0	1
8	1	1	0	1	0	1
10	1	1	0	1	0	1

Failure Scenario 2: The fault direction is set to $\Theta = [22110]$

$$y_l = \Xi(u_l^* + \Theta f) = \Xi u_l^* + \Xi \Theta f \neq \Xi u_l^*, \forall f \neq 0$$

It can be seen that y is affected by f and its fault level in this kind of fault, so this kind of failure scenario is identified as quality-related fault.

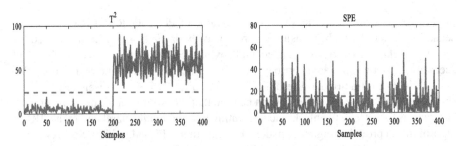

Fig. 7. PLS detection diagram for Failure Scenario 2 when f = 6

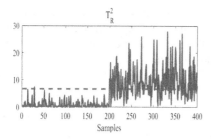
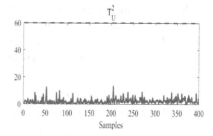

Fig. 8. IPCR detection diagram for Failure Scenario 2 when f = 6

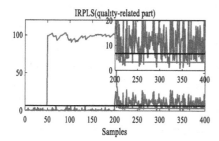
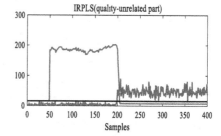

Fig. 9. IRPLS detection diagram for Failure Scenario 2 when f = 6

Figure 7, 8 and 9 are the detection diagrams of PLS, IPCR and IRPLS for fault scenario 2 when the fault intensity is 6, respectively. It can be seen that the alarm of IRPLS in quality-related subspace exceeds that of PLS and IPCR, which is more in line with the actual situation. In addition, the red line in Fig. 9 is lower than the black line, so the alarm rate of IRPLS is also higher than that of RPLS.

Table 2. FDRs of fault scenario 2 under different fault intensities

Fault magnitude	PLS		IPCR		IRPLS	
	T^2	*SPE*	T_R^2	T_U^2	T_y^2	T_u^2
2	0	0.56	0.055	0	0	0
4	0.17	0.805	0.23	0	0.055	0
6	0.815	0.585	0.73	0	0.865	0.935
8	1	1	0.885	0	0.985	0.975
10	1	1	1	0	0.995	1
20	1	1	1	0	1	1

Table 2 shows the detection rates of quality-related faults by PLS, IPCR and IRPLS methods under different fault intensities. It can be seen that when the fault is at a lower level, the detection capabilities of PLS, IPCR and IRPLS all need to be improved.

With the gradual increase of fault intensity, the performance differences of these three fault detection methods appear. When the fault intensity rises to 6, the detection ability of IRPLS begins to exceed that of PLS and IPCR. It can be concluded that IRPLS outperforms PLS and IPCR in terms of linear quality related fault detection.

B. Nonlinear numerical case

In this section, a nonlinear numerical case [11] is introduced to verify the performance of the three algorithms in the nonlinear system. The specific model is described as follows:

$$u_1 \sim N(1, 0.01^2), u_2 \sim N(1, 0.01^2) \tag{51}$$

$$u_3 = \sin(u_1) + d_1 \tag{52}$$

$$u_4 = u_1^2 - 3u_1 + 4 + d_2 \tag{53}$$

$$u_5 = u_2^2 + \cos(u_2^2) + 1 + d_3 y = u_3^2 + u_3 u_4 + u_1 + o \tag{54}$$

where $d_j \sim N(0, 0.001^2)(j = 1, 2, 3), o \sim N(0, 0.005^2)$.

It can be seen that variables 1, 3 and 4 are directly or indirectly related to quality indicator y, and faults occurring in them are considered as quality-related faults. Variables 2 and 5 are not related to y, so the failures occurring in them are considered to be quality-unrelated.

In this experiment, 960 normal data were selected to establish PLS, IPCR and IRPLS models, and 960 test data were used to verify the model performance of these methods. Window length $h = 100$, weighting factor $\lambda = 1.06$. The fault is introduced in the 481st sample. The fault is set as the following four forms, and the fault level is $f = 0.1$, $f = 0.001, f = 1$ and $f = 0.01$ respectively.

Failure Scenario 1: $u_2 = u_2^* + f$
Failure Scenario 2: $u_2 = u_2^* + (i - 480)f$
Failure Scenario 3: $u_1 = u_1^* + f$
Failure Scenario 4: $u_1 = u_1^* + (i - 480)f$

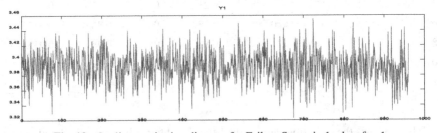

Fig. 10. Quality monitoring diagram for Failure Scenario 1 when f = 1

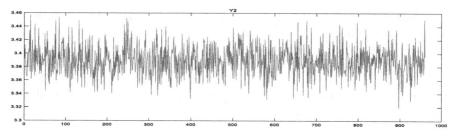

Fig. 11. Quality monitoring diagram for Failure Scenario 2 when f = 10

Figure 10 and Fig. 11 are the quality monitoring charts for quality-unrelated failure scenarios 1 and 2 at different levels. It can be seen that when these two faults occur and the grade changes, the quality does not change, so it can be inferred that these two faults are quality-independent faults.

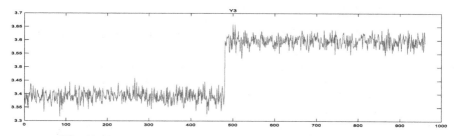

Fig. 12. Quality monitoring diagram for Failure Scenario 3 when f = 1

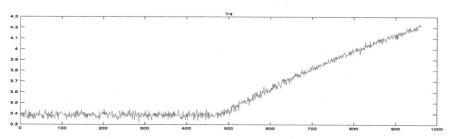

Fig. 13. Quality monitoring diagram for Failure Scenario 4 when f = 1

Figures 12, 13 are the quality monitoring charts for quality-related failure scenarios 3 and 4 at different intensities. As you can see, the quality changes rapidly after these two types of faults occur, so fault scenarios 3 and 4 bit quality-related failures.

According to the above analysis, the failure scenarios 1 and 2 are quality-unrelated faults, while the fault scenarios 3 and 4 are quality-related faults. The four fault levels are set as tiny levels to verify the ability of the algorithm to detect minor faults in nonlinear systems.

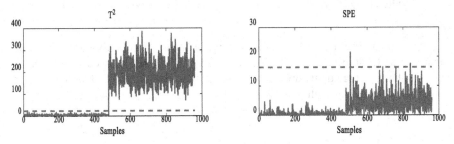

Fig. 14. PLS detection diagram for Failure Scenario 1 when f = 1

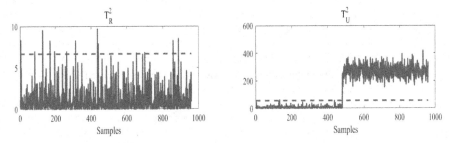

Fig. 15. IPCR detection diagram for Failure Scenario 1 when f = 1

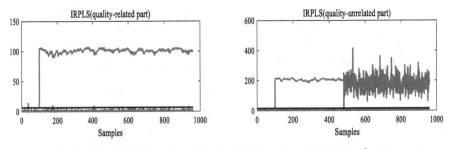

Fig. 16. IRPLS detection diagram for Failure Scenario 1 when f = 1

Figures 14, 15 and 16 are the detection diagrams of PLS, IPCR and IRPLS for fault scenario 1 when the fault intensity is 1, respectively. As can been seen, all three methods are completely alert in the quality-unrelated subspace. However, PLS misjudged this kind of fault as a quality-related fault by a large number of alarms in the quality-related subspace, which was not in line with the actual situation. While IPCR had a small number of false positives and IRPLS had no false positives.

Table 3. FDRs of different fault scenarios under different fault intensities

Fault Scenario	Type	magnitude	PLS		IPCR		IRPLS	
			T^2	SPE	T_R^2	T_U^2	T_y^2	T_u^2
1	Step	0.1	1	0	0.0083	1	0	1
2	ramp	0.001	0.9125	0.65	0.0104	0.9063	0	0.9146
3	Step	1	1	1	1	1	1	1
4	ramp	0.01	0.9875	0.973	0.9700	0.9700	0.9875	0.9813

Table 3 shows the fault detection rates of PLS, IPCR and IRPLS for four fault scenarios under different fault intensities. Obviously, for the quality-unrelated fault scenario 1 and scenario 2, the false positive rate of IRPLS algorithm in the KPI-related subspace is 0, and both PLS and IPCR have different degrees of false positive. The alarm rate of IRPLS in the quality-related subspace is also higher than that of PLS and IPCR. For quality-related fault scenarios 3 and 4, IRPLS still has the highest alarm rate in the quality-related subspace. In summary, IRPLS has the most superior detection results for non-linear and minor faults.

C. Tennessee process simulation

The TE model is set up by the Eastman Chemical Company, which are widely used to validate the property of process monitoring methods [22], the specific reaction process is as shown in Fig. 17.

The process is composed of reactor, condenser, compressor, separator and stripper. In this process, four gas components A, C, D, E and an inert component B participate in the reaction to generate two liquid main products G and H and a liquid by-product F. The reaction is closed-loop and irreversible, and the reaction process can be expressed as follows

$$A + C + D\ (E) \rightarrow G\ (H)$$
$$A + E \rightarrow F \qquad\qquad (55)$$
$$3D \rightarrow 2F$$

The whole process is divided into two parts. The first part consists of 41 measurement variable modules, which are further divided into 22 continuous process variables (XMEAS (1–22)) and 19 analytical variables (XMEAS(23–41)), and the second part consists of 12 operational variable modules (XMV(1–12)).In general, 11 operational variables and 22 continuous process variables are selected to construct the input matrix. The module representing the final product G or H can be used as the quality variable, and the sampling interval is 3 min.

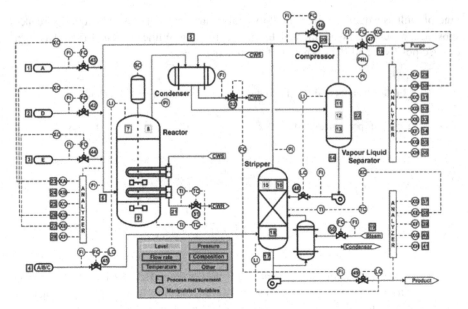

Fig. 17. TE Process Flowchart

21 faults were set in the TE process, including 15 known faults and 6 unknown faults [9]. The data set including a total of 22 training sets and the same number of test sets corresponding to the corresponding fault and one fault-free case under normal working conditions, which were collected within 48 h of operation time, and were widely used in the field of process monitoring [23]. In order to verify 15 kinds of known faults, this paper selects data sets corresponding to faults and data sets under fault-free conditions for simulation verification. The number of samples in the training set and the number of samples in the test set are 480 and 960 respectively, and the number of modeling training collected under normal working conditions is 500.In this paper, the failure was introduced after the 160th sample.

Figure 18 shows the detection rate of IRPLS algorithm for different quality-related faults with different weighting factors. It can be seen that when the weighting factor is 1.06, the fault detection rate is generally the highest, so in the TE model: $\lambda = 1.06$, $h = 100$.

According to prior knowledge, 15 known fault types are divided into quality-related fault (IDV(1), IDV(2), IDV(6), IDV(8), IDV(10), IDV(12), IDV(13)) and quality-unrelated fault (IDV(3), IDV(4), IDV(9), IDV(11), IDV(14), IDV(15)). As shown in Fig. 19, after the occurrence of fault IDV (14), the trend of quality variable is similar to that under normal working conditions without significant changes, which also proves that IDV(14) is quality-unrelated fault. Figures 20, 21 and 22 are the detection diagrams of PLS, IPCR and IRPLS for quality-unrelated faults IDV(14) respectively. It is obvious that both PLS and IPCR have varying degrees of alarm in the quality-related subspace, which does not help us identify the correct type of fault. However, in Fig. 22, IRPLS

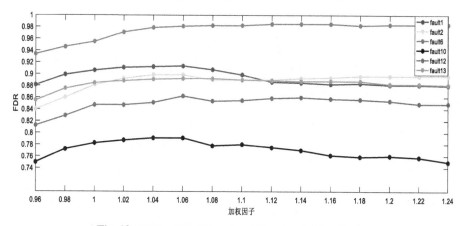

Fig. 18. FDRs of IRPLS under different weighting factors

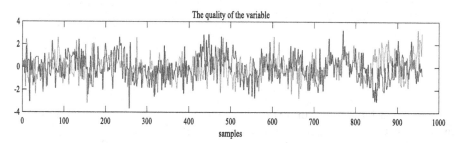

Fig. 19. Changes of molar ratio under different working conditions

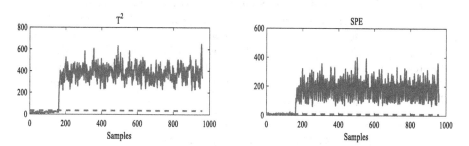

Fig. 20. PLS detection diagram for IDV(14)

only alerts in quality-related subspace and does not alarm in quality-unrelated subspace, indicating that IDV (14) is quality-unrelated fault.

FAR is introduced to evaluate the performance of the algorithm together with FDR:

$$FAR = \frac{N_w}{N_t} \tag{56}$$

where N_t is the total number of samples, and N_w is the number of false alarms.

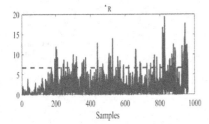
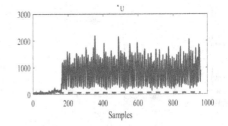

Fig. 21. IPCR detection diagram for IDV(14)

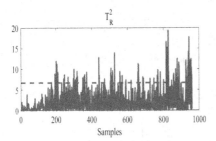
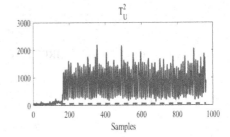

Fig. 22. IRPLS detection diagram for IDV(14)

Table 4 and Table 5 show the FDRs of quality-related faults and the FARs of quality-unrelated faults by the three methods respectively. As can be seen in Table 4, the detection ability of IPCR for fault 8 and fault 10 is slightly insufficient, while IRPLS and PLS have no obvious short board, which can provide a lot of alarms for all quality-related faults detected. Table 5 illustrates that IRPLS has the lowest far and the KPI-unrelated fault detection performance is the best. And for some faults such as IDV (3), IDV (14),IRPLS can achieve zero false alarm. In addition, it is worth mentioning that the high FAR of PLS for quality-unrelated faults means that it will misjudge quality-related faults as quality-related faults, which reduces the credibility of PLS for FDR of quality-related faults. It can be concluded that IRPLS has the highest FDR for quality-related faults and the lowest FAR for quality-unrelated faults.

Table 4. FDRs of quality-related faults

Fault ID	Fault Description	Fault detection rate		
		PLS	IPCR	IRPLS
1	A/C Feed Ratio, B Composition constant	0.9988	0.9063	0.9138
2	B composition A/C Ration Constant	0.9863	0.8838	0.8988
6	A Feed Loss Step	1	0.9913	0.9813

(continued)

Table 4. (*continued*)

Fault ID	Fault Description	Fault detection rate		
		PLS	IPCR	IRPLS
8	A, B, C Feed composition	0.985	0.6788	0.7925
10	C Feed temperature	0.8913	0.46	0.7850
12	condenser cooling water inlet temperature	0.9950	0.8413	0.8525
13	Reaction kinetics	0.9538	0.9038	0.8925

Table 5. FARs of quality-unrelated faults

Fault ID	Fault Description	Fault alarm rate		
		PLS	IPCR	IRPLS
3	D Feed Temperature (step)	0.0938	0.1363	0
4	Reactor cooling water inlet temperature	1	0.11	0.045
9	D Feed temperature (Random variation)	0.0663	0.075	0.005
11	Reactor cooling water inlet temperature	0.8213	0.1025	0.0413
14	Reactor cooling water valve	1	0.1	0
15	Condenser cooling water valve	0.16	0.105	0.0838

In addition, there is a class of known faults named regression faults, such as faults 5 and 7. After this kind of fault occurs, the feedback mechanism inside the system will be adjusted quickly to make the quality return to normal within a certain period of time. Whether this process can be monitored can reflect the following of the algorithm.

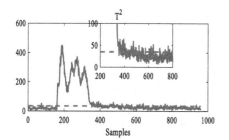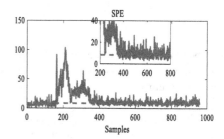

Fig. 23. PLS detection diagram for IDV (5)

Figure 26 shows the variation of the molar ratio of component G in stream 9 under different conditions. The blue solid line is the quality under normal conditions, and the green solid line is the quality under fault 5 conditions. It can be seen that the quality returns to normal after 400 samples. As can be seen from Fig. 25, IRPLS first gives a large

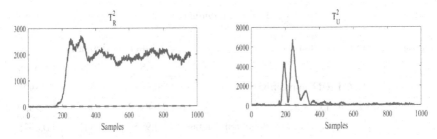

Fig. 24. IPCR detection diagram for IDV (5)

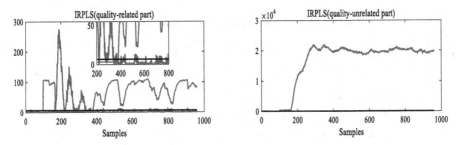

Fig. 25. IRPLS detection diagram for IDV (5)

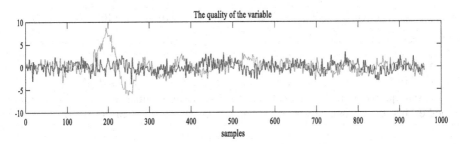

Fig. 26. Diagram of molar ratio change of component G in stream 9

number of alarms in the quality-related subspace, and then returns to normal quickly without any alarms. The presence of this fault can also be continuously monitored in the quality-unrelated subspace. However, neither Fig. 23 representing PLS nor Fig. 24 representing IPCR can give practical decisions. It can be concluded that IRPLS is better than PLS and IPCR in detecting regressive faults, and has stronger following ability, which is more suitable for industrial practice.

5   Conclusion

A quality-related fault detection method named IRPLS is proposed in this paper. In this method, the quality variables are decomposed and the relationship between the quality variables and the process variable space is established to reconstruct the process variables so as to better describe the quality variables. Corresponding test statistics are designed and compared with the introduced adaptive thresholds to help produce more reliable decisions, which improves the shortcomings of standard PLS in the detection of quality-related faults. By comparing with PLS and IPCR in numerical examples and TE processes, it is concluded that IRPLS has higher detection accuracy for quality-related and quality-unrelated faults as well as minor faults, and has the best tracking performance for specific types of faults, which means it is more suitable for modern industrial processes.

Funding. This works is partly supported by the Education Committee Project of Liaoning, China under Grant LJKZ1011 and LJ2019003.

References

1. Qin, S.J.: Statistical process monitoring: basics and beyond. J. Chemometr. **17**(8–9), 480–502 (2003)
2. Liang, S., Zhang, S., Huang, Y., et al.: Data-driven fault diagnosis of FW-UAVs with consideration of multiple operation conditions. ISA Trans. **126**, 472–485 (2022)
3. Rezamand, M., Kordestani, M., Carriveau, R., et al.: A new hybrid fault detection method for wind turbine blades using recursive PCA and wavelet-based PDF. IEEE Sens. J. **20**, 2023–2033 (2020)
4. Pandit, R., Infield, D., Dodwell, T.: Operational variables for improving industrial wind turbine yaw misalignment early fault detection capabilities using data-driven techniques. IEEE Trans. Inst. Meas. **70**, 1–8 (2021)
5. Wang, K., Chen, J., Song, Z.: Performance analysis of dynamic PCA for closed-loop process monitoring and its improvement by output oversampling scheme. IEEE Trans. Control Syst. Technol. **27**(1), 378–385 (2019)
6. Qin, Y., Yan, Y., Ji, H., et al.: Recursive correlative statistical analysis method with sliding windows for incipient fault detection. IEEE Trans. Ind. Electron. **69**, 4185–4194 (2021)
7. Wang, G., Yin, S.: Enhanced quality-related fault detection approach based on OSC and M-PLS. IEEE Trans. Ind. Inf. 1 (2015)
8. Li, G., Qin, S.J., Zhou, D.: Geometric properties of partial least squares for process monitoring. Automatica **46**(1), 204–210 (2010)
9. Zhou, D., Li, G., Qin, S.J.: Total projection to latent structures for process monitoring. AIChE J. NA-NA (2009)
10. Yin, S., Ding, S.X.: Study on modifications of PLS approach for process monitoring. IFAC Proc. **44**, 12389–12394 (2011)
11. Peng, K., Zhang, K., Li, G.: Quality-related process monitoring based on total kernel PLS model and its industrial application. Math. Probl. Eng. **2013**, 1–14 (2013)
12. Zhang, Y., Sun, R., Fan, Y.: Fault diagnosis of nonlinear process based on KCPLS reconstruction. Chemom. Intell. Lab. Syst. **140**, 49–60 (2015)
13. Said, M., Abdellafou, K.B., Taouali, O.: Machine learning technique for data-driven fault detection of nonlinear processes. J. Intell. Manuf. **31**(4), 865–884 (2019)
14. Li, J., Yan, X.: Process monitoring using principal component analysis and stacked autoencoder for linear and nonlinear coexisting industrial processes. J. Taiwan Inst. Chem. Eng. **112**, 322–329 (2020)
15. Sun, C., Hou, J.: An improved principal component regression for quality-related process monitoring of industrial control systems. IEEE Access **5**, 21723–21730 (2017)

16. Jang, K., Hong, S., Kim, M., et al.: Adversarial autoencoder based feature learning for fault detection in industrial processes. IEEE Trans. Ind. Inf. **18**(2), 827–834 (2021)

17. Zamani, H., Bahrami, H.R., Garris, P.A., Mohseni, P.: Compressed principal component regression (C–PCR) algorithm and FPGA validation. IEEE Trans. Circ. Syst. II Express Briefs **67**(12), 3512–3516 (2020)

18. Lahdhiri, H., Taouali, O.: Reduced rank KPCA based on GLRT chart for sensor fault detection in nonlinear chemical process. Measurement **169**, 108342 (2021)

19. Xidonas, P., Tsionas, M., Zopounidis, C.: On mutual funds-of-ETFs asset allocation with rebalancing: sample covariance versus EWMA and GARCH. Ann. Oper. Res. **284**(1), 469–482 (2018). https://doi.org/10.1007/s10479-018-3056-z

20. Bakdi, A., Kouadri, A.: A new adaptive PCA based thresholding scheme for fault detection in complex systems. Chemom. Intell. Lab. Syst. **162**, 83–93 (2017)

21. Song, B., Shi, H.: Fault detection and classification using quality-supervised double-layer method. IEEE Trans. Ind. Electron. **65**(10), 8163–8172 (2018)

22. Adeli, M., Mazinan, A.H.: High efficiency fault-detection and fault-tolerant control approach in Tennessee Eastman process via fuzzy-based neural network representation. Complex Intell. Syst. **6**(1), 199–212 (2019). https://doi.org/10.1007/s40747-019-0094-3

23. Sun, Y., Qin, W., Zhuang, Z., Xu, H.: An adaptive fault detection and root-cause analysis scheme for complex industrial processes using moving window KPCA and information geometric causal inference. J. Intell. Manuf. **32**(7), 2007–2021 (2021). https://doi.org/10.1007/s10845-021-01752-9

A Novel Stochastic Event-Based Feedback Watermark for Replay Attack Detection

Xudong Zhao$^{(\boxtimes)}$, Xinyu Wang, Fengde Xu, and Yuhan Wang

Key Laboratory of Intelligent Control and Optimization for Industrial Equipment,
Dalian University of Technology, Dalian 116024, China
xdzhaohit@gmail.com

Abstract. The security of cyber physical systems (CPSs) is the premise of resource sharing in modern industry, which has attracted considerable attention of researchers. Many effective methods have been proposed to defend CPSs, among which physical watermark is one prevailing approach which can enhance the replay attack detection capability of CPSs. In order to make the watermarks work more effective, a novel stochastic event-based feedback physical watermark is proposed in this paper to detect replay attacks. We formulate first the problem taking into account the Kalman filter, the linear quadric Gaussian (LQG) optimal controller and the χ^2 detector. Then, we characterize the LQG performance loss and the probability of adding a physical watermark in two different scenarios: the system operates with and without replay attacks. It is proved that the probability of adding a watermark signal will increase when replay attacks exist. Furthermore, we discuss the performance of the χ^2 detector under the framework of our approach. Finally, numerical simulations are verified the theoretical results.

Keywords: CPSs security · Stochastic event-based feedback physical watermark · Replay attacks

1 Introduction

Cyber physical systems integrate distributed networks of smart sensors and computational elements with physical plants, which achieve better efficiency and productivity than traditional control systems [1]. However, the wide usage of communication networks may bring many drawbacks in security, such as the Stuxnet Worm on Iranian centrifuges and the attack on Venezuelan hydropower stations, leading to a serious depression of the economy or even threaten the national security. Therefore, it is in an urgent need to model and analyze the CPSs security.

This work is supported by the National Natural Science Foundation of China (U21A20477, 61722302, 61573069, 62203064), the Fundamental Research Funds for the Central Universities (DUT19ZD218, DUT22ZD402), the Liaoning Revitalization Talents Program under Grant XLYC1907140, and National Major Science and Technology Project (J2019-V-0010-0105).

H. R. Karimi and N. Wang (Eds.): S-Cube 2022, LNICST 487, pp. 107–119, 2023.
https://doi.org/10.1007/978-3-031-34899-0_7

Unsurprisingly, the CPSs security has been extensively studied in recent years. The work [2] has considered two main kinds of attacks, i.e., injection attacks and denial of service (DoS) attacks. Compared with DoS attacks, the injection attacks require comprehensive information about the system, making them more difficult to be detected. Therefore, in the following, we concentrate on injection attacks, where the attackers alter sensor measurements and affect date integrity.

Replay attacks are the main classes of injection attacks, which need to replay the previous sensor measurements for the purpose of deceiving the CPSs. It should be pointed out that replay attacks have the ability to bypass passive detection methods in regardless of the knowledge of the system. However, adding physical watermarks is a particular active detection method, which is helpful to defend against replay attacks first provided in [3]. According to the work [3], the authors in work [4] have extended the results by presenting a more general watermarks scheme, and proposed a Cross-Correlator to detect replay attacks. In addition, Mo et al. [5] also have designed the correlated physical watermarks using stationary Gaussian processes. Weerakkody et al. [6] have focused on the physical watermarks in the presence of data packet dropouts in the system. In work [7], the authors have been concerned with finding an algorithm that can generate watermarks to detect replay attacks in the fact of unknown system parameters. However, the above physical watermarks on the one hand can detect replay attacks easily, but, on the other hand, they would like to degrade the control performance to a certain degree. In order to reduce the loss of control performance, Fang et al. [8] have been interesting in obtaining a periodic schedule to add watermarks. Besides, the authors [9] have paid attention to a multiplicative sensor watermarks. Furthermore, Miao et al. [10,11] have developed a sub-optimal scheme to add watermark signals over a finite time horizon by resorting to the game theoretic approach.

It is obvious that most of the physical watermarks are closely relevant to the time evolutions, while few work focuses on event-based physical watermarks. Also, event-based method is a hot spot and widely used to reduce the communication cost [12,13]. When the predefined condition is met, the sensor measurements are immediately transmitted to the remote estimator over the wireless communication network. Therefore, we find that the event scheduler can utilize real-time data and provide more information for decision whether to add a watermark signal. Motivated by the above, we provide in the paper an event-based feedback watermark, which, on the one hand, improve the detection rate subject to replay attacks, and on the other hand, ensure system performance.

In this paper, a novel stochastic event-based feedback physical watermark is proposed for detecting replay attacks. The system performances are studied after adding the physical watermarks. In addition, our watermarks are proved to effectively improve detection rates of χ^2 detector. The main contributions of this paper can be divided into the following:

1. We propose a novel stochastic event-based feedback physical watermark, and prove that the probability of adding a watermark is a constant without replay attacks. In such scenario, we also investigate the system performance loss.
2. We provide the boundary of the probability of launching a watermark under replay attacks. We show that the probability of launching a watermark increases in the case of replay attacks exist.
3. We show the effectiveness of stochastic event-based feedback physical watermarks for detecting replay attacks.

The rest of this paper is organized as follows: Sect. 2 setup the problem taking into account the Kalman filter, the LQG controller and the χ^2 detector. Section 3 proposes a stochastic event-based feedback watermark and characterizes the system performances without replay attacks. Section 4 shows the validity of our proposed watermarks under replay attacks. Section 5 gives some numerical simulations to show the effectiveness of our watermarks, followed by the conclusion in Sect. 6.

2   Problem Setup

We introduce a linear time invariant (LTI) system:

$$x_{k+1} = Ax_k + Bu_k + w_k, \tag{1}$$
$$y_k = Cx_k + v_k \tag{2}$$

where x_k, u_k and y_k are the system state, control input and the sensor measurement, respectively. The initial state $x_0 \sim \mathcal{N}(0, \Sigma)$, while w_k and v_k are mutually independent, w_k and v_k are independent identically distributed (i.i.d.) Gaussian variables with covariance Q and R, respectively. Furthermore, we assume that (A, C) is detectable and $\left(A, Q^{\frac{1}{2}}\right)$ is stabilizable.

A Kalman filter is used to provide optimal state estimate of state x_k:

$$\hat{x}_{0|-1} = 0, P_{0|-1} = \Sigma, \tag{3}$$
$$\hat{x}_{k+1|k} = A\hat{x}_{k|k} + Bu_k, \tag{4}$$
$$P_{k+1|k} = AP_{k|k}A^T + Q, \tag{5}$$
$$K_k = P_{k|k-1}C^T(CP_{k|k-1}C^T + R)^{-1}, \tag{6}$$
$$\hat{x}_{k|k} = \hat{x}_{k|k-1} + K_k(y_k - C\hat{x}_{k|k-1}), \tag{7}$$
$$P_{k|k} = P_{k|k-1} - K_kCP_{k|k-1}, \tag{8}$$

It should be pointed out that the gain K_k will converge exponentially if (A, C) is detectable [14]. Hence, the filter can be expressed as a fixed gain estimator:

$$P \triangleq \lim_{k \to \infty} P_{k|k-1}, K \triangleq PC^T(CPC^T + R)^{-1}, \tag{9}$$

$$\hat{x}_{k+1|k} = A\hat{x}_{k|k} + Bu_k, \tag{10}$$
$$\hat{x}_{k|k} = \hat{x}_{k|k-1} + K(y_k - C\hat{x}_{k|k-1}). \tag{11}$$

Using $\hat{x}_{k|k}$ generated by the Kalman filter, the controller wants to minimize LQG cost:

$$J = \lim_{M \to \infty} \mathbb{E}\{\frac{1}{M}[\sum_{k=0}^{M-1}(x_k^T W x_k + u_k^T U u_k)]\}, \tag{12}$$

where $W \succ 0$ and $U \succ 0$. The optimal control input adopts a steady-state strategy:

$$u_k^* = -(B^T S B + U)^{-1}B^T S A \hat{x}_{k|k} = L \hat{x}_{k|k}, \tag{13}$$

where S is the unique positive definite matrix satisfies the following Riccati equation:

$$S = A^T S A + W - A^T S B(B^T S B + U)^{-1}B^T S A. \tag{14}$$

The cost function in this case becomes a constant:

$$J = trace(SQ) + trace[(A^T S A + W - S)(P - KCP)]. \tag{15}$$

2.1 χ^2 Detector

χ^2 detector is very commonly used for anomaly detection in the system [14], which utilizes the statistical properties of the Kalman filter innovation:

Lemma 1. *The innovation* $z_i = y_i - C\hat{x}_{i|i-1} \sim \mathcal{N}(0, \mathscr{P})$ *is a i.i.d. Gaussian random variable where* $\mathscr{P} = CPC^T + R$ *[15].*

Let

$$g_k = \sum_{i=k-\mathscr{K}+1}^{k} z_i^T \mathscr{P}^{-1} z_i \underset{\mathscr{H}_1}{\overset{\mathscr{H}_0}{\lessgtr}} \eta, \tag{16}$$

where $\mathscr{K}$ is the window size and η is the threshold. $\mathscr{H}_1$ denotes replay attack exists and $\mathscr{H}_0$ is on the contrary. From Lemma 1, it is trivial to show that g_k has a χ^2 distribution with $m\mathscr{T}$ degrees of freedom when the system is operating normally.

Define the false alarm and detection rate as α_k and β_k, respectively:

$$\alpha_k \triangleq Pr(g_k > \eta|\mathscr{H}_0), \beta_k \triangleq Pr(g_k > \eta|\mathscr{H}_1). \tag{17}$$

2.2 Replay Attack and Physical Watermark

In this paper, we concentrate on replay attack. The malicious entities can record all sensor measurements and arbitrarily modify them into y_k's. We have the following results from work [4]:

Lemma 2. *If* $\mathscr{A} \triangleq (A + BL)(I - KC)$ *is stable*

$$\lim_{k \to \infty} \beta_k = \alpha_k. \tag{18}$$

On the contrary, if it is unstable

$$\lim_{k \to \infty} \beta_k = 1 \tag{19}$$

This lemma shows that an attacker can fool the χ^2 detector if and only if $\mathscr{A}$ is stable. Therefore, we assume that $\mathscr{A}$ is stable in the rest of this article. In addition, physical watermarks are added to defend against such attacks,

$$u_k = u_k^* + \gamma_k \Delta u_k, \qquad (20)$$

where $\gamma_k = 1$ means adding a physical watermark at time k and $\gamma_k = 0$ is the opposite, $\Delta u_k \sim \mathcal{N}(0, \mathscr{Q})$ is the watermark that follows the i.i.d. Gaussian distribution, and for all k, it is independent of u_k^*, w_k and v_k. It is worth noting that in the existing approaches such as [3,4], the watermark is always added, i.e., $\gamma_k \equiv 1$. However, the LQG cost of this approach is too high. In the next section, we will use a stochastic event-based approach to design γ_k.

3 Stochastic Event-Based Feedback Physical Watermarks

It is well known that adding physical watermarks can improve the detection rate by sacrificing control performances when the system is subject to replay attacks. However, existing watermarks are added based on time intervals. Since the watermarks will be added even when the system is under normal operation, resulting in excessive sacrifice of system performances.

In this section, we propose a stochastic event-based feedback physical watermark. To be more specific, at each step k, the computer center produces an i.i.d. variable ζ_k, which obeys a uniform distribution between $[0,1]$, and furthermore compares it with the function φ_k:

$$\varphi_k = \exp\{-\frac{1}{2} \sum_{i=k-\mathcal{K}+1}^{k} z_i^T Y z_i\}, \qquad (21)$$

where $\mathcal{K}$ is the window size and $Y \succ 0$. The computer centre chooses to add a physical watermark if and only if $\varphi_k < \zeta_k$. Then γ_k is obtained by:

$$\gamma_k = \begin{cases} 0, & \text{with prob.}\varphi_k, \\ 1, & \text{with prob.}1 - \varphi_k. \end{cases} \qquad (22)$$

It should be pointed out that when the system is operating normal, the probability of adding a physical watermark is a constant. Furthermore, the probability of adding a watermark $1 - \varphi_k$ will increase when replay attacks exist, which will be proved in the following article.

Furthermore, we add a feedback channel to increase the watermark covariance (see Fig. 1). At present, the watermark can be expressed as $f(g_k)\gamma_k \Delta u_k$ where $f(\cdot) : \mathbb{R}^+ \rightarrow [0, \delta]$. The bound δ is to prevent an excessive watermark signal. Notably, if Y is large enough and $f(g_k) \equiv 1$, we will obtain the time-based watermarks.

In the rest of this article, both the $\mathscr{K}$ and $\mathcal{K}$ are set to 1. However, it is easy to extend our results to more general cases by state extension. We first focus on the situation where the system operates without replay attacks. The next theorem shows the probability of adding a watermark:

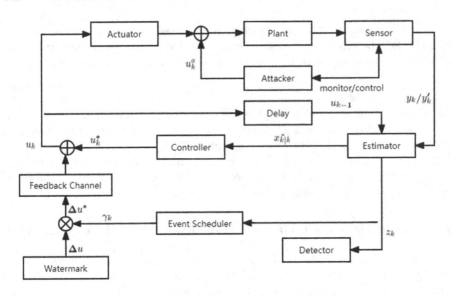

Fig. 1. System diagram

Theorem 1. *In the absence of replay attacks, the probability of adding a watermark is a constant*

$$\gamma = Pr(\gamma_k = 1) = 1 - \frac{1}{|I + Y\mathscr{P}|^{\frac{1}{2}}}. \tag{23}$$

Proof.

$$
\begin{aligned}
Pr(\gamma_k = 0) &= \mathbb{E}[\varphi_k] = \int_{\mathbb{R}^m} \varphi_k p(z_k) dz_k \\
&= \frac{1}{(2\pi)^{m/2}|\mathscr{P}|^{\frac{1}{2}}} \int_{\mathbb{R}^m} exp\{-\frac{1}{2}z_k^T Y z_k\} exp\{-\frac{1}{2}z_k^T \mathscr{P}^{-1} z_k\} dz_k \\
&= \frac{1}{|I + Y\mathscr{P}|^{\frac{1}{2}}},
\end{aligned} \tag{24}
$$

Thus,

$$Pr(\gamma_k = 1) = 1 - \frac{1}{|I + Y\mathscr{P}|^{\frac{1}{2}}}. \tag{25}$$

From work [4], we know that

Lemma 3.

$$J' = J + trace[(U + B^T SB)\mathscr{Q}], \tag{26}$$

where J' is the LQG performance after adding a physical watermark at each time step, and $\mathscr{Q}$ is the watermark covariance.

Then we can obtain the LQG performance with our watermarks by the following theorem:

Theorem 2. *The LQG performance with stochastic event-based feedback physical watermarks is:*

$$J' \leq J + \Delta J, \tag{27}$$

where $\Delta J = \hat{q} trace[(U + B^T SB)\mathcal{Q}]$, *and* $\hat{q} = \mathbb{E}[f(g_0)^2]$.

Proof.

$$Cov(f(g_k)\gamma_k \Delta u_k) = \mathbb{E}[f(g_k)^2 \gamma_k]\mathcal{Q} \leq \mathbb{E}[f(g_k)^2]\mathcal{Q}. \tag{28}$$

Combining $Cov(f(g_k)\gamma_k \Delta u_k)$ with Lemma 3, we complete the proof.

We will verify the effectiveness of detecting replay attacks with our stochastic event-based feedback physical watermarks in the next section.

4 Detection Performance

We will consider the case where replay attacks exist in the following. According to the work [3], the attack model can be represented by the following system dynamics:

$$x'_{k+1} = Ax'_k + Bu'_k + w'_k, \tag{29}$$
$$y'_k = Cx'_k + v'_k, \tag{30}$$
$$\hat{x}'_{k+1|k} = A\hat{x}'_{k|k} + Bu'_k, \tag{31}$$
$$\hat{x}'_{k|k} = \hat{x}'_{k|k-1} + K(y'_k - \hat{x}'_{k|k-1}), \tag{32}$$
$$u'_k = L\hat{x}'_{k|k} + f(g'_k)\gamma'_k \Delta u'_k, \tag{33}$$

where γ'_k is the indication variable when the system operate without replay attacks and $\Delta u'_k \sim \mathcal{N}(0, \mathcal{Q})$. $\hat{x}_{k+1|k}$ and $\hat{x}'_{k+1|k}$ can be rewritten:

$$\hat{x}_{k+1|k} = \mathscr{A}\hat{x}_{k|k-1} + (A + BL)Ky'_k + Bf(g^a_k)\gamma_k \Delta u_k. \tag{34}$$
$$\hat{x}'_{k+1|k} = \mathscr{A}\hat{x}'_{k|k-1} + (A + BL)Ky'_k + Bf(g'_k)\gamma'_k \Delta u'_k. \tag{35}$$

Let $\hat{x}_{0|-1} - \hat{x}'_{0|-1} \triangleq \zeta$. Then the innovation of Kalman filter when replay attacks exist can be expressed as:

$$z^a_k = y'_k - C\hat{x}_{k|k-1}$$
$$= z'_k - C\mathscr{A}^k\zeta - C\sum_{i=0}^{k-1}\mathscr{A}^{k-i-1}B(f(g^a_i)\gamma_i \Delta u_i - f(g'_i)\gamma'_i \Delta u'_i), \tag{36}$$

The next theorem shows the upper bound of $\mathbb{E}[f(g^a_k)^2]$ when the replay attacks exist.

Theorem 3. *Define* $q(\cdot) \triangleq f(\cdot)^2$. *We assume that* $q(\cdot)$ *is a monotonically increasing truncation function and the watermark is added at each time step* k *when the replay attacks exist, since using this method the* $\mathbb{E}[q(g_k^a)]$ *is the largest, and the upper bound of* $\mathbb{E}[q(g_k^a)]$ *is* $\bar{q}$ *and* $\bar{q} \geq \hat{q}$.

Proof. It is worth noted that Δu_i is independent of $f(g_j^a)$ when $j \leq i$ and the vectors of the virtual system for all k. The proof can refer to the proof of Theorem 3 in work [16], so it is omitted here.

The following theorem gives the upper and lower bounds of the probability of adding a physical watermark when the replay attacks exist.

Theorem 4. *The probability of adding a watermark will increase when replay attacks exist. The bounds of* $Pr(\gamma_k = 1)$ *are given as follows:*

$$\lim_{k \to \infty} Pr(\gamma_k = 1) \leq 1 - \frac{1}{|I + Y\mathscr{H}|^{\frac{1}{2}}}, \tag{37}$$

$$\lim_{k \to \infty} Pr(\gamma_k = 1) \geq \gamma, \tag{38}$$

where

$$\mathscr{H} = \mathscr{P} + C\mathscr{M}C^T + C\mathscr{N}C^T, \tag{39}$$

$\mathscr{M}$ *and* $\mathscr{N}$ *are the solutions of the following Lyapunov equations, respectively*

$$\mathscr{M} - \bar{q}B\mathscr{Q}B^T = \mathscr{A}\mathscr{M}\mathscr{A}^T, \tag{40}$$

$$\mathscr{N} - \hat{q}B\mathscr{Q}B^T = \mathscr{A}\mathscr{N}\mathscr{A}^T. \tag{41}$$

Proof. Define $\tilde{\gamma}_k \triangleq (\gamma_1, \gamma_1', ..., \gamma_k, \gamma_k')$. It can be seen from (36) that when k is large enough, the expectation of z_k^a will converge to 0, so $z_k^a \sim \mathcal{N}(0, \Pi_k(\tilde{\gamma}_{k-1}))$, where

$$\Pi_k(\tilde{\gamma}_{k-1}) = \mathscr{P} + C\sum_{i=0}^{k-1}\{\mathbb{E}[q(g_i^a)\gamma_i]\mathscr{A}^{k-i-1}B\mathscr{Q}B^T(\mathscr{A}^{k-i-1})^T \tag{42}$$

$$+ \mathbb{E}[q(g_i')\gamma_i']\mathscr{A}^{k-i-1}B\mathscr{Q}B^T(\mathscr{A}^{k-i-1})^T\}C^T.$$

The probability of not adding a watermark:

$$Pr(\gamma_k = 0) = \mathbb{E}_{\tilde{\gamma}_{k-1}}\left[\int_{\mathbb{R}^m} \varphi_k p(z_k^a) dz_k^a\right]$$

$$= \mathbb{E}_{\tilde{\gamma}_{k-1}}\left[\frac{1}{(2\pi)^{m/2}|\Pi_k(\tilde{\gamma}_{k-1})|^{\frac{1}{2}}}\right.$$

$$\left. \times \int_{\mathbb{R}^m} exp\{-\frac{1}{2}z_k^{aT}Yz_k^a\}exp\{-\frac{1}{2}z_k^{aT}\Pi_k(\tilde{\gamma}_{k-1})^{-1}z_k^a\}dz_k^a\right] \tag{43}$$

$$= \mathbb{E}_{\tilde{\gamma}_{k-1}}\left[\frac{1}{|I + Y\Pi_k(\tilde{\gamma}_{k-1})|^{\frac{1}{2}}}\right].$$

Combining (42) and Theorem 3, we have

$$\Pi_k(\tilde{\gamma}_{k-1}) \geq \mathscr{P}$$

$$\Pi_k(\tilde{\gamma}_{k-1}) \leq \mathscr{P} + C \sum_{i=0}^{k-1} \{\bar{q}\mathscr{A}^{k-i-1}B\mathscr{Q}B^T(\mathscr{A}^{k-i-1})^T \tag{44}$$

$$+ \hat{q}\mathscr{A}^{k-i-1}B\mathscr{Q}B^T(\mathscr{A}^{k-i-1})^T\}C^T = \mathscr{H}.$$

Then we can acquire that

$$\lim_{k\to\infty} Pr(\gamma_k = 0) \leq \frac{1}{|I + Y\mathscr{P}|^{\frac{1}{2}}} \tag{45}$$

$$\lim_{k\to\infty} Pr(\gamma_k = 0) \geq \frac{1}{|I + Y\mathscr{H}|^{\frac{1}{2}}}. \tag{46}$$

which finishes the proof.

In the next theorem, we analyze the performance of the χ^2 detector based on stochastic event-based feedback physical watermarks. We will show the utility of our watermarks by proving the improvement in detection rate.

Theorem 5. *When the system operates without replay attacks,*

$$\mathbb{E}[g_k] = m. \tag{47}$$

When the replay attacks exist,

$$\lim_{k\to\infty} \mathbb{E}[g_k] \leq m + trace(C^T\mathscr{P}^{-1}C\mathscr{M})$$

$$+ trace(C^T\mathscr{P}^{-1}C\mathscr{N}), \tag{48}$$

$$\lim_{k\to\infty} \mathbb{E}[g_k] \geq m. \tag{49}$$

Proof. When the system operates without replay attacks, it is trivial to prove

$$\mathbb{E}[z_k^T\mathscr{P}^{-1}z_k] = trace(\mathscr{P}^{-1}\mathbb{E}(z_k z_k^T)) = m. \tag{50}$$

When the replay attacks exist, from (44)

$$\mathscr{P} \leq \lim_{k\to\infty} Cov(z_k^a) \leq \mathscr{P} + C\mathscr{M}C^T + C\mathscr{N}C^T. \tag{51}$$

Hence, we can obtain that

$$\lim_{k\to\infty} \mathbb{E}[z_k^{aT}\mathscr{P}^{-1}z_k^a] = \lim_{k\to\infty} trace(\mathscr{P}^{-1}\mathbb{E}(z_k^a z_k^{aT}))$$

$$\leq m + trace(C^T\mathscr{P}^{-1}C\mathscr{M}) + trace(C^T\mathscr{P}^{-1}C\mathscr{N}), \tag{52}$$

$$\lim_{k\to\infty} \mathbb{E}[z_k^{aT}\mathscr{P}^{-1}z_k^a] = \lim_{k\to\infty} trace(\mathscr{P}^{-1}\mathbb{E}(z_k^a z_k^{aT}))$$

$$\geq m. \tag{53}$$

5   Numerical Example

In this section, we will demonstrate the effectiveness of stochastic event-based feedback physical watermarks by comparing with the ordinary watermarks [3]. For simplicity, we analyze the detection of replay attacks on the following system:

$$A = \begin{bmatrix} 1 & 1 \\ 0 & 1 \end{bmatrix}, B = \begin{bmatrix} 0 \\ 1 \end{bmatrix}, C = \begin{bmatrix} 1 & 0 \end{bmatrix}, Q = 0.8I, R = 1, W = I, U = 1.$$

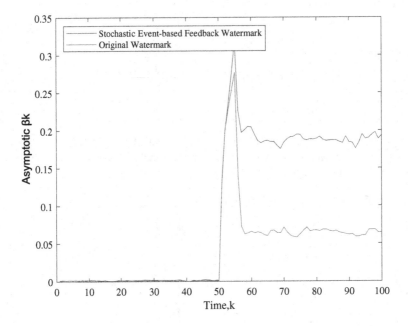

Fig. 2. Detection rates under replay attacks

The eigenvalues of $\mathscr{A}$ can be calculated as -0.339 and -0.105. Hence the system is vulnerable to replay attacks. The window sizes $\mathscr{K}$ (the χ^2 detector) and $\mathcal{K}$ (the event trigger) are set to be 5 and $f(g_k) = \sqrt{g_k}$ with upper bound $\delta = 5$, which means that the output of the χ^2 detector can be used directly. In this case, $\hat{h} = m\mathscr{T} = 5$.

Based on the above parameters, it is easy to get that $J = 23.1$. In order to better compare with the original watermarks, we set the LQG cost J' the same as $J' = 1.47J$, and the detection rates of χ^2 detector for different watermarks will be displayed. Attackers record the sensor readings from time 1 to time 50 and replay them from time 51 to time 100. In addition, the false alarm rate $\alpha_k = 0.001$. Each result takes an average of 5000 experiments. Firstly, we set $Y = 1.25\mathscr{P}^{-1}$. The covariance of our watermarks $\mathscr{Q} = 0.41$ and the covariance of ordinary watermarks $\mathscr{Q} = 1.922$. It is worth pointing out that we use this form of Y since the event scheduler can directly use g_k. We can know that when using

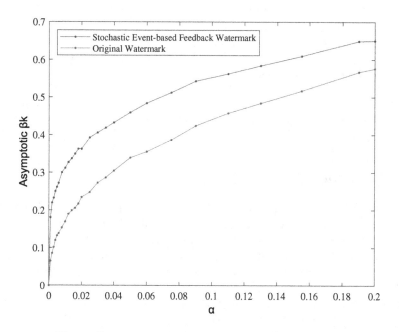

Fig. 3. Receiver operating characteristic (ROC) curves

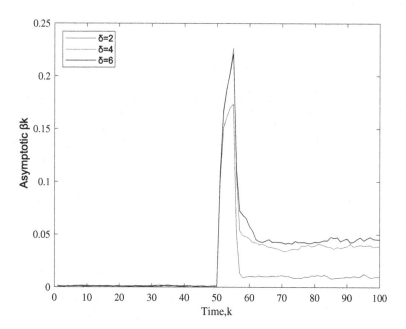

Fig. 4. Relationship between bound δ and asymptotic β_k

the stochastic event-based feedback physical watermarks, the detection rate is higher under the same performance loss according to Fig. 2. Then the ROC curves for different watermark approaches are drawn in Fig. 3. From Fig. 2 and Fig. 3, it can be immediately concluded that our watermarks are more effective than the ordinary watermarks.

Finally, we intend to study the impact of the bound δ. We set $Y = 1.25 \mathscr{P}^{-1}$ and $\mathscr{Q} = 0.2$ with $\delta = 2, 4, 6$, respectively. Figure 4 shows that a larger δ can improve the detection rate. However, it is also easy to undermine the certainty of the system.

6   Conclusion

A novel stochastic event-based feedback watermark is proposed in this paper to defend against replay attacks. Firstly, the probability of adding a watermark and the LQG performance loss when the system operates without replay attacks are analyzed. Secondly, the asymptotic upper and lower bounds of the probability of adding a stochastic event-based feedback watermark in the presence of replay attacks are discussed, and it is proved that the probability of adding a physical watermark will increase when replay attacks exist. Furthermore, the utility of our watermarks is proved by calculating the detection rate of the χ^2 detector. Finally, several numerical simulations illustrate that our method is more effective than the ordinary watermarks. In future work, we will consider parameter optimization and feedback function design.

References

1. Zhang, X.-M., Han, Q.-L., Yu, X.: Survey on recent advances in networked control systems. IEEE Trans. Industr. Inf. **12**(5), 1740–1752 (2015)
2. Cardenas, A.-A., Amin, S., Sastry, S.: Secure control: Towards survivable cyber-physical systems. In: 28th International Conference on Distributed Computing Systems Workshops, pp. 495–500 (2008)
3. Mo, Y., Sinopoli, B.: Secure control against replay attacks. In: 47th annual Allerton Conference On Communication, Control, and Computing (Allerton), pp. 911–918 (2009)
4. Mo, Y., Chabukswar, R., Sinopoli, B.: Detecting integrity attacks on SCADA systems. IEEE Trans. Control Syst. Technol. **22**(4), 1396–1407 (2013)
5. Mo, Y., Weerakkody, S., Sinopoli, B.: Physical authentication of control systems: designing watermarked control inputs to detect counterfeit sensor outputs. IEEE Control Syst. Mag. **35**(1), 93–109 (2015)
6. Weerakkody, S., Ozel, O., Sinopoli, B.: A Bernoulli-Gaussian physical watermark for detecting integrity attacks in control systems. In: 55th Annual Allerton Conference on Communication, Control, and Computing (Allerton), pp. 966–973 (2017)
7. Liu, H., Yan, J., Mo, Y.: An on-line design of physical watermarks. In: IEEE Conference on Decision and Control (CDC), pp. 440–445 (2018)
8. Fang, C., Qi, Y., Cheng, P.: Cost-effective watermark based detector for replay attacks on cyber-physical systems. In: 11th Asian Control Conference (ASCC), pp. 940–945 (2017)

9. Ferrari, R.-M., Teixeira, A.-M.: Detection and isolation of replay attacks through sensor watermarking. IFAC-PapersOnLine **50**(1), 7363–7368 (2017)
10. Miao, F., Pajic, M., Pappas, G.-J.: Stochastic game approach for replay attack detection. In: 52nd IEEE Conference on Decision and Control, pp. 1854–1859 (2013)
11. Miao, F., Zhu, Q., Pajic, M.: A hybrid stochastic game for secure control of cyber-physical systems. Automatica **93**, 55–63 (2018)
12. Shi, L., Johansson, K.-H., Qiu, L.: Time and event-based sensor scheduling for networks with limited communication resources. IFAC Proceed. Vol. **44**(1), 13263–13268 (2011)
13. Han, D., Mo, Y., Wu, J.: Stochastic event-triggered sensor schedule for remote state estimation. IEEE Trans. Autom. Control **60**(10), 2661–2675 (2015)
14. Bertsekas, D.: Dynamic programming and optimal control: Volume I. Athena scientific (2012)
15. Mehra, R.-K., Peschon, J.: An innovations approach to fault detection and diagnosis in dynamic systems. Automatica **7**(5), 637–640 (1971)
16. Zhao, X., Liu, L., Karimi, H.-R.: Detection against replay attack: a feedback watermark approach. In: International Summit Smart City 360°, pp. 702–715 (2022)

A Cascade Finite-Time Nonlinear Extended State Observer for Active Disturbance Rejection Control

Zhicheng Gao$^{(\boxtimes)}$, Qiang Ding, and Xudong Zhao

Key Laboratory of Intelligent Control and Optimization for Industrial Equipment,
Dalian University of Technology, Dalian, China
gaozc@mail.dlut.edu.cn

Abstract. Extended state observer(ESO) is a class of high-gain observers and plays a significant role in output feedback control theory for uncertain nonlinear systems. However, it faces a challenge in industrial applications when the output is corrupted by high-frequency measurement noise, which means the core parameter, referred to as bandwidth, cannot be too large. It faces a trade-off between convergence rate and noise suppression. In this paper, A new cascade finite-time nonlinear ESO(FTNESO) combining cascade structure and finite-time nonlinear observer, which provides extra degree of freedom to design the controller, is proposed to improve the estimation performance in the presence of measurement noise. Based on the proposed cascade FTESO, an active disturbance rejection control scheme(ADRC) is established, and the controller is applied to the nonlinear gas turbine model to show its effectiveness.

Keywords: cascade · finite-time · nonlinear ESO · measurement noise · load varying

1 Introduction

Gas turbines play a significant role in the industrial field and are used on many occasions. However, in recent years, the structure of gas turbines has become more complicated, and they always work under complex conditions, so the controllers are challenging to design [1]. The traditional controller applied in the gas turbine system is a proportional integral derivative (PID) controller. It is a classical control structure and easy to design but leads to poor control accuracy or robustness.

Due to its simple structure and model-independent characteristics, ADRC is becoming popular in the gas turbine control field. In [2], Jiang et al. adopted

This work is supported by the National Natural Science Foundation of China (61722302, 61573069, 62203064), the Liaoning Revitalization Talents Program (XLYC1907140), National Major Science and Technology Project(J2019-V-0010-0105) and the Fundamental Research Funds for the Central Universities (DUT19ZD218).

H. R. Karimi and N. Wang (Eds.): S-Cube 2022, LNICST 487, pp. 120–132, 2023.
https://doi.org/10.1007/978-3-031-34899-0_8

ADRC in gas turbine control systems, compared ADRC with PID, and concluded that ADRC is superior to classical PID for its inherent robustness. Sun et al. proposed an increment cascade ADRC structure that could deal with gas turbine speed and power turbine speed simultaneously [3]. Du et al. [4] combined an ADRC with a bumpless transfer controller and improved control quality in the natural gas supply system of the gas turbine.

ADRC was proposed naturally from PID by Han [5]. Furthermore, Gao put forward linear ADRC (LADRC), using the method of pole assignment, introducing the parameter called "bandwidth" to simplify parameters adjusting [6]. To a considerable extent, the core component of ADRC is the extended state observer (ESO); the performance of ADRC depends on the accuracy and speed of ESO. However, the observer theory has its drawbacks which means it faces a trade-off between tracking speed and measurement noise suppression [7]. In [8] Lakomy K et al. proposed a new paradigm called cascade ESO, which is composed of several simple ESOs, to improve the observer's performance considering the existence of measurement noise; each level can filter part of the noise with a relatively small bandwidth. Moreover, the total result is a combination of each level. However, with extra cascade levels, the phase lag becomes more pronounced and deteriorates the accuracy of the controller.

One of the most direct ways to deal with this drawback is to improve the convergence rate of ESO. Dai et al. replaced traditional ESO with high-order sliding mode observer (HOSMO) in a class of nonlinear systems and proved the stability of the closed-loop system [9]. Humaidi et al. in [10] used another finite-time nonlinear ESO, depending on a particular nonlinear function, and came to similar effects. Another approach proposed by Wei et al. is adding a phase-leading network to a classical ESO [11], called phase-leading ESO (PESO). They provided an effective way to estimate dynamic responses without introducing extra nonlinearities or increasing the order.

This paper proposes a new ADRC based on a cascade finite-time nonlinear extended state observer. First, an FTNESO is designed to guarantee finite-time convergence of the state observers. Then, it is combined with a cascade structure to filter measurement noise. At last, the proposed controller is verified by two examples and applied to a gas turbine. The main contributions of this paper are summarized below:

1) A cascade FTNESO-based ADRC structure was introduced to improve dynamic performance.
2) A classical system example was considered, and the advantages of the proposed controller were verified by comparison.
3) An nonlinear model of a gas turbine was established and controlled by the proposed controller.

2   Preliminaries

Before the proposed cascade finite-time nolinear extend state observer based ADRC is explained, we first recall some existing preliminary results.

2.1 Standard ESO and Cascade ESO

First, the algorithm of standard ESO is established for a nonlinear dynamical system. The dynamical system is described by the following state-space model:

$$\begin{cases} \dot{x}(t) = A_n x(t) + B_n[bu(t) + f(x,t) + d(t)], \\ y(t) = C_n^T x(t) + w(t), \end{cases} \tag{1}$$

where $x = [x_1, x_2, \cdots, x_n]^T \in \mathbb{R}^n$ is the state, $d \in \mathbb{R}$ is an external disturbance, $u \in \mathbb{R}$ is the control input, $y \in \mathbb{R}$ is the measured output, $w \in \mathbb{R}$ denotes the measurement noise, $f \in \mathbb{R}$ represents lumped dynamics of the controlled system, b is the bounded uncertain nonzero control gain, and matrices A_n, B_n and C_n are given by

$$A_n = \begin{bmatrix} 0 & 1 & \cdots & 0 \\ \vdots & \vdots & \ddots & \vdots \\ 0 & 0 & \cdots & 1 \\ 0 & 0 & \cdots & 0 \end{bmatrix} \in \mathbb{R}^{n \times n}, B_n = \begin{bmatrix} 0 \\ \vdots \\ 0 \\ 1 \end{bmatrix} \in \mathbb{R}^{n \times 1},$$

$$C_n = \begin{bmatrix} 1 & 0 & \cdots & 0 \end{bmatrix}^T \in \mathbb{R}^{n \times 1}.$$

Based on the standard ESO method, let $F(t) \triangleq f(x,t) + d(t) + (b - b_0)u$, which is also called total disturbance, be the extended state x_{n+1}, where b_0 is the nonzero nominal value of the control gain b, we can expand the n order system to $n + 1$ order, with its state called z. Assume that the total disturbance $F(t)$ and its derivative $\dot{F}(t)$ are bounded, then the standard ESO design is expressed by the dynamics of the extended state estimate $z := \xi \in \mathbb{R}^{n+1}$, i.e.,

$$\dot{\xi} = A_{n+1}\xi + d_{n+1}b_0 u + L_{n+1}(y - C_{n+1}^T \xi), \tag{2}$$

where $d_{n+1} \triangleq [0, \cdots, 1, 0]^T \in \mathbb{R}^{n+1}$, and $L_{n+1} \triangleq [k_1\omega_1, k_2\omega_1^2, \cdots, k_{n+1}\omega_1^{n+1}]^T \in \mathbb{R}^{n+1}$ is the observer gain vector determined by parameter $\omega_1 \in \mathbb{R}_+$ and coefficients $k_i \in \mathbb{R}_+$ for $i \in \{1, 2, \cdots, n+1\}$. Moreover, the coefficient $k_i, i = 1, 2, \cdots, n+1$, is selected such that the following polynomial is Hurwitz:

$$\lambda^{n+1} + k_1\lambda^n + \cdots + k_n\lambda + k_{n+1}.$$

The observation error can be defined as $\tilde{\xi} \triangleq z - \xi$, while its dynamics can be calculated as

$$\dot{\tilde{\xi}} = (A_{n+1} - L_{n+1}C_{n+1}^T)\tilde{\xi} + B_{n+1}\dot{F} - L_{n+1}w. \tag{3}$$

However, the standard ESO suffers a trade-off between the speed of state reconstruction and the suppression of noise. Specifically, as is discussed in [12], we can select a large ω_1 to guarantee a fast convergence speed, while the impact of noise $w(t)$ is also amplified, and on the contrary, the smaller the parameter ω_1, the slower the convergence, and the less sensitive to noise.

In order to deal with the problem, a cascade ESO is proposed in [8], which decomposes the unknown total disturbance into a predefined number of parts based on certain frequency, and using a series of cascaded observers to reconstruct them respectively. In detail, the first level of cascade ESO uses a relatively low ω_1 to ensure only the precise estimation of the first element of state, i.e., $C_{n+1}^T z$. Following elements of the extended state, depending on further derivatives of the first one, usually are more dynamic, thus are not estimated precisely by the first level of ESO. So, the estimated state z_{n+1} will not correctly represent the total disturbance, denoting residual total disturbance as $\tilde{F} = F - z_{n+1}$, which could cause a poor control precision. Then next level observer is proposed with a larger ω_1 to guarantee a more accurate evaluation of the remaining elements of state. So by increasing the level of cascade ESO to arbitrary value p, such that $p \geq 2$, we could get a precise estimation of all the elements of state.

Based on the method proposed in [8], a cascade ESO with p level is described as

$$\dot{\xi}_1 = A_{n+1}\xi_1 + d_{n+1}b_0 u + L_{1,n+1}(y - C_{n+1}^T \xi_1),$$

$$\dot{\xi}_i = A_{n+1}\xi_i + d_{n+1}(b_0 u + B_{n+1}^T \sum_{j=1}^{i-1} \xi_j) \tag{4}$$

$$+ L_{i,n+1}C_{n+1}^T(\xi_{i-1} - \xi_i),$$

for $i \in \{2, \cdots, p\}$, $L_{i,n+1} = [k_1\omega_i, k_2\omega_i^2, \cdots, k_{n+1}\omega_i^{n+1}]^T$, where $\omega_i = \alpha\omega_{i-1}$ for $\alpha > 1$. So we only need to determine the first parameter ω_1. Finally, the extend state estimate should be expressed as

$$\hat{z} := \xi_i + B_{n+1}B_{n+1}^T \sum_{j=1}^{i-1} \xi_j. \tag{5}$$

The core idea of the cascade ESO is summarized as: observering the total disturbance with several levels, each level employs a larger bandwidth to estimate residual total disturbance left from the previous level, and get the precise estimation by combining all levels.

2.2 Nonlinear ESO

Compared with the linear ESO, the nonlinear ESO (NESO) has many advantages, such as guarantees fast-convergence, more robust to noise etc., for NESO always employs nonlinear function, which can ensure "big error, small gain or small error, big gain". As is proposed in [13], using an appropriate nonlinear function $f_{ci}(e)$ to construct NESO and choosing the parameter correctly, we could prove that the observation error dynamic has the following characteristics:

(1) converges to zero in finite-time if the derivative of the total disturbance F equals to zero, i.e., $\dot{F}(t) = 0$;
(2) can be bounded by a close region G_0, if $\dot{F}(t)$ is bounded, i.e., $|\dot{F}(t)| \leq W$.

The most commonly used nonlinear function in NESO is $fal(\cdot)$, given as

$$fal(e, \alpha, \delta) = \begin{cases} \dfrac{e}{\delta^{1-\alpha}} & |e| \leq \delta, \\ |e|^{\alpha}sgn(e) & |e| > \delta, \end{cases} \tag{6}$$

where δ is a small number which aims to express the length of the linear part. Based on $fal(\cdot)$ function, a classical nonlinear ESO is given by Han [14].

3   Main Results

In this section, inspired by [8,10], we will propose a new ESO algorithm combining a finite-time NESO and cascade ESO. And based on the proposed ESO, an improved ADRC algorithm is established.

3.1   New Finite-Time NESO

As is discussed above, a new finite-time NESO (FTNESO) is proposed here. The FTNESO has the following advantages when compared to standard ESO:

(1) ensure finite time convergence;
(2) are more flexible to deal with the peaking phenomenon;
(3) has a saturation-like profile.

For ninlinear dynamical system (1), the proposed new FTNESO is designed as

$$
\begin{aligned}
e &= y - C_{n+1}^T \xi \\
\dot{\xi} &= A_{n+1}\xi + d_{n+1}b_0 u + CL_{n+1}\mathcal{G}(\omega_1 e)e,
\end{aligned} \tag{7}
$$

where $L_{n+1} = [k_1\omega_1, k_2\omega_1^2, \cdots, k_{n+1}\omega_1^{n+1}]^T \in \mathbb{R}^{n+1}$ is the same as a standard ESO, $C = diag\{c_1, c_2, \cdots, c_{n+1}\} \in \mathbb{R}^{n+1 \times n+1}$ is a diagonal matrix, which is used to help further suppress peaking phenomenon of ESO, and the parameters $c_i, i = 1, 2, \cdots, n+1$ are chosen such that $c_1 > c_2 > \cdots > c_{n+1} > 0$. The nonlinear function $\mathcal{G}(\cdot) : \mathbb{R} \to \mathbb{R}$ is defined as

$$
\mathcal{G}(\omega_1 e) = K_\alpha |\omega_1 e|^{\alpha-1} + K_\beta |\omega_1 e|^\beta, \tag{8}
$$

where $K_\alpha, K_\beta, \alpha$ and β are the positive design parameters among 0 and 1. Similar to $fal(\cdot)$ function (6), the proposed nonlinear function $\mathcal{G}(\cdot)$ also has a saturation-like profile that ensure the feature of "small error, large gain, and large error, small gain", and it is an odd function in terms of the error e, while e is closer to zero, the value of $\mathcal{G}(\cdot)$ is larger, i.e., $\mathcal{G}_{min} < \mathcal{G}(\omega_1 e) < \infty$.

Based on the new FTNESO (7), the observation error $\tilde{\xi}$ is given by:

$$
\dot{\tilde{\xi}} = A_{n+1}\tilde{\xi} + B_{n+1}\dot{F} - CL_{n+1}\mathcal{G}(\omega_1 e)(C_{n+1}^T\tilde{\xi} + w). \tag{9}
$$

Particularly, if we select C as a $n+1$-order identity matrix, and assume $\mathcal{G}(\cdot)$ degenerate to a constant, i.e., $\mathcal{G}(\omega_1 e) \equiv 1$, which means the parameters in (8) are chosen as $\alpha = 1; \beta = 0; K_\alpha + K_\beta = 1$, then the NESO (7) is deteriorated to standard ESO (2).

As is shown in [13], using Filippov sense and self-stable region approach, we can prove that the new NESO is globally asymptotically stable, and converge to the extend state of system (1) in finite time if the measurement noise $w(t)$ can be ignored, i.e., $\tilde{\xi} = 0$ for all $t > t_f$.

3.2   New Cascade Finite-Time NESO for ADRC

A classical ADRC diagram is composed of three modules: a tracking differentiator (TD), a linear extend state observer (LESO), and a state error feedback (SEF). In brief, TD is a relatively independent part, and is employed to track the reference input and get its derivative, which will be used in SEF module. SEF is designed to provide a stable and effective output signal based on state error feedback control and total disturbance feedforward cancelling. The SEF commonly adopted is:

$$u = u_0 - \frac{\hat{z}_{n+1}}{b_0},$$

$$u_0 = \sum_{i=1}^{n}(v_i - \hat{z}_i),$$

(10)

where $v_i, i \in \{1, 2, \cdots, n\}$ are the derivatives of reference signal given by TD, i.e., $v_1 \to r, v_2 \to \dot{r}, \cdots, v_n \to r^{n-1}$, and r is the reference. Apparently, the first part of control signal u is given by state error feedback and the latter comes from total disturbance feedforward.

It is analyzed and verified in [10] that the observation errors of classical cascade ESO is bounded under non-zero measurement noise. Here, for the sake of fast convergence and peaking phenomenon suppression, in this section, FTNESO (7) is used as a component in cascade ESO, i.e., taking place of standard ESO in each level of cascade ESO. So the proposed p-level cascade FTNESO is expressed as:

$$e_1 = y - C_{n+1}^T \xi$$
$$\dot{\xi}_1 = A_{n+1}\xi_1 + d_{n+1}b_0 u + CL_{n+1}\mathcal{G}(\omega_1 e_1)e_1,$$

$$e_i = C_{n+1}^T(\xi_{i-1} - \xi_i)$$

(11)

$$\dot{\xi}_i = A_{n+1}\xi_i + d_{n+1}(b_0 u + B_{n+1}^T \sum_{j=1}^{i-1}\xi_j)$$

$$+ CL_{i,n+1}\mathcal{G}(\omega_i e_i)e_i,$$

for $i \in \{2, \cdots, p\}$, and the matrices $L_{i,n+1}$ are the same as (4). The description of extend state estimate is consistent with (5). The matrix C in each level, used to weaken peaking phenomenon, could be selected as a constant matrix to reduce parameters' adjusting. Also, if C is degenerate to identity matrix and $\mathcal{G}(\omega_1 e) \equiv 1$, cascade FTESO is deteriorated to cascade ESO.

Ignoring the measurement noise $w(t)$, we could prove, using the method given by [8], that each level of the cascade ESO is globally asymptotically stable and converge to state z in finite time, which means each level of cascade structure converges fast and ensures rapid response to various fluctuation. A block diagram of ADRC control structure with the proposed cascade FTNESO is shown in Fig. 1.

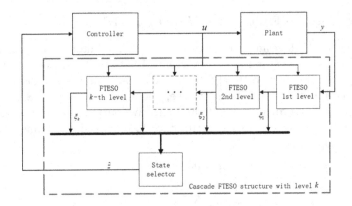

Fig. 1. the proposed cascade FTNESO

3.3   Simulation and Verification

In order to verify the effectiveness of proposed cascade FTNESO based ARDC
in terms of control precision and measurement noise attenuation, its result is
compared with a standard ESO based ADRC and a classical cascade ESO based
ADRC. The following motion control test bed system, i.e., second order time-
varying single-input single-output system is considered:

$$\ddot{y} = (-1.41\dot{y} + 23.2T_d) + 23.2u, \tag{12}$$

and torque disturbance is set as $T_d = 5sin(t) + 1$, or written in state-space form:

$$\begin{cases} \dot{x}(t) = A_2 x(t) + B_2[bu + f(x) + d(t)], \\ y = C_2^T x(t) + w(t), \end{cases} \tag{13}$$

with system state $x = \begin{bmatrix} x_1 \\ x_2 \end{bmatrix}$, where $b = 23.2$, $f(x) = -1.41x_1$, $d(t) = 23.2T_d$,
and $w(t)$ is band-limited white noise caused by sensors with power $1e^{-6}$. The
sampling frequency is set to 1000 HzHz. For comparison, the cascade level p is
set as 3.

Sim1. Firstly, we assume the control gain b is accurately known, then $b_0 = b = 23.2$, and total disturbance is generalized as $F(t) = -1.41x_1 + 23.2T_d$. The
total disturbance estimation, controller output and system output controlled by
these three controller (i.e., standard ESO based ADRC, classical cascade ESO
based ADRC and FTNESO based ARDC) is given in Fig. 2. The parameters are
summarized in Table 1. The coefficient $k_i, i = 1, 2, 3$ in observer gain matrix L_3
is selected as $k_1 = 3, k_2 = 3, k_3 = 1$ by pole placement technique, i.e., assigning
all observer eigenvalues at $-\omega_1$.

Considering the system output, the control signal and reconstructed total disturbance, we can find that, the standard ESO with parameter $\omega_1 = 150$, which

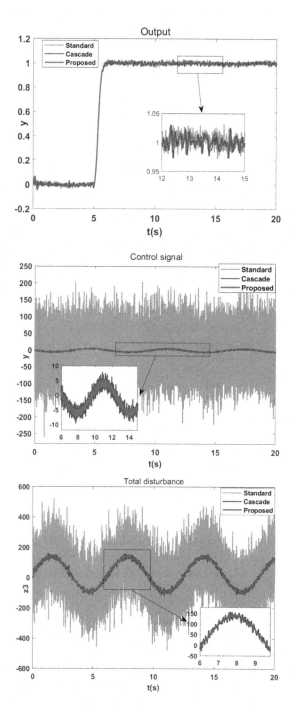

Fig. 2. performance comparison between three controllers with given $b_0 = b = 23.2$

Table 1. Observer structures and parameters used in the comparison

	ω_1	ω_2	ω_3
Standard ESO	150		
Cascaded ESO	35	$1.1\omega_1$	$1.1^2\omega_1$
Proposed FTESO	60	$1.1\omega_1$	$1.1 * 1.2\omega_1$
	$K_\alpha = 0.999; \alpha = 0.3013; k_\beta = 0.38; \beta = 0.305$		

is also known as observer bandwidth, is severely polluted by measurement noise, i.e., its observed total disturbance varying rapidly, and consumes more control energy to obtain similarly output results. It is not difficult to understand, as is analyzed in [7], with a large observer bandwidth, the tracking speed is accelerated, means the observer error declines rapidly, while the noise is amplified simultaneously, and the higher order of state to be estimate, the amplification effect is more obvious. While the rest two cascade methods show better tracking performance and smaller oscillation frequency, additionally,the FTESO has better noise suppression ability. To compare the advantages and disadvantages of the two cascade methods, we consider two internal criteria given in [11], which can represent tracking accuracy and energy consuming, i.e., $\int_0^T t|r - y(t)| \, dt$ and $\int_0^T u(t)^2 \, dt$, and simulation time is set as $T = 5s$. The results are shown in Table 2.

Table 2. Assessment based on selected integral quality criteria in $Sim1$

Criterion	$\int_0^T t|r - y(t)| \, dt$	$\int_0^T u(t)^2 \, dt$
Standard ESO	3.689	50041.1
Cascaded ESO	3.470	308.6
Proposed FTESO	3.222	283.7

Hence, from Table 2, compared to classical cascade ESO based ADRC, the proposed FTNESO based ADRC are more precise in reference signal tracking and more energy saving, which means also more friendly to actuators and dynamical system.

Sim2. Consider SISO system (12) again, for in many cases the control gain b is probably time-varying or not precisely known, but based on prior knowledge we assume that the nominal value b_0 is 15. Then the total disturbance can be summarized as $F(t) = -1.41x_1 + 23.2T_d + (b - b_0)u$. If we don't adjust the controller structure and control parameters, this is reasonable for the controller should be robust against various working condition changes in practical application, then the advantages of proposed cascade FTNESO based ADRC are more apparent. The responses and state estimations are shown in Fig. 3. Same as before, the internal criteria,i.e., tracking accuracy and energy consuming are exhibited in Table 3.

Table 3. Assessment based on selected integral quality criteria in $Sim2$

Criterion	$\int_0^T t|r - y(t)|\, dt$	$\int_0^T u(t)^2\, dt$
Standard ESO	4.612	83969.5
Cascaded ESO	4.022	535.9
Proposed FTESO	3.157	300.4

From the results we see obviously that the effect of classical cascade ESO based ADRC deteriorated rapidly, the tracking performance even worse than standard ESO based ADRC. Whereas the proposed cascade FTNESO still observer system state and total disturbance effectively with previous bandwidth for its fast convergence merit. In fact in this simulation, if the parameter b_0 is selected as 12 or smaller, which is quiet possible in practical application, for the control gain might affected by external interference and vary in a large region, the classical cascade ESO based ADRC even cannot ensure state convergence. While on the other hand, the proposed cascade FTNESO based ADRC also show great performance.

4 Application in Gas Turbine

Gas turbine has a complicated structure and composes of many thermodynamic models, turbomachinery models, sensor models, actuator models and heat exchange models. Recently years, ADRC is applied in gas turbine to achieve better dynamical performance and disturbance rejection ability.

In classical ADRC controller, while considering measurement noise, with a large observer bandwidth to observe system states and total disturbance rapidly, the control signal will therefore fluctuate violently. In this section, we will apply the new proposed cascade FTNESO based ADRC into the gas turbine model to filter measurement noise as much as possible and retain its disturbance rejection ability. For comparison, a classical ADRC controller is also established.

In order to verify the disturbance rejection ability and noise suppression ability of cascade FTNESO based ADRC adopted in gas turbine. in this paper, gas turbine component-level model built with T-MATS toolbox and controller simulations is set up in MATLAB. The reference speed is set to 6400 r/min, the load varies in the form of sine wave between 100% and 40% at 10s on the gas turbine. A band-limited white noise with power $4.5e^{-4}$ is used to simulate the measurement noise.

The performance of classical ADRC and cascade FTNESO based ADRC are compared and the results are shown in Fig. 4. Two criteria discussed above, tracking accuracy and energy consuming are compared in Table 4. To distinguish

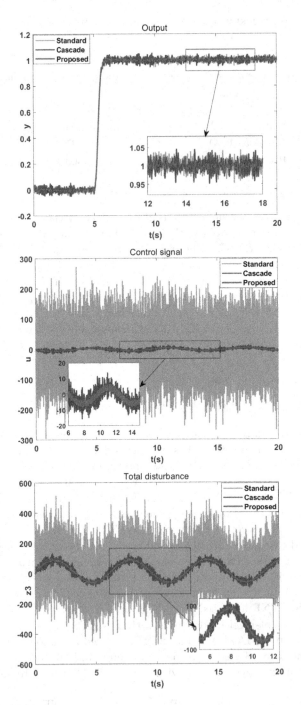

Fig. 3. performance comparison between three controllers with unknown $b = 23.2$ and nominal $b_0 = 15$

these two controllers, here we introduce another criterion [14], i.e., vibration amplitude of control input$((\int_0^T |\dot{u}(t)|\, dt))$.

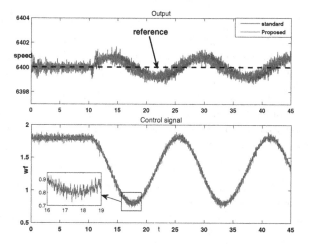

Fig. 4. performance comparison in gas turbine model

Table 4. Assessment based on selected criteria in gas turbine

Criterion	$\int_0^T t|r-y(t)|\, dt$	$\int_0^T u(t)^2\, dt$	$\int_0^T |\dot{u}(t)|\, dt$
Standard ADRC	545.1	99.50	127.4
Proposed ADRC	515.0	99.44	26.3

We could find clearly that our proposed cascade FTNESO based ADRC shows better dynamic performance and with less fluctuations.

5 Conclusion

This paper proposes a new active disturbance rejection controller based on cascade finite-time nonlinear extended state observer for a kind of nonlinear system with uncertainty both from measurement noise and inner load fluctuation. The new FTNESO-based ADRC has a faster response to handle the uncertainties caused by the load varying and a more substantial inhibition effect on measurement noise. A SISO model is established to verify the superiority of the proposed controller compared to the other two classical controllers. Then, the controller is used in a strongly nonlinear gas turbine model and proved to work effectively. Further work includes simplifying parameter adjustment.

References

1. Sun, R., Shi, L., Yang, X.: A coupling diagnosis method of sensors faults in gas turbine control system. Energy **205**, 117999 (2020)
2. Jiang, J.-P., Zhang, Q., Wang, L.-P.: Research on modeling and simulation of active disturbance rejection controller for gas turbine. In: Applied Mechanics and Materials, pp. 507–510. Trans Tech Publications Ltd (2012)
3. Sun, L., Wang, R., Sun, J., Zhang, H.: Subsystem disturbance rejection control of turbo-shaft engine/helicopter based on cascade ADRC. J. Beijing Univ. Aeronaut. Astronaut. **37**(10), 1312 (2011)
4. Du, J.-W., Sui, Y.-F., Wen, S.-X., Hao, G.-C., Du, X., Sun, X.-M.: Bumpless Transfer Control for Gas Turbine. IFAC-PapersOnLine **54**(10), 488–493 (2021)
5. Han, J.: From PID to active disturbance rejection control. IEEE Trans. Industr. Electron. **56**(3), 900–906 (2009)
6. Gao, Z.-Q.: Scaling and bandwidth-parameterization based controller tuning. In: ACC, pp. 4989–4996. (2003)
7. Khalil, H.-K., Praly, L.: High-gain observers in nonlinear feedback control. Int. J. Robust Nonlinear Control **24**(6), 993–1015 (2014)
8. Lakomy, K., Madonski, R.: Cascade extended state observer for active disturbance rejection control applications under measurement noise. ISA Trans. **109**, 1–10 (2021)
9. Dai, C., Yang, J., Wang, Z., Li, S.: Universal active disturbance rejection control for non-linear systems with multiple disturbances via a high-order sliding mode observer. IET Control Theory Appl. **11**(8), 1194–1204 (2017)
10. Humaidi, A.J., Ibraheem, I.K.: Speed control of permanent magnet DC motor with friction and measurement noise using novel nonlinear extended state observer-based anti-disturbance control. Energies **12**(9), 1651 (2019)
11. Wei, W., Zhang, Z., Zuo, M.: Phase leading active disturbance rejection control for a nanopositioning stage. ISA Trans. **116**, 218–231 (2021)
12. Ahrens, J.-H., Khalil, H.-K.: High-gain observers in the presence of measurement noise: a switched-gain approach. Automatica **45**(4), 936–943 (2009)
13. Huang, Y., Han, J.: Analysis and design for the second order nonlinear continuous extended states observer. Chin. Sci. Bull. **45**(21), 1938–1944 (2000)
14. Lakomy, K., et al.: Active disturbance rejection control design with suppression of sensor noise effects in application to DC-DC buck power converter. IEEE Trans. Industr. Electron. **69**(1), 816–824 (2021)

Fixed-Time Disturbance Observer-Based Power Control of Wave Power Generation System

Chao Bai[1] and Ning Wang[2](✉)

[1] School of Marine Electrical Engineering, Dalian Maritime University, Dalian, China

[2] School of Marine Engineering, Dalian Maritime University, Dalian, China
n.wang.dmu.cn@gmail.com

Abstract. In this paper, the current tracking control problem of direct-drive wave power generation system disturbed by complex environment is solved by designing finite-time controller(FTC) and backstepping sliding mode controller (BSMC). In order to realize the maximum power tracking control of the directly driven wave energy converter (DWEC), a fixed-time observer (FTDO) is designed to quickly compensate for environmental disturbances, and a backstepping sliding mode control strategy based on FTDO (FTDO-BSMC) is proposed to accurately track the current. Finally, Numerical simulation and comparison demonstrate the feasibility and superiority of the proposed scheme.

Keywords: direct-drive wave energy conversion · maximum wave energy tracking · fixed-time disturbance observer · back-stepping sliding mode control

1 Introduction

In recent years, the problem of energy shortages has become increasingly prominent, and the ocean contains huge amounts of energy. The low energy absorption efficiency of wave energy converters (WECs) has become a bottleneck problem in promotion and application [1–3]. As a type of wave energy power generation device, Permanent magnet linear generator (PMLG) is used to directly convert the moving wave energy into electrical energy [4]. Compared with other forms of multi-stage conversion links, it reduces power loss and improves the wave energy of the entire device. At present, in order to improve the efficiency of wave energy, researchers have carried out maximum power control research. Through mechanical control or electrical control, the wave energy conversion system can resonate with waves.

Supported by organization National Natural Science Foundation of China (Grant 52271306) Innovative Research Foundation of Ship General Performance (Grant 31422120).

© ICST Institute for Computer Sciences, Social Informatics and Telecommunications Engineering 2023
Published by Springer Nature Switzerland AG 2023. All Rights Reserved
H. R. Karimi and N. Wang (Eds.): S-Cube 2022, LNICST 487, pp. 133–145, 2023.
https://doi.org/10.1007/978-3-031-34899-0_9

Two classical theories of amplitude-phase control and complex-conjugate control for power control of wave power generation. In the amplitude-phase control, the motion of the floating body and the wave must meet certain amplitude and phase conditions to reach the resonance state and improve the output power [5–8]. However, in this control method, the natural frequency of the system is related to the wave period. For the actual sea state, it is difficult to always meet the phase condition of reaching the resonance state, and the applicability is poor when the wave frequency bandwidth changes greatly. It is suitable for wave Sea conditions with a unique dominant frequency and a small frequency variation range. In complex conjugate control, the system damping force is related to the speed and displacement of the floating body, which can be divided into two parts: linear damping force and elastic damping force. The optimal velocity of the floating body can be obtained when the system damping is equal to the conjugate of the impedance within the WEC system. At this time, the floating body motion phase and the wave motion phase still differ by 90°. The system dynamics model is equivalent to the second-order resonant circuit of inductance-capacitance-resistance, and the response form of the system is similar to the series resonance of the resonant circuit [9]. However, when it is constrained by the system motion stroke, force and output power limit, its practicality is poor in the sea area with high wave energy density and frequent sea state changes. The hill-climbing method has a simple structure and few system model parameters, so it is also used in wave power generation systems [10,11]. However, the control response speed of the hill-climbing method is greatly affected by the inertia of the system, and the disturbance step size is not easy to select. If the step size is too large, oscillation will occur near the maximum power point, resulting in energy loss. If the step size is too small, the arrival speed will be too slow, which will affect the dynamic performance of the system, so it needs to be improved. In [12–14] , a control method of changing the disturbance step size is proposed. In the case of sudden wave changes, the variable step length control method can effectively improve the anti-jamming capability of the maximum power tracking of the system, and quickly re-tracking to near the maximum power point.

Nonlinear control and intelligent control have also been developed and applied in wave power generation systems with nonlinear and strong coupling. Model predictive control and neural network-based model predictive control have been widely used in wave power generation because they do not need to rely on accurate mathematical models [15–20]. However, there is still the problem of relying on historical data, and a large amount of ocean data needs to be obtained, which is constrained by the cost problem. Sliding mode control (SMC) can solve the state and input delay problems of the system very well [10,21,22]. However, nonlinear disturbances are ignored. For unknown disturbances, observers were used to improve control performance. In [23–25], considering the system state measurements and the state-dependent disturbances are not available for feedback purposes, an observer-based adaptive control strategy has been proposed. In [26–29] a finite-time disturbance observer is proposed, in which the disturbance of the system can be observed and compensated for in a finite time.

In this paper, the system dynamics model is combined with the linear motor kinematics model, the control model of the whole system is established, and a fixed-time disturbance observer (FTDO) is designed to quickly compensate for internal and external disturbances. Unlike the finite-time perturbation observer, the fixed-time observer does not depend on the initial observation error, and the observation effect is better. At the same time, a finite-time control strategy [30,31] and a fixed-time disturbance observer-based backstepping sliding-mode control strategy (FTDO-BSMC) are designed for the d-axis current and the q-axis current, respectively, to improve the anti-disturbance and response speed of the control system and achieve the maximum wave can be captured.

2   Preliminaries and Problem Description

2.1   Lemma

Lemma 1. The following system:

$$\dot{x}(t) = f(x(t)) \tag{1}$$

where f(·)is continuous and f(0)=0
 Suppose there is a positive definite function V satisfies:

$$V + kV^\alpha \leq 0 \tag{2}$$

where $k > 0$ and $\alpha \in (0, 1)$,then the system(1) is stable in finite time.

Lemma 2. If there is a continuous radially bounded function V satisfies:

1) $V(x) = 0 \Leftrightarrow x = 0$,
2) For any $x(t)$ can satisfy the inequality $\dot{V}(x) \leq -\gamma_1 V^\alpha(x) - \gamma_2 V^\beta(x)$, where γ_1, γ_2 , α and β. are all positive constants,and $0 < \alpha < 1, \beta > 1$, then the original system can converge to zero in a fixed time, and the convergence time T satisfies:

$$T \leq T_{\max} = \frac{1}{\gamma_1 (1 - \alpha)} + \frac{1}{\gamma_2 (\beta - 1)} \tag{3}$$

It can be seen from the above formula that the convergence time of the system is only related to the system parameters γ_1, γ_2, α and β.

2.2   Problem Description

The float of the direct-drive wave energy conversion (DWEC) moves with the waves and uses the linear generator to collect wave energy. Due to the special structure of the linear generator, there is no intermediate energy conversion link, which can effectively improve the utilization rate of wave energy. However, the marine environment is relatively complex. Due to the effect of wind and waves on the float, it is difficult for the float to remain in a vertical state all the time, which will cause

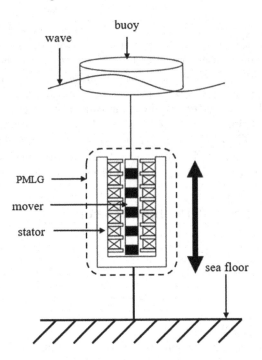

Fig. 1. Structure of direct-drive wave power generation device.

interference to the maximum wave energy tracking of DWEC. Therefore, an effective estimation of the interference is necessary to achieve accurate tracking of the maximum wave energy significant. Figure 1 shows the structure diagram of the direct-drive wave power generation device. Under the driving of the wave, the permanent magnet and the coil will produce relative motion to convert the mechanical energy of the wave into electrical energy.

The kinematic equation of the device is:

$$m\ddot{x} = F_e - F_g + F_r + F_b - mg \tag{4}$$

where m is the mass of the DWEC system, x is the mover displacement in the vertical direction, F_e is the wave excitation force, F_g is the anti-electromagnetic force of the linear motor, F_r and F_b are the radiation force and the static buoyancy of the float, respectively, which are expressed as:

$$F_r = -m_a\ddot{x} - R_a\dot{x} \tag{5}$$

$$F_b = -\kappa_1 x + mg \tag{6}$$

$$F_g = R_g\dot{x} + \kappa_2 x \tag{7}$$

Among them, m_a is the additional mass, R_a is the external damping, $\kappa_1 = \rho g S$ is the buoyancy coefficient, ρ is the seawater density, g is the gravitational acceleration, S is the contact surface between the float and the wave, R_g is the internal damping of the linear motor, and κ_2 is the elastic coefficient of the linear motor.

Combining (5)–(7), we have:

$$M\ddot{x} = F_e - (R_a + R_g)\dot{x} - (\kappa_1 + \kappa_2)x \tag{8}$$

where $M = m + m_a$ is the total mass of DWEC.

DWEC output power is:

$$P_g = \frac{F_e^2}{8R_a}\left(\left|1 - \frac{R_a - R_g - j(\omega M - \frac{\kappa}{\omega})}{R_a + R_g + j(\omega M - \frac{\kappa}{\omega})}\right|\right) \tag{9}$$

The modeling equations of device dynamics in two stationary coordinate systems are:

$$\begin{cases} \frac{di_d}{dt} = -\frac{R_s}{L_s}i_d + \frac{2\pi}{\lambda}vi_q - \frac{1}{L_s}u_d \\ \frac{di_q}{dt} = -\frac{R_s}{L_s}i_q - \frac{2\pi}{\lambda}vi_d + \frac{2\pi\psi_f}{\lambda L_s}v - \frac{1}{L_s}u_q \end{cases} \tag{10}$$

where i_d and i_q are the current components of the dq-axis, respectively.

The back electromagnetic force of the generator can also be expressed as:

$$F_g = 3\pi\frac{\psi_f i_q + (L_d - L_q)\,i_d i_q}{2\lambda} \tag{11}$$

where L_d and L_q are the inductances of the dq-axis, respectively.

It can be seen from the above formula that the anti-electromagnetic force F_g can be changed by changing the current component of the dq-axis. Therefore, the DWEC control model can be constructed by taking into account the unknown disturbances Δ existing in the actual marine environment and combining the dynamic and kinematic equations.

Combined with (8)–(11), the control model of the entire DWEC system is:

$$\begin{cases} \dot{i}_d = -\ell_s i_d + \alpha_2 vi_q - \frac{1}{L_s}u_d \\ \dot{x} = v \\ \dot{v} = D_1 + D_2 + \frac{\alpha_1(\psi_f + \ell_{dq}i_d)i_q}{M} + \Delta \\ \dot{i}_q = -\ell_s i_q - \alpha_2 vi_d + \frac{\alpha_2}{L_s}\psi_f v - \frac{1}{L_s}u_q \end{cases} \tag{12}$$

where v is the mover speed of the linear motor, $D_1 = -\frac{R_a}{M}v - \frac{\kappa_1}{M}x, D_2 = \frac{F_e}{M}, \alpha_1 = \frac{3\pi}{2\lambda}, \ell_{dq} = L_d - L_q, \ell_s = \frac{R_s}{L_s}$.

3 Power Control System Design

3.1 Disturbance Observer Design

To design the observer, first define the variable $D = v_f - \chi$,

$$\dot{\chi} = \lambda_1 D + \lambda_2 D^\alpha + \lambda_3 D^\beta + \lambda_4 sign\,(D) -$$
$$D_1 - D_2 - \frac{\alpha_1(\psi_f + \ell_{dq}i_d)i_q}{M} \tag{13}$$

Among them, $\lambda_i \in \mathbf{R}$ (i=1,2,3,4) is the positive definite diagonal matrix to be designed, each element in matrix λ_4 satisfies $\lambda_4 \geq \delta$, α and β are positive numbers, satisfies: $0 < \alpha < 1, \beta > 1$.

According to (12) and (13), the derivative of D can be obtained by:

$$\dot{D} = \dot{v}_f - \dot{\chi}$$
$$= D_1 + D_2 + \frac{\alpha_1(\psi_f + \ell_{dq} i_d) i_q}{M} + \Delta -$$
$$\lambda_1 D - \lambda_2 D^\alpha - \lambda_3 D^\beta - \lambda_4 sign(D) - D_1 - D_2 \qquad (14)$$
$$-\frac{\alpha_1(\psi_f + \ell_{dq} i_d) i_q}{M}$$
$$= -\lambda_1 D - \lambda_2 D^\alpha - \lambda_3 D^\beta - \lambda_4 sign(D) + \Delta$$

Choose $\hat{\Delta}$ as follows:

$$\hat{\Delta} = \lambda_1 D + \lambda_2 D^\alpha + \lambda_3 D^\beta + \lambda_4 sign(D) \qquad (15)$$

Define the observation error $\tilde{\Delta} = \hat{\Delta} - \Delta$, and the specific expression is:

$$\tilde{\Delta} = \hat{\Delta} - \Delta$$
$$= \lambda_1 D + \lambda_2 D^\alpha + \lambda_3 D^\beta + \lambda_4 sign(D) +$$
$$D_1 + D_2 + \frac{\alpha_1(\psi_f + \ell_{dq} i_d) i_q}{M} - \dot{v}_f \qquad (16)$$
$$= \dot{\chi} - \dot{v}_f$$
$$= -\dot{D}$$

It can be seen from (16) that if Π converges, $\tilde{\Delta}$ can be guaranteed to converge.

3.2   D-Axis Current Loop-Finite Time Controller

In order to improve the output power, the d-axis adopts the zero vector control method, and the sliding-mode control surface of the d-axis is designed as:

$$s_d = i_d + k_{id} x_e \qquad (17)$$

where $k_{id} > 0$, $x_e = x - x_d$ is the displacement error and x_d is the wave reference displacement.

The first derivative of the d-axis sliding mode control surface is:

$$\dot{s}_d = \dot{i}_d + k_{id} v_e \qquad (18)$$

The d-axis voltage control law is designed as:

$$u_d = L_s(-\varsigma_s i_d + \gamma_2 v i_q + k_{id} v_e + \eta_1 sign(s_d)) \qquad (19)$$

where η_1 is the designed constant.

3.3   Q-Axis Current Loop - Backstepping Sliding Mode Controller

Combined with the q-axis current tracking system, the tracking error is defined as:

$$x_e = x - x_d, v_e = v - v_d \qquad (20)$$

where x_d is the wave reference velocity and v_d is the wave reference velocity.

The current control law of the q-axis is designed by the backstepping method as:

$$\begin{cases} \dot{x}_e = v_e \\ \dot{v}_e = D_1 + D_2 + \frac{\alpha_1 \psi_f}{M} i_q - \dot{v}_d + \Delta \\ \dot{i}_q = -\ell_s i_q - \alpha_2 v i_d + \frac{\alpha_2}{L_s} \psi_f v - \frac{1}{L_s} u_q \end{cases} \tag{21}$$

$$i_q^* = -\frac{M}{\alpha_1 \psi_f}(D_1 + D_2 - \dot{v}_d + k_{iq} v_e + \Delta) \tag{22}$$

Substituting (22) into (21), the error dynamic equation is:

$$\begin{cases} \dot{x}_e = v_e \\ \dot{v}_e = D_1 + D_2 + \frac{\alpha_1 \psi_f}{M} i_q - \dot{v}_d + \Delta \\ i_{qe} = -\ell_s i_q + \frac{\gamma_2}{L_s} \psi_f v - \frac{1}{L_s} u_q - \alpha_2 v i_d + \frac{M}{\alpha_1 \psi_f} \\ (D_1 + D_2 - \dot{v}_d + k_{iq} v_e + \Delta) \end{cases} \tag{23}$$

where $i_q = i_q^* - i_q$.

In order to eliminate the current tracking error, the sliding mode control surface is designed:

$$s_q = i_{qe} + x_e \tag{24}$$

For the q-axis current tracking error (23), an integral sliding mode control surface is designed:

$$s_q = i_{qe} + k_{s_q} \int_0^t x_e dt - \frac{M k_{iq}}{\gamma_1 \psi_f} x_e - k_2 \int_0^t i_{qe} dt \tag{25}$$

For the q-axis integral sliding mode control surface, the voltage control law of the integral sliding mode control surface is designed as:

$$\begin{aligned} u_q = \frac{M L_s}{\alpha_1 \psi_f}(\mathcal{D}_1 + \mathcal{D}_2 - \dot{v}_d - k_{iq} v_e + \hat{\Delta}) - \ell_s L_s i_q - \\ \alpha_1 L_s v_d i_d + \alpha_1 \psi_f v - k_{s_q} x_e + \frac{M k_{iq}}{\alpha_1 \psi_f} v_e - k_2 i_{eq} \\ + L_s \eta_2 sign(s_q) \end{aligned} \tag{26}$$

4 Stability Analysis

Assumption 1 : Δ in (12) is bounded, and $||\Delta|| \leq \delta < \infty$, where δ is a known constant.

Theorem 1 : Under Assumption 1, the constructed disturbance observer can accurately estimate the unknown disturbance Δ within the stable time, and the estimation error is zero.

Proof: Choose the following Lyapunov function:

$$V_d = \frac{1}{2} D^T D \tag{27}$$

According to formula (12), the derivative of V_d can be obtained:

$$
\begin{aligned}
\dot{V}_d &= D^T \dot{D} \\
&= D^T \left(-\lambda_1 D - \lambda_2 D^\alpha - \lambda_3 D^\beta - \lambda_4 sign\left(D\right) + \Delta \right) \leq \\
&-\lambda_1 \left(D^T D \right) - \lambda_2 \left(D^T D \right)^{\frac{\alpha+1}{2}} - \lambda_3 \left(D^T D \right)^{\frac{\beta+1}{2}} \leq \\
&- \lambda_{\min}\left(\lambda_2\right) \left(D^T D \right)^{\frac{\alpha+1}{2}} - \lambda_{\min}\left(\lambda_3\right) \left(D^T D \right)^{\frac{\beta+1}{2}} = \\
&-2^{\frac{\alpha+1}{2}} \lambda_{\min}\left(\lambda_2\right) \left(\tfrac{1}{2} D^T D\right)^{\frac{\alpha+1}{2}} - 2^{\frac{\beta+1}{2}} \lambda_{\min}\left(\lambda_3\right) \left(\tfrac{1}{2} D^T D\right)^{\frac{\beta+1}{2}} \\
&= -2^{\frac{\alpha+1}{2}} \lambda_{\min}\left(\lambda_2\right) \left(V_d\right)^{\frac{\alpha+1}{2}} - -2^{\frac{\beta+1}{2}} \lambda_{\min}\left(\lambda_2\right) \left(V_d\right)^{\frac{\beta+1}{2}}
\end{aligned}
\tag{28}
$$

According to Lemma 2, it can be seen that the system Π is globally stable in fixed time, and the convergence time satisfies:

$$
T_0 \leq T_{\max} = \frac{2^{\frac{1-\alpha}{2}}}{\lambda_{\min}\left(\lambda_2\right)\left(1-\alpha\right)} + \frac{2^{\frac{1-\beta}{2}}}{\lambda_{\min}\left(\lambda_3\right)\left(\beta-1\right)}
\tag{29}
$$

According to the definition of V_d, when $t \geq T_0$, $V_d \equiv 0$, $\dot{V}_d \equiv 0$, $\dot{\Pi} \equiv 0$, then:

$$
\hat{\Delta} = 0, t \geq T_0
\tag{30}
$$

Theorem 2 : FTDO-BSMC considers the model (12) that satisfies the hypothesis 1. Under the action of the disturbance observer (15), control laws (22), (26), the unknown external disturbance to the system can be observed in a fixed time. At the same time, the error signals x_e, v_e, i_{qe} can be stabilized to zero, and the actual state can also track the expected value under the action of the controller.

Proof: The proof process is divided into two steps. First, it is proved that the d-axis current converges on the sliding mode surface in a finite time, and then it is proved that the displacement, velocity tracking error and q-axis current tracking error are after reaching the designed non-singular terminal sliding mode surface. Asymptotically stable converges to zero.

Step 1: For the d-axis current tracking control subsystem, choose the following Lyapunov function:

$$
V_1 = \frac{1}{2} s_d^2
\tag{31}
$$

Taking the derivative of the above formula, we can get:

$$
\begin{aligned}
\dot{V}_1 &= s_d \dot{s}_d \\
&= s_d(-\ell_s i_d + \gamma_2 v i_q - \tfrac{1}{L_s} u_d)
\end{aligned}
\tag{32}
$$

Substituting the voltage control law (22) into the above formula, we can get:

$$
\begin{aligned}
\dot{V}_1 &= s_d(-k_1 s_d - \eta_1 sign(s_d)) \\
&= -k_1 s_d^2 - \eta_1 \left| s_d \right|
\end{aligned}
\tag{33}
$$

According to Lemma 1, the tracking error of the d-axis current tracking system can converge to zero within a finite time.

Step 2: For the q-axis current tracking system, establish the following Lyapunov function:

$$V_2 = \frac{1}{2}v_e^2 + \frac{1}{2}s_q^2 \tag{34}$$

Taking the derivative of (32), we get:

$$\dot{V}_2 = v_e\dot{v}_e + s_q\dot{s}_q \tag{35}$$

Step 3: Considering the entire DWEC maximum wave energy tracking control system, design the Lyapunov function:

$$V = V_1 + V_2 \tag{36}$$

Combining the disturbance observer (15) and the control law (19), (22), we get:

$$\dot{V} = -\eta_1\,|s_d| - k_1s_d^2 - k_{iq}v_e^2 - k_2s_q^2 - \eta_2\,|s_q| \tag{37}$$

It can be known from the above formula that $\dot{V} \leq 0$. According to Lyapunov stability theory and Barbalat's lemma, when $t \rightarrow \infty$, x_e and v_e converge to zero. The whole system is asymptotically stable under the FTDO-BSMC control scheme.

5   Simulation Studies

In order to verify the effectiveness and feasibility of the proposed control strategy, this paper uses the direct-drive wave power generation device in the literature [5] for simulation research.

Comparing with the equivalent circuit method and sliding mode control (SMC) to verify the effectiveness of the proposed control model and control scheme. This control scheme proposes a high-level control model. The traditional equivalent circuit method is used to obtain the ideal q-axis current value , and then the control process is transformed into a high-level model virtual control quantity for direct control, which is conducive to improving the accuracy of device control. The reference displacement of the direct-drive wave energy power generation device is as follows:

$$x_d = sin\,(0.2t + 3)\,cos\,(0.5t + 8) \tag{38}$$

The unknown disturbance is:

$$\Delta = \frac{20\sin(\frac{2t}{3} + 5)\cos 0.5t\cos(\frac{t}{3})}{M} \tag{39}$$

As shown in Fig. 2, the designed fixed-time disturbance observer can effectively estimate the unknown disturbance in the marine environment, improve the tracking performance and suppress the disturbance. As shown in Fig. 3, the designed d-axis finite-time controller has a faster response speed than SMC in

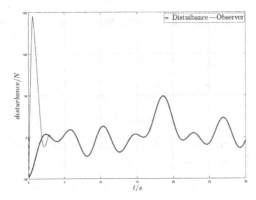

Fig. 2. Observation result of disturbance.

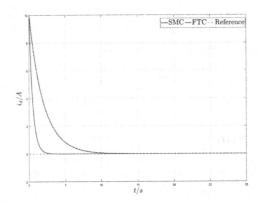

Fig. 3. Desired and actual states for i_d.

the zero vector control strategy, which reduces the reactive power loss of the direct-drive wave power generation system to a certain extent. The active power output of the system is improved. The simulation results are shown in Fig. 4 to 6. Figure 4 shows the tracking results of displacement and velocity and the tracking errors of displacement and velocity under different control strategies. It can be seen that, compared with sliding mode control and backstep sliding mode control, the proposed backstep sliding mode control strategy based on fixed time disturbance observer has smaller tracking error and tracking effect, which ensures that the float is in the running process. It can be in the same direction as the wave excitation force to achieve the purpose of resonance. Figure 5 shows the tracking effect of the q-axis current under three different control strategies. It can be seen that the proposed FTDO-BMSC control strategy can accurately track the reference current due to the interference suppression and compensation brought by the observer. The tracking error is almost zero, so that the back electromagnetic force of the linear generator can be controlled to achieve the condition of maximum power output. Figure 6 shows the energy capture of the

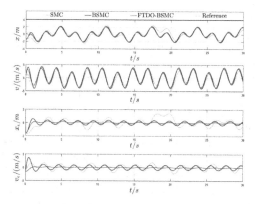

Fig. 4. Desired and actual states for x and v.

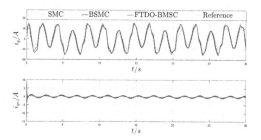

Fig. 5. Desired and actual states for i_q.

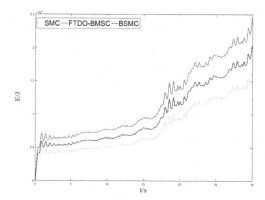

Fig. 6. Wave energy capture results under different control strategies.

direct-drive wave power generation system under different control strategies. It can be seen that compared with the other two control strategies, the proposed method can achieve the maximum wave energy capture, thereby improving the output power, which verifies the effectiveness of the algorithm.

6 Conclusion

In this paper, a backstepping sliding-mode control scheme based on a fixed-time disturbance observer is proposed to solve the power control problem of a direct-drive wave energy conversion (DWEC) under unknown disturbances in actual marine conditions. A fixed-time observer is designed to obser-ve and compensate the disturbance existing in the wave power generation system, which improves the anti-interference of the whole device. A finite-time controller is designed for the d-axis current loop, which reduces the unnecessary power loss of the device and improves the power generation efficiency. A backstepping sliding mode controller is designed for the q-axis current loop to achieve accurate current tracking. In the overall control, the float and the wave achieve the purpose of resonance, and the purpose of maximum power output is achieved. After a rigorous Lyapunov stability analysis, the stability of the entire FTDO-BSMC scheme was proved. The simulation results show the feasibility and effectiveness of the proposed control strategy.

References

1. Lopez, I., Andreu, J., Ceballos, S., Alegria, I.M.D., Kortabarria, I.: Review of wave energy technologies and the necessary power-equipment. Renew Sustain. Energy Rev. **27**, 413–434 (2013)
2. Khan, N., Kalair, A., Abas, N., Haider, A.: Review of ocean tidal, wave and thermal energy technologies. Renew. Sustain. Energy Rev. **72**, 590–604 (2017)
3. Sheng, W.: Wave energy conversion and hydrodynamics modelling technologies: a review. Renew. Sustain. Energy Rev. **109**, 482–498 (2019)
4. Ahamed, R., Mckee, K., Howard, I.: Advancements of wave energy converters based on power take off (PTO) systems: a review. Ocean Eng. **204**, 107248 (2020)
5. de O. Falco, A.F.: Phase control through load control of oscillating-body wave energy converters with hydraulic PTO system. Ocean Eng. **35**(3–4), 358–366 (2008)
6. Henriques, J., Gato, L., Falco, A.F.O., Robles, E., Fa, F.X.: Latching control of a floating oscillating-water-column wave energy converter. Renew. Energy **90**, 229–241 (2016)
7. Teillant, B., Gilloteaux, J.C., Ringwood, J.V.: Optimal damping profiles for a heaving buoy wave energy converter. IFAC Proceed. Vol. **43**(20), 360–365 (2010)
8. Babarit, A., Guglielmi, M., Clement, A.H.: Declutching control of a wave energy converter. Ocean Eng. **36**(12–13), 1015–1024 (2009)
9. Wilson, D.G., Bacelli, G., Robinett, R.D., Korde, U.A., Abdelkhalik, O., Glover, S.F.: Order of magnitude power increase from multi-resonance wave energy converters. In: OCEANS 2017 - Anchorage, pp. 1–7 (2017)
10. Amon, E.A., Brekken, T.K.A., Schacher, A.A.: Maximum power point tracking for ocean wave energy conversion. IEEE Trans. Ind. Appl. **48**(3), 1079–1086 (2012). https://doi.org/10.1109/TIA.2012.2190255
11. Xiao, X., Huang, X., Kang, Q.: A hill-climbing-method-based maximum-power-point-tracking strategy for direct-drive wave energy converters. IEEE Trans. Ind. Electron. **63**(1), 257–267 (2015)
12. Zhao, A., et al.: A flower pollination method based global maximum power point tracking strategy for point-absorbing type wave energy converters. Energies **12**(7), 1343 (2019)

13. Lettenmaier, T., Von Jouanne, A., Brekken, T.: A new maximum power point tracking algorithm for ocean wave energy converters. Int. Jo. Marine Energy **17**, 40–55 (2017)

14. Yue, X., Geng, D., Chen, Q., Zheng, Y., Gao, G., Xu, L.: 2-D lookup table based MPPT: Another choice of improving the generating capacity of a wave power system. Renew. Energy **179**, 625–640 (2021)

15. Valerio, D., Mendes, M.J.G.C., Beirao, P., da Costa, J.S.: Identification and control of the AWS using neural network models. Appl. Ocean Res. **30**(3), 178–188 (2008)

16. Li, L., Wang, H., Gao, Y.: Development of a real-time latching control algorithm based on wave force prediction. IEEE J. Ocean. Eng. **46**(2), 583–593 (2021)

17. Wang, N., Er, M.J., Sun, J.C., Liu, Y.C.: Adaptive robust online constructive fuzzy control of a complex surface vehicle system. IEEE Trans. Cybern. **46**(7), 1511–1523 (2015)

18. Wang, N., Qian, C., Sun, J.C., Liu, Y.C.: Adaptive robust finite-time trajectory tracking control of fully actuated marine surface vehicles. IEEE Trans. Control Syst. Technol. **24**(4), 1454–1462 (2015)

19. Zhan, S., Li, G., Bailey, C.: Economic feedback model predictive control of wave energy converters. IEEE Trans. Ind. Electron. **67**(5), 3932–3943 (2020)

20. Zhan, S., Li, G., Na, J., He, W.: Feedback noncausal model predictive control of wave energy converters. Control. Eng. Pract. **85**(1), 110–120 (2019)

21. Zhan, S., Na, J., Li, G., Wang, B.: Adaptive model predictive control of wave energy converters. IEEE Trans. Sustain. Energy **11**(1), 229–238 (2018)

22. Dalala, Z.M., Zahid, Z.U., Yu, W., Cho, Y.: Design and analysis of an MPPT technique for small-scale wind energy conversion systems. IEEE Trans. Energy Convers. **28**(3), 756–767 (2013)

23. Ybs, A., Ias, B., Al, C.: Smooth second-order sliding modes: Missile guidance application. Automatica **43**(8), 1470–1476 (2007)

24. Wang, N., Su, S.F.: Finite-time unknown observer-based interactive trajectory tracking control of asymmetric underactuated surface vehicles. IEEE Trans. Ind. Inform. **16**(99), 1–10 (2021)

25. Wang, N., Deng, Z.: Finite-time fault estimator based fault-tolerance control for a surface vehicle with input saturations. IEEE Trans. Industr. Inf. **16**(2), 1172–1181 (2020)

26. Wang, N., Er, M.J.: Self-constructing adaptive robust fuzzy neural tracking control of surface vehicles with uncertainties and unknown disturbances. IEEE Trans. Control Syst. Technol. **23**(3), 991–1002 (2014)

27. Wang, N., Karimi, H.R., Li, H., Su, S.F.: Accurate trajectory tracking of disturbed surface vehicles: a finite-time control approach. IEEE/ASME Trans. Mechatron. **24**(3), 1064–1074 (2019)

28. Wang, N., Ahn, C.K.: Coordinated trajectory-tracking control of a marine aerial-surface heterogeneous system. IEEE/ASME Trans. Mechatron. **26**(6), 3198–3210 (2021)

29. Wang, N., Zhang, Y., Ahn, C.K., Xu, Q.: Autonomous pilot of unmanned surface vehicles: Bridging path planning and tracking. IEEE Trans. Veh. Technol. **71**(3), 2358–2374 (2022)

30. Wang, N., Jia, Y., Fu, S.: Spring-resonance-assisted maximal power tracking control of a direct-drive wave energy converter. Trans. Inst. Meas. Control. **43**(13), 3024–3030 (2021)

31. Wang, N., Er, M.J.: Direct adaptive fuzzy tracking control of marine vehicles with fully unknown parametric dynamics and uncertainties. IEEE Trans. Control Syst. Technol. **24**(5), 1845–1852 (2016)

Disturbance Observer-Based Fast Fixed-Time Nonsingular Terminal Sliding-Mode Formation Control for Autonomous Underwater Vehicles

Hongde Qin, Jinshuai Si[✉], and Liyang Gao

Harbin Engineering University, Harbin 150001, China
sijinshuai0820@163.com

Abstract. In this paper, a disturbance observer-based fixed-time formation control method is studied for autonomous underwater vehicles with actuator faults, model uncertainties and external disturbances. Firstly, the leader-follower strategy is combined with the artificial potential field method to obtain the formation configuration. Then, a fast fixed-time disturbance observer is designed to deal with unknown composite disturbances. Further, based on the disturbance observer and fixed-time nonsingular terminal sliding-mode surface, a novel fast fixed-time formation control method is proposed. Finally, simulation results show the effectiveness of the proposed method.

Keywords: Autonomous underwater vehicles · Formation control · Nonsingular fixed-time terminal sliding-mode · Fixed-time disturbance observer

1 Introduction

In the past decade, autonomous underwater vehicles (AUV) have attracted wide attention due to its outstanding performance in underwater oil exploration, underwater surveillance and minesweeping. When performing tasks, the team cooperation of multiple AUVs is often more efficient than that of a single AUV. At the same time, in order to complete the task efficiently, advanced control methods are crucial [1–3]. Therefore, it is essential to study the formation control of AUVs. The common formation methods of AUV include leader-follower method [4], behavior-based method [5], artificial potential field method [6] and virtual structure [7], which the leader-follower method is the most widely used [8, 9]. Since different control methods have their own different advantages, two different formation control methods can be combined to enhance their respective advantages. In [10], Wu proposed a control method combining artificial potential field (APF) and leader-follower, which achieved the desired formation structure without collision.

In order to ensure fast and accurate control effect, the sliding mode control (SMC) is often used [11–18]. The traditional sliding mode control can only guarantee the asymptotic stability or finite-time stability of the system, which the convergence time cannot be calculated [19]. In [20], Polyakov proposed fixed-time control for the first time, which can make the system stable in a fixed time without considering the initial conditions.

H. R. Karimi and N. Wang (Eds.): S-Cube 2022, LNICST 487, pp. 146–163, 2023.
https://doi.org/10.1007/978-3-031-34899-0_10

In [21], two fixed-time formation control methods for multi-robot formation systems with undirected topology and directed topology were presented. In [22], a new control algorithm based on fixed-time control and switching control method was presented for multi-agent systems with first-order and second-order dynamic models, which can achieve the distributed consensus for multi-agent in a fixed time.

The multi-AUV formation system is susceptible to external disturbances and the unmodeled dynamics of the system, which poses a huge challenge to achieve stable formation effect [23]. At present, the main methods to cope with disturbances include neural network and disturbance observer [24–32]. Based on the study of traditional nonlinear disturbance observer, a disturbance estimator is used in formation control method to achieve accurately estimation of disturbances. In [33], a fixed-time disturbance estimator was proposed for USV systems with actuator saturation and dead zone, which can accurately estimate unknown disturbances. In [34], a fixed-time integral sliding-mode disturbance estimator was devised to deal with disturbances, which greatly improved the robustness of the system and was not limited by the initial conditions of the system.

Driven by the above observations, we design a multi-AUV formation control algorithm based on a fixed-time disturbance observer considering actuator fault, model uncertainties and unknown disturbances. Firstly, the desired formation configuration is obtained by combining leader-follower and APF. Then, actuator fault, unmodeled dynamics and unknown disturbances are considered as composite disturbances, and a fixed time disturbance observer is proposed to estimate them accurately. Finally, based on the fixed-time theory and sliding-mode control, a novel formation control method is proposed, which realizes the desired formation structure in a fixed time. The contributions of this article are summarized as follows:

(1) By combining the leader-follower with artificial potential field strategy, the desired formation configuration can be obtained.
(2) A fixed-time disturbance observer is designed to cope with complex disturbances, which enhances the robustness of the entire system.
(3) A new fixed-time formation control method is presented based on a fixed-time nonsingular terminal sliding-mode surface, which reaches the formation configuration.

2 Preliminaries and Problem Formulation

2.1 Preliminaries

Lemma 1. Inspired by [35], if the following system satisfies

$$\dot{z} = -\frac{1}{N(z)}\left(\alpha_0 sig^{1+\kappa}(z) + \beta_0 sig^{\frac{\ell}{q}}(z)\right) \tag{1}$$

where $\kappa = \left(\frac{m}{2n}\right)(1 + \text{sgn}(|z| - 1)). \alpha_0 > 0$, $\beta_0 > 0$, $0 < a < 1$, $b > 0$ are four scalars. $c > 0$ is an even integer. $m > 0$, $n > 0$, $p > 0$, $q > 0$ are odd integers satisfying $m > n$, $p < q$ and $N(z) = a + (1 - a)\exp(-b|z|^c), \begin{cases} c, & |z| \geq 1 \\ 1, & |z| < 1 \end{cases}$. The convergence time of the system is

$$T < \frac{n}{\alpha_0 m} + \frac{q}{\alpha_0(q - p)}\ln\left(1 + \frac{\alpha_0}{\beta_0}\right) \tag{2}$$

Remark 1. Compared with [35], the fixed-time stable system has faster convergence performance. In detail, the $N(z)$ is smaller than the $N(z)$ proposed in [35] when $|z| < 1$, which means that when the state of the system approaches the equilibrium point, the convergence rate is improved. Therefore, it is demonstrated that the system is faster than [35].

2.2 Problem Formulation

2.2.1 Leader-Follower Strategy Based on APF.

Considering the formation configuration, we choose the leader-follower strategy based on APF. The position information of i-th AUV relative to the leader l is

$$\dot{\eta}_i - \dot{\eta}_l = -\nabla_{\eta i} J(\eta) \tag{3}$$

where η_l is the position information of the leader. The net potential function is denoted as $J(\eta)$, which represents the interaction between AUVs and it is shown as

$$J(\eta) = \sum_{i=1}^{N} J_a(\|\eta_i - \eta_l\|) - J_r(\|\eta_i - \eta_l\|) \tag{4}$$

where $J_a(\bullet)$ denotes the attractive potential field and $J_r(\bullet)$ denotes the repulsive potential field. The formation configuration is restricted by artificial potential field. $J_a(\bullet)$ and $J_r(\bullet)$ are shown as

$$J_a(\bullet) = \frac{1}{2}a\|\bullet\|^2 \tag{5}$$

$$J_r(\bullet) = -\frac{1}{2}bc \exp\left(-\frac{\|\bullet\|^2}{c}\right) \tag{6}$$

where a, b, c are three constants, which are relevant to the distance between the follower and the leader. In this paper, when $\|\eta_i - \eta_l\| = d$ and $J_a(\bullet) = J_r(\bullet)$ are satisfied, the unique minimum value is obtained. Meanwhile, the net gradient potential field is zero, and the formation configuration is realized. The potential field gradient is shown as

$$\nabla J_a(\bullet) = a(\eta_i - \eta_l) / \|(\eta_i - \eta_l)\| \tag{7}$$

$$\nabla J_r(\bullet) = -\left[b(\eta_i - \eta_j) \times e^{-\|\eta_i - \eta_j\|^2 / c}\right] \tag{8}$$

$$\nabla_{\eta i} J(\bullet) = \nabla J_a(\bullet) + \nabla J_r(\bullet) \tag{9}$$

where $\nabla J_a(\bullet)$ is the attractive force to reach formation configuration and $\nabla J_r(\bullet)$ represents the repulsive force to avoid collision.

2.2.2 AUV Dynamics

The kinematics and dynamics equations of i-th AUV are shown as

$$\dot{\boldsymbol{\eta}}_i = \boldsymbol{R}(\psi_i)\boldsymbol{v}_i \tag{10}$$

$$\boldsymbol{M}_i\dot{\boldsymbol{v}}_i + \boldsymbol{C}(\boldsymbol{v}_i)\boldsymbol{v}_i + \boldsymbol{D}(\boldsymbol{v}_i)\boldsymbol{v}_i = \boldsymbol{\tau}_i + \boldsymbol{\tau}_{di} \tag{11}$$

where $\boldsymbol{\eta}_i = \begin{bmatrix} x_i, & y_i, & \psi_i \end{bmatrix}^{\mathrm{T}}$ represents the position information, $\boldsymbol{v}_i = [u_i, \ v_i, \ r_i]^{\mathrm{T}}$ represents the velocity information, $\boldsymbol{M}_i$, $\boldsymbol{C}(\boldsymbol{v}_i)$ and $\boldsymbol{D}(\boldsymbol{v}_i)$ represent inertia matrix, Coriolis matrix and damping matrix, respectively. $\boldsymbol{\tau}_i = [\tau_{iu}, \ \tau_{iv}, \ \tau_{ir}]^{\mathrm{T}}$ denotes control inputs, $\boldsymbol{\tau}_{di}$ indicates external disturbance. $\boldsymbol{R}(\psi_i)$ represents the rotation matrix and is expressed as $\boldsymbol{R}(\psi_i) = \begin{bmatrix} \cos(\psi_i) & -\sin(\psi_i) & 0 \\ \sin(\psi_i) & \cos(\psi_i) & 0 \\ 0 & 0 & 1 \end{bmatrix}$. $\boldsymbol{R}^{\mathrm{T}}(\psi_i)\boldsymbol{R}(\psi_i) = \boldsymbol{I}$, $\dot{\boldsymbol{R}}(\psi_i) = \boldsymbol{R}(\psi_i)\boldsymbol{S}(r)$, $\forall\psi_i \subseteq$ $[0, 2\pi]$, and $\boldsymbol{R}^{\mathrm{T}}(\psi_i)\boldsymbol{S}(r)\boldsymbol{R}(\psi_i) = \boldsymbol{R}(\psi_i)\boldsymbol{S}(r)\boldsymbol{R}^{\mathrm{T}}(\psi_i) = \boldsymbol{S}(r)$, where $\boldsymbol{S}(r) = \begin{bmatrix} 0 & -r & 0 \\ r & 0 & 0 \\ 0 & 0 & 0 \end{bmatrix}$

For actuator faults, the control input $\boldsymbol{\tau}_i$ is defined as

$$\boldsymbol{\tau}_i = \boldsymbol{\tau}_{Ai} + [(\boldsymbol{E}(t) - \boldsymbol{I})\boldsymbol{\tau}_{Ai} + \overline{\boldsymbol{\tau}}_i] = \boldsymbol{\tau}_{Ai} + \boldsymbol{\tau}_{Fi} \tag{12}$$

where $\boldsymbol{\tau}_{Ai}$ is the actual control input and $\overline{\boldsymbol{\tau}}_i$ is the additional bias fault. $\boldsymbol{E}(t) = \mathrm{diag}\{e_1, e_2, e_3\}$ indicates the effective coefficient matrix of the actuator. When $e_i = 1$ and $\overline{\boldsymbol{\tau}}_i = 0$, it represents that the actuator is working normally; when $e_i = 0$, it represents that the actuator is working normally. In this paper, $e_i > 1$ is considered.

According to Eqs. (10)–(12), the model is written as

$$\boldsymbol{M}_{\eta i}(\boldsymbol{\eta}_i)\ddot{\boldsymbol{\eta}}_i + \boldsymbol{C}_{\eta i}(\boldsymbol{\eta}_i, \dot{\boldsymbol{\eta}}_i)\dot{\boldsymbol{\eta}}_i + \boldsymbol{D}_{\eta i}(\boldsymbol{\eta}_i, \dot{\boldsymbol{\eta}}_i)\dot{\boldsymbol{\eta}}_i = \boldsymbol{\tau}_{\eta i} + \boldsymbol{R}(\psi_i)\boldsymbol{\tau}_{di} + \boldsymbol{R}(\psi_i)\boldsymbol{\tau}_{Fi} \tag{13}$$

where $\boldsymbol{M}_{\eta i}(\boldsymbol{\eta}_i) = \boldsymbol{R}(\psi_i)\boldsymbol{M}_i\boldsymbol{R}^{\mathrm{T}}(\psi_i)$, $\boldsymbol{C}_{\eta i}(\boldsymbol{\eta}_i, \dot{\boldsymbol{\eta}}_i) = \boldsymbol{R}(\psi_i)(\boldsymbol{C}_i - \boldsymbol{M}_i\boldsymbol{S})\boldsymbol{R}^{\mathrm{T}}(\psi_i)$, $\boldsymbol{\tau}_{\eta i} = \boldsymbol{R}(\psi_i)\boldsymbol{\tau}_{Ai}$, $\boldsymbol{D}_{\eta i}(\boldsymbol{\eta}_i, \dot{\boldsymbol{\eta}}_i) = \boldsymbol{R}(\psi_i)\boldsymbol{D}_i\boldsymbol{R}^{\mathrm{T}}(\psi_i)$.

In general, accurate model parameters are often unavailable. Therefore, the parameter matrix can be divided into two parts.

$$\boldsymbol{M}_{\eta i}(\boldsymbol{\eta}_i) = \hat{\boldsymbol{M}}_{\eta i}(\boldsymbol{\eta}_i) + \Delta\boldsymbol{M}_{\eta i}(\boldsymbol{\eta}_i) \tag{14}$$

$$\boldsymbol{C}_{\eta i}(\boldsymbol{\eta}_i, \dot{\boldsymbol{\eta}}_i) = \hat{\boldsymbol{C}}_{\eta i}(\boldsymbol{\eta}_i, \dot{\boldsymbol{\eta}}_i) + \Delta\boldsymbol{C}_{\eta i}(\boldsymbol{\eta}_i, \dot{\boldsymbol{\eta}}_i) \tag{15}$$

$$\boldsymbol{D}_{\eta i}(\boldsymbol{\eta}_i, \dot{\boldsymbol{\eta}}_i) = \hat{\boldsymbol{D}}_{\eta i}(\boldsymbol{\eta}_i, \dot{\boldsymbol{\eta}}_i) + \Delta\boldsymbol{D}_{\eta i}(\boldsymbol{\eta}_i, \dot{\boldsymbol{\eta}}_i) \tag{16}$$

where $\hat{\boldsymbol{M}}_{\eta i}(\boldsymbol{\eta}_i)$, $\hat{\boldsymbol{C}}_{\eta i}(\boldsymbol{\eta}_i, \dot{\boldsymbol{\eta}}_i)$, and $\hat{\boldsymbol{D}}_{\eta i}(\boldsymbol{\eta}_i, \dot{\boldsymbol{\eta}}_i)$ represent the nominal terms and $\Delta\boldsymbol{M}_{\eta i}(\boldsymbol{\eta}_i)$, $\Delta\boldsymbol{C}_{\eta i}(\boldsymbol{\eta}_i, \dot{\boldsymbol{\eta}}_i)$, $\Delta\boldsymbol{D}_{\eta i}(\boldsymbol{\eta}_i, \dot{\boldsymbol{\eta}}_i)$ represent the uncertain terms.

Through the above equations, we get

$$\hat{\boldsymbol{M}}_{\eta i}(\boldsymbol{\eta}_i)\ddot{\boldsymbol{\eta}}_i + \hat{\boldsymbol{C}}_{\eta i}(\boldsymbol{\eta}_i, \dot{\boldsymbol{\eta}}_i)\dot{\boldsymbol{\eta}}_i + \hat{\boldsymbol{D}}_{\eta i}(\boldsymbol{\eta}_i, \dot{\boldsymbol{\eta}}_i)\dot{\boldsymbol{\eta}}_i = \boldsymbol{\tau}_{\eta i} + \boldsymbol{d}'_i \tag{17}$$

where d'_i represents the uncertainty of the lumped system

$$d'_i = R(\psi_i)\tau_{di} + R(\psi_i)\tau_{Fi} - \Delta M_{\eta i}(\eta_i)\ddot{\eta}_i - \Delta C_{\eta i}(\eta_i, \dot{\eta}_i)\dot{\eta}_i - \Delta D_{\eta i}(\eta_i, \dot{\eta}_i)\dot{\eta}_i \quad (18)$$

Consider the desired position information $\eta_i^d = \eta_l - \int_0^t \nabla_{\eta i} J(\eta)$ and define the formation position error $\eta_{ei} = \eta_i - \eta_i^d$ and auxiliary error $\omega_{ei} = \dot{\eta}_i - \dot{\eta}_i^d$. Therefore, let $x_{1i} = \eta_{ei}$, $x_{2i} = \omega_{ei}$, the kinematics and dynamics equations can be modified as

$$\begin{cases} \dot{x}_{1i} = x_{2i} \\ \dot{x}_{2i} = u_i + d_i - \hat{M}_{\eta i}^{-1}(\eta_i)\left(\hat{C}_{\eta i}(\eta_i, \dot{\eta}_i)\dot{\eta}_i + \hat{D}_{\eta i}(\eta_i, \dot{\eta}_i)\dot{\eta}_i\right) - \ddot{\eta}_i^d \end{cases} \quad (19)$$

where $u_i = \hat{M}_{\eta i}^{-1}(\eta_i)\tau_{\eta i}$ is transformed control input, $d_i = \hat{M}_{\eta i}^{-1}(\eta_i)d'_i$ is composite disturbance.

3 Main Results

The composite disturbance and the convergence rate of the system will affect the efficiency of formation task. In order to improve the efficiency of formation task, a new fixed-time formation control method is proposed by combining a fixed-time observer with the improved sliding-mode surface, which is also the main result of this paper.

3.1 Fixed-Time Disturbance Observer Design and Analysis

The existence of composite disturbance will affect the state of the system. If we cannot deal with the composite disturbance well, it will have a negative impact on the formation result. Therefore, in order to ensure that the system has good performance in the presence of composite disturbance, a new fixed-time disturbance observer is designed to estimate this composite disturbance d_i in this part. An auxiliary system is designed as

$$x_{fi} = \gamma_1 \int_0^t \left[u_i - \hat{M}_{\eta i}^{-1}(\eta_i)\left(\hat{C}_{\eta i}(\eta_i, \dot{\eta}_i)\dot{\eta}_i + \hat{D}_{\eta i}(\eta_i, \dot{\eta}_i)\dot{\eta}_i\right) - \ddot{\eta}_i^d - x_{fi}\right]d\tau - \gamma_1 x_{2i} \quad (20)$$

where x_{fi} is the auxiliary system, and $\gamma_1 > 0$ is the control parameter. Taking the derivative of (20), we get

$$\dot{x}_{fi} = -\gamma_1 x_{fi} - \gamma_1 d_i \quad (21)$$

$$y_{1i} = \gamma_2 x_{fi} \quad (22)$$

where y_{1i} denotes the output of (22) and $\gamma_2 > 0$ denotes a gain parameter.

The estimation of x_{fi} is designed as $\hat{x}_{fi}$

$$\dot{\hat{x}}_{fi} = -\gamma_3\gamma_2\hat{x}_{fi} + \gamma_2^{-1}y_{1i} + \gamma_3 y_{1i} + \frac{1}{N(\tilde{x}_{fi})}\left(\lambda_1 sig^{k_1}(\tilde{x}_{fi}) + \lambda_2 sig^{k_2}(\tilde{x}_{fi})\right) \quad (23)$$

where $\tilde{x}_{fi} = x_{fi} - \hat{x}_{fi}$ is estimation error, and $\gamma_3 > 0$ is a control gain parameter. $N(\tilde{x}_{fi}) = a_1 + (1 - a_1)\exp(-b_1|\tilde{x}_{fi}|^{c_1})$, $\begin{cases} c_1, & |\tilde{x}_{fi}| \geq 1 \\ 1, & |\tilde{x}_{fi}| < 1 \end{cases}$, $k_1 = 1 + \left(\frac{m_1}{2n_1}\right)(1 + \text{sgn}(|\tilde{x}_{fi}| - 1))$, $k_2 = \frac{p_1}{q_1}$, $\lambda_1 > 0$, $\lambda_2 > 0$, $0 < a_1 < 1$, $b_1 > 0$, $c_1 > 0$ are five constants. $m_1 > n_1 > 0$, $0 < p_1 < q_1$ are four odd integers.

Lemma 2. Based on the proposed auxiliary system (20), the estimation error will converge to the origin in a fixed time, and the convergence time T_0 is

$$T_0 < \frac{1}{\lambda_1\mu_1} + \frac{1}{\lambda_1(1-\omega_1)}\ln\left(1 + \frac{\lambda_1}{2^{(\omega_1-1)/2}\lambda_2}\right) \tag{24}$$

where $\mu_1 = \frac{m_1}{n_1}$, $\omega_1 = \frac{p_1}{q_1}$.

Proof. Consider the Lyapunov function $V_1 = \frac{1}{2}\tilde{x}_{fi}^T\tilde{x}_{fi}$, and the derivative of V_1 satisfies

$$\begin{aligned}
\dot{V}_1 &= \tilde{x}_{fi}^T\dot{\tilde{x}}_{fi} = \tilde{x}_{fi}^T\left(\dot{x}_{fi} - \dot{\hat{x}}_{fi}\right) \\
&= \tilde{x}_{fi}^T\left(-\gamma_1 x_{fi} - \gamma_1 d_i + \gamma_3\gamma_2\hat{x}_{fi} - \gamma_2^{-1}\gamma_2 x_{fi} - \gamma_3\gamma_2 x_{fi}\right) \\
&\quad - \tilde{x}_{fi}^T\frac{1}{N(\tilde{x}_{fi})}\left(\lambda_1 \text{sig}^{k_1}(\tilde{x}_{fi}) + \lambda_2 \text{sig}^{k_2}(\tilde{x}_{fi})\right) \\
&= \tilde{x}_{fi}^T\left(-\gamma_3\gamma_2\tilde{x}_{fi} - \frac{1}{N(\tilde{x}_{fi})}\left(\lambda_1 \text{sig}^{k_1}(\tilde{x}_{fi}) + \lambda_2 \text{sig}^{k_2}(\tilde{x}_{fi})\right)\right) \\
&\leq -\tilde{x}_{fi}^T\frac{1}{N(\tilde{x}_{fi})}\left(\lambda_1 \text{sig}^{k_1}(\tilde{x}_{fi}) + \lambda_2 \text{sig}^{k_2}(\tilde{x}_{fi})\right) \\
&\leq -\sum_{j=1}^{3}\frac{1}{N(\tilde{x}_{fi,j})}\left(\lambda_1|\tilde{x}_{fi,j}|^{k_1+1} + \lambda_2|\tilde{x}_{fi,j}|^{k_2+1}\right) \\
&\leq -\frac{1}{N(\tilde{x}_{fi})}\lambda_1(2V_1)^{(k_1+1)/2} - \frac{1}{N(\tilde{x}_{fi})}\lambda_2(2V_1)^{(k_2+1)/2}
\end{aligned} \tag{25}$$

when $|\tilde{x}_{fi}| \geq 1$, one has

$$\dot{V}_1 \leq -\frac{1}{N(\tilde{x}_{fi})}\lambda_1(2V_1)^{(\mu_1+1)/2} - \frac{1}{N(\tilde{x}_{fi})}\lambda_2(2V_1) \tag{26}$$

when $|\tilde{x}_{fi}| < 1$, one has

$$\dot{V}_1 \leq -\frac{1}{N(\tilde{x}_{fi})}\lambda_1(2V_1) - \frac{1}{N(\tilde{x}_{fi})}\lambda_2(2V_1)^{(\omega_1+1)/2} \tag{27}$$

Therefore, the error of the auxiliary system can converge to the origin in a fixed time.

$$T_0 < \frac{1}{\lambda_1\mu_1} + \frac{1}{\lambda_1(1-\omega_1)}\ln\left(1 + \frac{\lambda_1}{2^{(\omega_1-1)/2}\lambda_2}\right) \tag{28}$$

Lemma 3. The estimated value of composite disturbance is defined as

$$\hat{d}_i = -(\gamma_1 \gamma_2)^{-1} \dot{y}_{1i} - \hat{x}_{fi} \tag{29}$$

Proof. Define the error $\tilde{d}_i = \hat{d}_i - d_i$. From (22), we have

$$d_i = -x_{fi} - \gamma_1^{-1} \dot{x}_{fi} \tag{30}$$

Then, combining Eqs. (29) and (30), we can further get

$$\tilde{d}_i = \hat{d}_i - d_i = -(\gamma_1 \gamma_2)^{-1} \dot{y}_{1i} - \hat{x}_{fi} + x_{fi} + \gamma_1^{-1} \dot{x}_{fi}$$
$$= -\gamma_1^{-1} \dot{x}_{fi} + \gamma_1^{-1} \dot{x}_{fi} - \hat{x}_{fi} + x_{fi} = \tilde{x}_{fi} \tag{31}$$

According to Lemma 2, we can obtain that $\tilde{d}_i$ tends to 0 for $t \geq T_0$. Therefore, the composite disturbance can accurately be observed by the proposed fixed-time disturbance observer. This means that the robustness of the system is greatly enhanced.

Remark 2. The proposed fixed-time disturbance observer in this part has the following advantages. On the one hand, the convergence rate of the observation error is improved, and the convergence time of the system is not affected by the initial conditions. On the other hand, we can observe the composite disturbance accurately without knowing prior information about it, which means that the observer can be better applied in practice.

3.2 Nonsingular Fast Fixed-Time Controller Design

The convergence rate is a very important performance index in the control system. The faster convergence rate can accomplish the formation task more efficiently. Therefore, based on the above analysis, a novel nonsingular fast fixed-time formation controller is designed.

Inspired by Lemma 1, the sliding-mode surface is designed as

$$S_i = x_{2i} + \frac{1}{N(x_{1i})} \left(\lambda_3 sig^{k_3}(x_{1i}) + \lambda_4 S_{ci} \right) \tag{32}$$

where $S_{i,j} = [S_{i,1}, S_{i,2}, S_{i,3}]^T$, $N(x_{1i}) = a_2 + (1 - a_2) \exp(-b_2 |x_{1i}|^{c_2})$, $\begin{cases} c_2, & |x_{1i}| \geq 1 \\ 1, & |x_{1i}| < 1 \end{cases}$, and $k_3 = 1 + \left(\frac{m_2}{2n_2}\right)(1 + sgn(|x_{1i}| - 1))$. $\lambda_3 > 0$, $\lambda_4 > 0$, $0 < a_2 < 1$, $b_2 > 0$ are four scalars. $c_2 > 0$ is an even integer. $m_2 > n_2 > 0$ are two odd integers. $S_{ci,j} = [S_{ci,1}, S_{ci,2}, S_{ci,3}]^T$ is designed as

$$S_{ci} = \begin{cases} sig^{k_4}(x_{1i}), & \text{if } \bar{S}_i = 0 \text{ or } \bar{S}_i \neq 0, |x_{1i}| \geq \phi \\ \sigma_1 x_{1i} + \sigma_2 x_{1i}^2 sgn(x_{1i}), & \text{if } \bar{S}_i \neq 0, |x_{1i}| < \phi \end{cases} \tag{33}$$

where $k_4 = \frac{p_2}{q_2}, 0 < \phi < 1. 0 < p_2 < q_2$ are two odd integers and $\sigma_1 = \left(2 - \frac{p_2}{q_2}\right) \phi^{\frac{p_2}{q_2} - 1}$, $\sigma_2 = \left(\frac{p_2}{q_2} - 1\right) \phi^{\frac{p_2}{q_2} - 2}, \bar{S}_i = x_{2i} + \frac{1}{N(x_{1i})} (\lambda_3 sig^{k_3}(x_{1i}) + \lambda_4 sig^{k_4}(x_{1i}))$.

Take the derivative of the sliding mode surface (32)

$$\dot{S}_i = \dot{x}_{2i} + \frac{1}{N^2(x_{1i})}\left[N(x_{1i})(\lambda_3 P_1 + \lambda_4 P_2)x_{1i} - \dot{N}(x_{1i})\left(\lambda_3 sig^{k_3}(x_{1i}) + \lambda_4 S_{ci}\right)\right]$$

$$= u_i + d_i - \hat{M}_{\eta i}^{-1}(\eta_i)\left(\hat{C}_{\eta i}(\eta_i, \dot{\eta}_i)\dot{\eta}_i + \hat{D}_{\eta i}(\eta_i, \dot{\eta}_i)\dot{\eta}_i\right) - \ddot{\eta}_i^d$$

$$+ \frac{1}{N^2(x_{1i})}\left[N(x_{1i})(\lambda_3 P_1 + \lambda_4 P_2)\dot{x}_{1i} - \dot{N}(x_{1i})\left(\lambda_3 sig^{k_3}(x_{1i}) + \lambda_4 S_{ci}\right)\right]$$

(34)

Combining the disturbance observer Eq. (29) and the sliding-mode surface (32), a fixed-time formation controller is presented

$$u_i = u_{i1} + u_{i2} \tag{35}$$

where

$$u_{i1} = -\left(\begin{array}{c} \hat{d}_i - \hat{M}_{\eta i}^{-1}(\eta_i)\left(\hat{C}_{\eta i}(\eta_i, \dot{\eta}_i)\dot{\eta}_i + \hat{D}_{\eta i}(\eta_i, \dot{\eta}_i)\dot{\eta}_i\right) - \ddot{\eta}_i^d \\ + \frac{1}{N^2(x_{1i})}\left[N(x_{1i})(\lambda_3 P_1 + \lambda_4 P_2)\dot{x}_{1i} - \dot{N}(x_{1i})\left(\lambda_3 sig^{k_3}(x_{1i}) + \lambda_4 S_{ci}\right)\right] \end{array}\right)$$

(36)

$$u_{i2} = -\frac{1}{N(S_i)}\left(\lambda_5 sig^{k_5}(S_i) + \lambda_6 sig^{k_6}(S_i)\right) \tag{37}$$

where $N(S_i) = a_3 + (1 - a_3)\exp\left(-b_3|S_i|^{c_3}\right)$,
$\begin{cases} c_3, & |S_i| \geq 1 \\ 1, & |S_i| < 1 \end{cases}$, $k_5 = 1 + \left(\frac{m_3}{2n_3}\right)(1 + sgn(|S_i| - 1))$, $k_6 = \frac{p_3}{q_3}$, $\lambda_5 > 0$, $\lambda_6 > 0$,
$0 < a_3 < 1$, $b_3 > 0$, $c_3 > 0$, $m_3 > n_3 > 0$, $q_3 > p_3 > 0$ are four odd integers.
$P_2 = \begin{cases} k_4 diag(|x_{1i}|^{k_4-1}), & \text{if } \bar{S}_i = 0 \text{ or } \bar{S}_i \neq 0, |x_{1i}| \geq \phi \\ \sigma_1 I_3 + 2\sigma_2 diag(|x_{1i}|), & \text{if } \bar{S}_i \neq 0, |x_{1i}| < \phi \end{cases}$, $P_1 = k_3 diag(|x_{1i}|^{k_3-1})$.

Theorem 1. Applying the proposed controller (35) to the kinematics and dynamics Eq. (19), the formation errors can convergence to the origin with the settling time T satisfying $T < \max(T_0, T_1) + T_2$, where T_1 and T_2 are shown as

$$T_1 < \frac{1}{\lambda_5 \mu_3} + \frac{1}{\lambda_5(1 - \omega_3)}\ln\left(1 + \frac{\lambda_5}{2^{(\omega_3-1)/2}\lambda_6}\right) \tag{38}$$

$$T_2 < \frac{1}{\lambda_3 \mu_2} + \frac{1}{\lambda_3(1 - \omega_2)}\ln\left(1 + \frac{\lambda_3}{2^{(\omega_2-1)/2}\lambda_4}\right) \tag{39}$$

where $\mu_2 = \frac{m_2}{n_2}$, $\omega_2 = \frac{p_2}{q_2}$, $\mu_3 = \frac{m_3}{n_3}$, $\omega_3 = \frac{p_3}{q_3}$.

Proof. According to the characteristics of sliding-mode control, we divide the proof process into two parts.

Part 1. Substituting (35) into (34), we have

$$\dot{S}_i = -\frac{1}{N(S_i)}\left(\lambda_5 sig^{k_5}(S_i) + \lambda_6 sig^{k_6}(S_i)\right) + d_i - \hat{d}_i \tag{40}$$

Considering the Lyapunov function $V_2 = \frac{1}{2}S_i^T S_i$, we can get

$$\dot{V}_2 = S_i^T \dot{S}_i = -S_i^T\left(\frac{1}{N(S_i)}\left(\lambda_5 sig^{k_5}(S_i) + \lambda_6 sig^{k_6}(S_i)\right) + \hat{d}_i - d_i\right)$$

$$\leq -\frac{1}{N(S_i)}\sum_{j=1}^{3}\left(\lambda_5|S_{i,j}|^{k_5+1} + \lambda_6|S_{i,j}|^{k_6+1}\right) - S_i^T d_e \qquad (41)$$

$$\leq -\frac{1}{N(S_i)}\lambda_5(2V_2)^{(k_5+1)/2} - \frac{1}{N(S_i)}\lambda_6(2V_2)^{(k_6+1)/2}$$

when $|S_i| \geq 1$, one has

$$\dot{V}_2 \leq -\frac{1}{N(S_i)}\lambda_5(2V_2)^{(\mu_3+1)/2} - \frac{1}{N(S_i)}\lambda_6(2V_2) \qquad (42)$$

when $|S_i| < 1$, we can obtain

$$\dot{V}_2 \leq -\frac{1}{N(S_i)}\lambda_5(2V_2) - \frac{1}{N(S_i)}\lambda_6(2V_2)^{(\omega_3+1)/2} \qquad (43)$$

Applying Lemma 1 and (41), we have $V_2 = 0$. According to Lemma 3, we have $\tilde{d}_i = 0$ when $t \geq T_0$. Therefore, the proposed sliding-mode surface can converge to the origin when $t \geq \max(T_0, T_1)$, and the fixed time T_1 satisfies

$$T_1 < \frac{1}{\lambda_5\mu_3} + \frac{1}{\lambda_5(1-\omega_3)}\ln\left(1 + \frac{\lambda_5}{2^{(\omega_3-1)/2}\lambda_6}\right) \qquad (44)$$

Part 2. When the sliding-mode surface reaches $S_i = 0$, we have

$$S_i = x_{2i} + \frac{1}{N(x_{1i})}\left(\lambda_3 sig^{k_3}(x_{1i}) + \lambda_4 sig^{k_4}(x_{1i})\right) = 0 \qquad (45)$$

Considering the Lyapunov function $V_3 = \frac{1}{2}x_{1i}^T x_{1i}$, we can get

$$\dot{V}_3 = x_{1i}^T \dot{x}_{1i} = x_{1i}^T \dot{x}_{2i} = -x_{1i}^T \frac{1}{N(x_{1i})}\left(\lambda_3 sig^{k_3}(x_{1i}) + \lambda_4 sig^{k_4}(x_{1i})\right)$$

$$\leq -\frac{1}{N(x_{1i,J})}\sum_{i=1}^{3}\left(\lambda_3|x_{1i,J}|^{k_3+1} + \lambda_4|x_{1i,J}|^{k_4+1}\right) \qquad (46)$$

$$\leq -\frac{1}{N(x_{1i})}\lambda_3(2V_3)^{(k_3+1)/2} - \frac{1}{N(x_{1i})}\lambda_4(2V_3)^{(k_4+1)/2}$$

when $|x_{1i}| \geq 1$, one has

$$\dot{V}_3 \leq -\frac{1}{N(x_{1i})}\lambda_3(2V_3)^{(\mu_2+1)/2} - \frac{1}{N(x_{1i})}\lambda_4(2V_3) \qquad (47)$$

when $|x_{1i}| < 1$, we can obtain

$$\dot{V}_3 \leq -\frac{1}{N(x_{1i})}\lambda_3(2V_3) - \frac{1}{N(x_{1i})}\lambda_4(2V_3)^{(\omega_2+1)/2} \qquad (48)$$

Similarly, according to Lemma 1, it is shown that the system state can converge to $R = \left\{ (x_{1i}, x_{2i}) : |x_{1i,j}| \le \phi, |x_{2i,j}| \le \frac{1}{N(x_{1i})}\lambda_3\phi^{k_3} + \frac{1}{N(x_{1i})}\lambda_4\phi^{k_4} \right\}$ in a fixed time T_2, and the convergence time T_2 satisfies

$$T_2 < \frac{1}{\lambda_3\mu_2} + \frac{1}{\lambda_3(1-\omega_2)} \ln\left(1 + \frac{\lambda_3}{2^{(\omega_2-1)/2}\lambda_4}\right) \tag{49}$$

The proof is completed.

Remark 3. The proposed control method has superior performance in this paper. It not only expedites the convergence rate of the whole system, but also improves the robustness of the system, which has a certain guiding significance for practical application. Moreover, the control method also has certain universality. For example, it can be applied to the control field of unmanned aerial vehicle. The difference between the two control objects is the difference of the models. We can apply it to the unmanned aerial vehicle as long as we make some adjustments to the proposed method.

4 Simulation Studies

To demonstrate the feasibility of the proposed controller method, the simulation study is conducted. The model parameter matrices are shown in [36]. The external disturbances $\hat{M}_{\eta i}^{-1}(\eta_i)R(\psi_i)\tau_{di} = [2\sin(0.1t), 1.5\sin(0.2t), \sin(0.05t)]^T$ and 20% uncertainties of the model parameters are taken into account. The control parameters are selected as $a = 0.1, b= 2.5, c= 3.5, \gamma_1=2, \gamma_2=\gamma_3 = 6, \lambda_1 = \lambda_2 = \lambda_3 = 0.01, \lambda_2 = \lambda_4 = \lambda_6 = 2, m_1 = m_2 = m_3 = 35, n_1 = n_2 = n_3 = 33, \phi = 0.001, p_1 = p_2 = p_3 = 9, q_1 = q_2 = q_3 = 15, a_1 = a_2 = a_3 = 0.8, b_1 = b_2 = b_3 = 10, c_1 = c_2 = c_3 = 2$. The initial values of AUV1 and AUV2 are chosen as $\eta_1=[-4, 3, 2]^T, v_1 = [0, 0, 0]^T, \eta_2=[-4, -3, 2]^T, v_2 = [0, 0, 0]^T$. The reference trajectory of the global leader is selected as $\eta_l = [0.1t, 2\cos(0.1t) - 2, 0.01t+2.5]^T$. The faults parameters are designed as $e_1 = \begin{cases} 1 & t \le 30 \\ 1.2 & \text{otherwise} \end{cases}, e_2 = \begin{cases} 1 & t \le 28 \\ 1.15 & \text{otherwise} \end{cases}, e_3 = \begin{cases} 1 & t \le 20 \\ 0.9 & \text{otherwise} \end{cases}$, $\overline{\tau}_i = [0.3, 0.4, 0.2]^T$. For any initial velocity $v_i = R^{-1}\omega_i$, and three different initial values are considered. Case 1: $\eta_1=[-4, 3, 2]^T, \omega_1 = [0, 0, 0]^T, \eta_2=[-4, -3, 2]^T, \omega_2 = [0, 0, 0]^T$. Case 2: $\eta_1=[-8, 2, 1.5]^T, \omega_1 = [0.01, 0.02, 0]^T, \eta_2=[-8, -2, 1.5]^T, \omega_2 = [0.02, 0.02, 0]^T$. Case 3: $\eta_1=[-6, 1, 1]^T, \omega_1 = [0.03, -0.01, 0.01]^T, \eta_2=[-6, -1, 1]^T, \omega_2 = [0.02, -0.02, 0.01]^T$.

Consider a formation configuration consisting of three AUVs, which are represented as "AUV1", "AUV2" and "AUV3", respectively. AUV3 acts as the leader to provide the desired trajectory information. Figure 1 shows the communication topology. The desired formation structure of AUVs is an isosceles triangle. The formation trajectories of three AUVs on the horizontal plane are shown in Fig. 2. It is obvious that the desired isosceles triangle formation configuration is achieved. The distances between AUV1 & AUV3 and AUV2 & AUV3 are shown in Fig. 3. The results show that the distance between the leader-follower members is 4m, which can be changed by adjusting the parameters of potential field function. Figures 4–7 demonstrate the convergence characteristics of the proposed control method under different initial states. It can be seen that the convergence time of the proposed algorithm is fixed and not limited by the initial state. The errors of position and velocity and the control input are shown in Figs. 8–10. It can be shown that the errors can converge to the origin in a fixed time. The composite disturbances and its estimation are shown in Figs. 11 and 12. It can be seen that the designed disturbance observer can accurately estimate the composite disturbances, which enhances the robustness of the system.

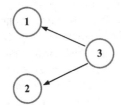

Fig. 1. Communication topology

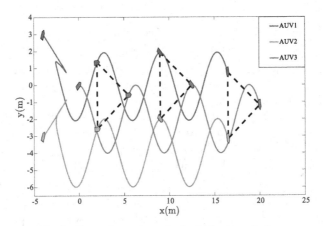

Fig. 2. Formation trajectories in the horizontal plane

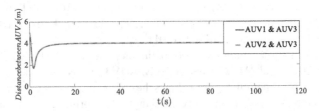

Fig. 3. Distance between the AUVs

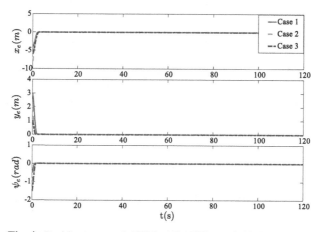

Fig. 4. Position errors of AUV1 under different initial conditions

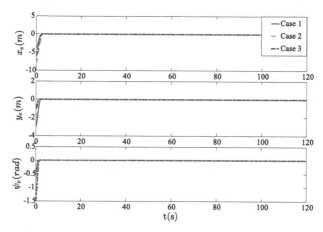

Fig. 5. Position errors of AUV2 under different initial conditions

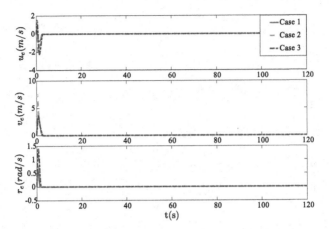

Fig. 6. Velocity errors of AUV1 under different initial conditions

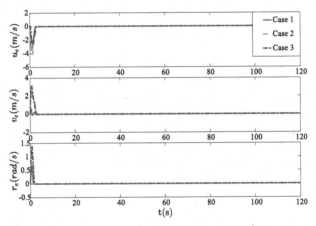

Fig. 7. Velocity errors of AUV2 under different initial conditions

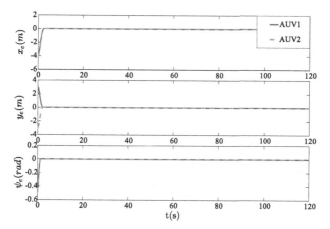

Fig. 8. Position errors of AUV1 and AUV2

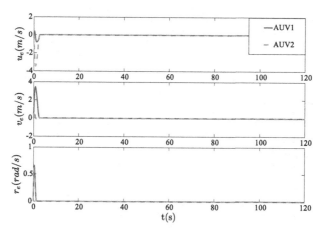

Fig. 9. Velocity errors of AUV1 and AUV2

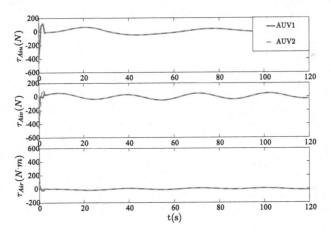

Fig. 10. Control inputs of AUV1 and AUV2

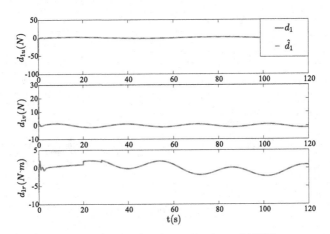

Fig. 11. The disturbance estimations of AUV1

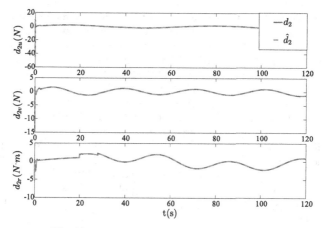

Fig. 12. The disturbance estimations of AUV2

5   Conclusion

In this paper, considering the problem of actuator faults, model uncertainties and unknown disturbances, a fast fixed-time formation control method is proposed. Specifically, the desired formation configuration can be obtained by properly adjusting the parameters of the artificial potential field function. Then, a fixed-time disturbance observer is designed for composite disturbances. Further, by combining disturbance observer and fast nonsingular terminal sliding-mode surface, a formation control method is designed. Eventually, the advantages and effectiveness of this method is verified by simulation.

References

1. Wang, N., Zhang, Y., Ahn, C., Xu, Q.: Autonomous pilot of unmanned surface vehicles: Bridging path planning and tracking. IEEE Trans. Veh. Technol. **71**(3), 2358–2374 (2022)
2. Gao, L., Qin, H., Li, P.: Disturbance observer-based finite-time exact bottom-following control for a BUV with input saturation. Ocean Eng. **266**, 112650 (2022)
3. Wang, N., Er, M., Sun, J., Liu, Y.: Adaptive robust online constructive fuzzy control of a complex surface vehicle system. IEEE Trans. Cybern. **46**(7), 1511–1523 (2016)
4. Cui, R., Shuzhi, S., Bernard, V., Yoo, S.: Leader–follower formation control of underactuated autonomous underwater vehicles. Ocean Eng. **37**(17), 1491–1502 (2010)
5. Balch, T., Arkin, R.: Behavior-based formation control for multirobot teams. IEEE Trans. Robot. Autom. **14**(6), 926–939 (1998)
6. Pashna, M., Yusof, R., Ismail, Z., Namerikawa, T., Yazdani, S.: Autonomous multi-robot tracking system for oil spills on sea surface based on hybrid fuzzy distribution and potential field approach. Ocean Eng. **207**, 107238 (2020)
7. Do, K.: Formation control of multiple elliptical agents with limited sensing ranges. Automatica **48**(7), 1330–1338 (2012)
8. Peng, Z., Wang, J., Wang, D.: Distributed containment maneuvering of multiple marine vessels via neurodynamics-based output feedback. IEEE Trans. Industr. Electr. **64**, 3831–3839 (2017)

9. Xu, J.: Fault tolerant finite-time leader–follower formation control for autonomous surface vessels with LOS range and angle constraints. Automatica **68**, 228–236 (2016)

10. Wu, T., Xue, K., Wang, P.: Leader-follower formation control of USVs using APF-based adaptive fuzzy logic nonsingular terminal sliding mode control method. J. Mech. Sci. Technol. **36**, 1–12 (2022). https://doi.org/10.1007/s12206-022-0336-y

11. Wang, N., Ahn, C.: Coordinated trajectory tracking control of a marine aerial-surface heterogeneous system. IEEE/ASME Trans. Mechatron. **26**(6), 3198–3210 (2021)

12. Yang, L., Yang, J.: Nonsingular fast terminal sliding-mode control for nonlinear dynamical systems. Int. J. Robust Nonlinear Control **21**(16), 1865–1879 (2011)

13. Wang, N., Karimi, H., Li, H., Su, S.: Accurate trajectory tracking of disturbed surface vehicles: a finite-time control approach. IEEE/ASME Trans. Mechatron. **24**(3), 1064–1074 (2019)

14. Chen, M., Shi, P., Lim, C.: Robust constrained control for MIMO nonlinear systems based on disturbance observer. IEEE Trans. Autom. Control **60**(12), 3281–3286 (2015)

15. Wang, N., Er, M.: Self-constructing adaptive robust fuzzy neural tracking control of surface vehicles with uncertainties and unknown disturbances. IEEE Trans. Control Syst. Technol. **23**(3), 991–1002 (2015)

16. Qiao, L., Bowen, Y., Wu, D., Zhang, W.: Design of three exponentially convergent robust controllers for the trajectory tracking of autonomous underwater vehicles. Ocean Eng. **134**, 157–172 (2017)

17. Qiao, L., Zhang, W.: Adaptive second-order fast nonsingular terminal sliding mode tracking control for fully actuated autonomous underwater vehicles. IEEE J. Oceanic Eng. **44**(2), 363–385 (2019)

18. Qiao, L., Zhang, W.: Trajectory tracking control of AUVs via adaptive fast nonsingular integral terminal sliding mode control. IEEE Trans. Industr. Inform. **16**(2), 1248–1258 (2020)

19. Wang, N., Su, S.: Finite-time unknown observer based interactive trajectory tracking control of asymmetric underactuated surface vehicles. IEEE Trans. Control Syst. Technol. **29**(2), 794–803 (2021)

20. Polyakov, A.: Nonlinear feedback design for fixed-time stabilization of linear control systems. IEEE Trans. Autom. Control **57**(8), 2106–2110 (2012)

21. Wang, C., Tnunay, H., Zuo, Z., Lennox, B., Ding, Z.: Fixed-time formation control of multirobot systems: design and experiments. IEEE Trans. Industr. Electron. **66**(8), 6292–6301 (2019)

22. Wang, N., Er, M.: Direct Adaptive fuzzy tracking control of marine vehicles with fully unknown parametric dynamics and uncertainties. IEEE Trans. Control Syst. Technol. **24**(5), 1845–1852 (2016)

23. Du, H., Wen, G., Wu, D., Cheng, Y., Lü, J.: Distributed fixed-time consensus for nonlinear heterogeneous multi-agent systems. Automatica **113**, 108797 (2020)

24. Wang, N., Gao, Y., Zhang, X.: Data-driven performance-prescribed reinforcement learning control of an unmanned surface vehicle. IEEE Trans. Neural Netw. Learn. Syst. **32**(12), 5456–5467 (2021)

25. Van, M.: An enhanced tracking control of marine surface vessels based on adaptive integral sliding mode control and disturbance observer. ISA Trans. **90**, 30–40 (2019)

26. Weng, Y., Wang, N.: Finite-time observer-based model-free time-varying sliding-mode control of disturbed surface vessels. Ocean Eng. **251**, 110866 (2022)

27. Wang, N., Qian, C., Sun, J., Liu, Y.: Adaptive robust finite-time trajectory tracking control of fully actuated marine surface vehicles. IEEE Trans. Control Syst. Technol. **24**(4), 1454–1462 (2016)

28. Lee, J., Chang, P., Jin, M.: Adaptive integral sliding mode control with time-delay estimation for robot manipulators. IEEE Trans. Industr. Electron. **64**(8), 6796–6804 (2017)

29. Weng, Y., Wang, N., Carlos, G.: Data-driven sideslip observer-based adaptive sliding-mode path-following control of underactuated marine vessels. Ocean Eng. **197**, 106910 (2020)

30. Cui, R., Chen, L., Yang, C., Chen, M.: Extended state observer-based integral sliding mode control for an underwater robot with unknown disturbances and uncertain nonlinearities. IEEE Trans. Industr. Electron. **64**(8), 6785–6795 (2017)

31. Kim, J., Joe, H., Yu, S., Lee, J., Kim, M.: Time-delay controller design for position control of autonomous underwater vehicle under disturbances. IEEE Trans. Industr. Electron. **63**(2), 1052–1061 (2016)

32. Wang, N., Gao, Y., Zhao, H., Ahn, C.: Reinforcement learning-based optimal tracking control of an unknown unmanned surface vehicle. IEEE Trans. Neural Netw. Learn. Syst. **32**(7), 3034–3045 (2021)

33. Guo, G., Zhang, P.: Asymptotic stabilization of USVs with actuator dead-zones and yaw constraints based on fixed-time disturbance observer. IEEE Trans. Veh. Technol. **69**(1), 302–316 (2020)

34. Wu, Y., Wang, Z., Huang, Z.: Distributed fault detection for nonlinear multi-agent systems under fixed-time observer. J. Franklin Inst. **356**(13), 7515–7532 (2019)

35. Cao, L., Xiao, B., Golestani, M., Ran, D.: Faster fixed-time control of flexible spacecraft attitude stabilization. IEEE Trans. Industr. Inform. **16**(2), 1281–1290 (2020)

36. Do, K., Pan, J.: Global robust adaptive path following of underactuated ships. Automatica **42**(10), 1713–1722 (2006)

Applications

A Deep Learning-Based Method for Drivers' Shoe-Wearing Recognition

Baoyue Hu$^{(\boxtimes)}$ and Xing Hu

University of Shanghai for Science and Technology, Shanghai, China
fanthal@163.com

Abstract. What types of shoes that the driver should be wear on driving is under the clear regulation. Non-standard shoe-wearing such as wearing high-heeled shoes, platform shoes, slippers or with bare feet will bring great safety risks and may lead to traffic accidents. According to statistics by traffic department, many traffic accidents are caused by irregular shoe-wearing. Although computer vision has been applied for monitoring driver's behavior in many aspects, such as driver's face, eye, and hand, there is still no computer vision-based method or hardware device on the vehicle that to monitor the driver's shoe-wearing. Therefore, if the driver's illegal shoe-wearing behavior can be identified before driving, it can play an important role in reducing the incidence of traffic accident. The main difficulties in drivers' shoe-wearing detection lie in the diversity of shoe types, the variety of foot postures, and the complexity of the detection environment. Therefore, the traditional computer vision method will be high error detection rate in such scenes. In this paper, a deep learning-based method for detecting abnormal shoe-wearing of drivers before driving is proposed. Different models such as SVM, Fast-RCNN, Faster-RCNN, YOLO v2, YOLO v3, YOLO v4 are used to identified drivers' shoe-wearing. To the best of our knowledge this is the first work that using the computer vision technology for automatic monitoring on drivers' shoe-wearing. The experimental results show the proposed method can identify the drivers' shoe wearing effectively and efficiently. It has high application value for improving traffic safety.

Keywords: YOLO v4 · Deep Learning · Computer Vision Technology · Shoe-Wearing Recognition

1 Introduction

1.1 A Subsection Sample

How drivers wear shoes while driving is clearly specified in traffic laws. Some irregular shoe-wearing behaviors, such as wearing high heels, slippers, platform shoes, and even bare feet, are not allowed while driving. Because in this shoe-wearing case, the driver often fails to jam on the brakes timely and effectively in the event of an emergency, which leads to traffic accidents. According to statistics, 60% of traffic accidents every

© ICST Institute for Computer Sciences, Social Informatics and Telecommunications Engineering 2023
Published by Springer Nature Switzerland AG 2023. All Rights Reserved
H. R. Karimi and N. Wang (Eds.): S-Cube 2022, LNICST 487, pp. 167–178, 2023.
https://doi.org/10.1007/978-3-031-34899-0_11

year are related to the drivers' irregular shoe-wearing [1]. However, the supervision of drivers' abnormal shoe-wearing is not as effective as other violations. The traffic cameras cannot monitor it effectively because the driver's feet are inside the cab. Even if the traffic police conduct an investigation of the vehicle, they will not be able to find the illegal shoe-wearing behavior if the driver does not get out of the car. What's more, it is difficult for the limited number of traffic police to monitor the large number of vehicles effectively.

With the development of computer vision and artificial intelligence technology, more and more supervision of drivers' violations is to use computer technology to achieve intelligence and automation. For example, not wearing a seat belt [2], holding a mobile phone with hands while driving [3], etc. can be detected by cameras installed above the road. However, since the drivers' feet are inside the cab, it is difficult to detect by the camera. Even the surveillance cameras installed inside the cab only focus on monitoring the drivers' face and hands. So far, there is no relevant in-vehicle equipment specifically used for monitoring the drivers' shoes. However, unlike shoe types identification in ordinary situations, the main difficulties in identifying the drivers' shoe-wearing behavior lies in the following points:

1) Diversity of the driver's foot posture.
2) Variety of driver's shoe types.
3) Light and occlusion problems in the cab. The existence of the above problems makes the traditional image processing and machine learning methods usually have a high recognition error rate.

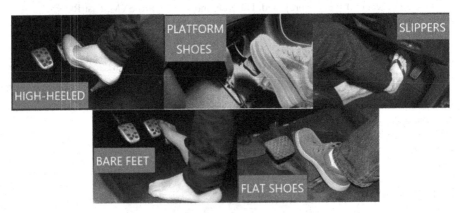

Fig. 1. Examples of Different Types of Shoes

This paper proposes a computer vision-based method of detection drivers' abnormal shoe-wearing to deal with these problems. The method proposed in this paper divides the drivers' shoe-wearing into two categories (as shown in Fig. 1): The first category is the types of shoes suitable for drivers to drive, including flat shoes, cloth shoes, leather shoes, etc. The other category is the types of shoes that are not suitable for driving, including slippers, high heels, platform shoes and bare feet, etc. The method captures pictures of the drivers' feet as they enter the cab with tiny cameras mounted inside the car doors. After that, use the captured pictures to train the deep neural network model, and output two types of labels which include legal shoe-wearing and illegal shoe-wearing. When it is detected that the type of shoes is illegal, the vehicle will be restricted from starting through the vehicle control system, and then the driver will be prompted to change to legal shoes by voice. This paper trains six neural network models of SVM, Fast-RCNN, Faster-RCNN, YOLO v2, YOLO v3 and YOLO v4 respectively. The results of the experiment show that the YOLO V4 model has the highest recognition rate. Meanwhile, it can meet the real-time requirements. To our best knowledge, this is the first work to automatically identify whether the driver's shoe-wearing is legal.

The main contributions of the paper are as follows:

1) We use the real data set to train the learning model and come to the conclusion that YOLO V4 model has the best performance in detection drivers' shoe-wearing behavior.
2) We construct a dataset for the identification of driver's abnormal shoe-wearing for the first time. The dataset contains a large number of legal and illegal shoe-wearing samples from real-world, which can be used for training deep learning models to get the most accurate conclusion.
3) The model proposed in this paper provides an effective method for the detection of drivers' shoe-wearing behavior in daily life, which can greatly reduce the incidence of traffic accidents.

This paper is organized as follows: The second paragraph describes the application of computer vision in driver-specific monitoring. The third paragraph describes the hardware of the proposed method in this paper and the flow chart of the algorithm. The fourth paragraph is the specific experimental content, which verifies the effectiveness of the method in this paper. The fifth paragraph concludes the paper.

2 Pertinent Literature

Since this paper propose a computer vision-based recognition method for driver's abnormal shoe-wearing for the first time, there is no similar related literature at present. However, there are many ways based on computer vision can be used to monitor drivers. This paper will review the related methods of driver's face and hand monitoring based on computer vision.

2.1 Computer Vision-Based Driver's Face Monitoring Method

Similar to driver's shoe recognition, in unconstrained face recognition, the face images may have many variations, such as low resolution, pose variation, complex light and motion blur, which will result the low recognition accuracy. Traditional face recognition algorithms, such as the Eigenfaces [4], Bayesian [5], support vector machine (SVM) based [6] can assist computers to complete basic face recognition. But for the more general case, such as unconstrained face matching, the traditional algorithms may not do well. As deep learning models exhibit the superior accuracy and robustness in extracting features, significant progress has been made in face recognition with the development of deep learning technology. Among the deep learning models, the convolutional neural network (CNN) has become the most popular one due to its excellent performance. Before the method proposed in this paper, deep learning models such as CNN [7] have been used for driver's face detection [8]. The driver's face detection often locates the face first, and the localization work is often indexed by the eyes or mouth [9]. If the accuracy of face recognition and classification needs to be guaranteed, it is necessary to ensure that the facial features of each person are extracted effectively as much as possible. The deep learning models provide us with ideas to solve these problems. Experiments show that the deep learning models can still extract the corresponding facial features well in complex situations, such as makeup considered eye status recognition for driver drowsiness [10], the anti-occlusion face recognition for drivers [11].

2.2 Computer Vision-Based Driver's Hands Monitoring Method

Different from the driver's facial recognition, the difficulty in monitoring driver's hands movements mainly lies in the diversity of postures. For this problem, it is often necessary to set a dataset with a sufficiently large sample size to solve it [12]. Because of the lack of driver's hand features, the classification of driver's behavior mainly relies on the large amount of existing data for training. The superior data processing ability of the deep learning models also makes it perform suitably in this problem [13, 17]. Before deep learning-based computer vision technology was used for driver behavior detection, methods for recognition and detection of different actions have been proposed. For example, RGB camera-based fallen person detection system was proposed with the emerging computer vision recognition algorithm YOLO [14]. The current mainstream method for driver's behavior detection is to pre-train the neural network through a dataset composed of a large number of samples, and then perform backpropagation and optimize the dataset according to the new images that are continuously captured. However, existing techniques utilizing image-feature-based for encoding such activity can sometimes misclassify crucial scenarios. The video-feature-based extraction was proposed then [15, 18]. Some efficient and accurate deep learning models like such as YOLO begin become popular and replace the traditional deep learning models like SVM, RCNN [16, 19].

3 Experimental Principles

3.1 System Structure

In this paper, the proposed deep learning-based method of detecting drivers' abnormal wearing of shoes relies on the assistance of miniature cameras and vehicle-mounted miniature computers. Its specific structure is shown in Fig. 2.

As shown in Fig. 2, when a driver is in the driver's seat, the miniature camera collects the images of the driver's feet and transmits the captured real-time images to the vehicle-mounted miniature computer. The vehicle-mounted miniature computer has already been equipped with a neural network that has been trained by a large number of samples. After receiving the real-time images, the vehicle-mounted miniature computer

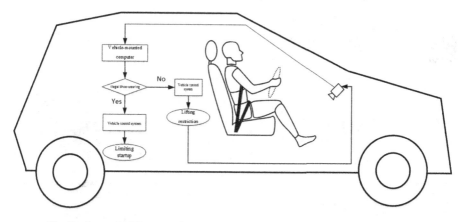

Fig. 2. Structure Diagram of Driver Abnormal Shoe Wearing Detection System

immediately starts to detect, identify and classify such images, and judges whether the driver's shoes are in line with the safe driving norms according to the detection results: if the driver is wearing high-heeled shoes, platform shoes, slippers or barefoot, the vehicle-mounted miniature computer will transmit a signal to the vehicle control system to limit the start of the car and issue an alarm to prevent the driver from driving wearing shoes with potential safety hazards; If the driver is wearing shoes such as flat shoes in line with the safe driving norms, the vehicle-mounted miniature computer will transmit an enabling signal to the vehicle control system to lift the startup restriction, so the driver can drive normally on the road.

3.2   Deep Learning Model

To describe the deep learning-based method of detecting drivers' abnormal wearing of shoes proposed in this paper more clearly, the network training algorithm, model, and structure used in the method are expounded here.

The proposed method is based on the YOLO V4 algorithm. Its main network architecture is shown in Fig. 3.

As shown in Fig. 3, the image standard input size of the network is 608 * 608, so the algorithm will preprocess the images before they enter the baseline network to scale their size to the standard size and uniformize them. In addition, Mosaic data enhancement, CmBN, and SAT [21] will also be performed on the images. To detect the abnormal shoe-wearing behaviors of drivers, the trained network is required to have high precision and high robustness. Therefore, sample data sets are processed by Mosaic for data enhancement, and sample images are randomly scaled, distributed, and spliced, which greatly improves detection speed and reduces memory requirements.

YOLO V4's backbone network (Backbone) is an improvement of YOLO V3's Dark-net53 network. Based on the network structure of YOLO V3, five CSP modules are added to the network of the YOLO V4 algorithm. In the course of processing input images and outputting feature maps, traditional computer vision detection methods usually use the DenseNet algorithm. Although this algorithm can complete the tasks of backpropagation

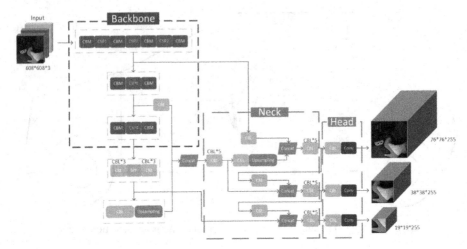

Fig. 3. YOLO v4 Network Architecture

and weight optimization, it will produce a lot of double counting during backpropagation, resulting in heavy workload and slow propagation and optimization speed. The CSP module divides the features of a basic image layer into two parts. One part is processed by the local Dense module and connected to the other part through a cross-stage hierarchical structure, which not only reduces the amount of computation but also ensures the accuracy of the overall structure.

Meanwhile, YOLO V4 uses the Mish activation function (as shown in Formula 1 below):

$$Mish = x * tan\ h(ln(1 + e^x)) \tag{1}$$

The image of the Mish activation function is shown in Fig. 4:

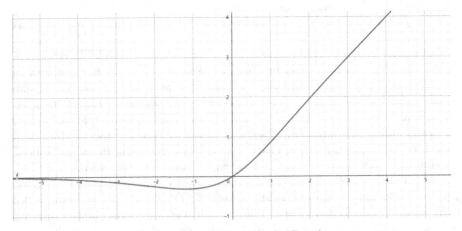

Fig. 4. Image of Mish Activation Function

Compared to the activation function of the previous version of the YOLO algorithm, the Mish activation function has a smoother curve and allows a smaller negative gradient, which ensures the integrity of feature information to a certain extent and has a better gradient descent effect. In addition, the linear function x and logarithmic function ln ensure that the gradient of tanh function doesn't approach 1 as it approaches positive or negative infinity, thus avoiding the saturation problem.

In the Neck part of the network architecture, YOLO V4 adopts SPP [22, 23] and FPN+PAN modules. In the Backbone part, YOLO V4 completes the preliminary shallow feature extraction before turning to the Neck part of the network for feature enhancement. The SPP module adopts the max-pooling mode of 1×1, 5×5, 9×9, and 13×13, and realizes Concat fusion and splicing of feature maps of different scales. The SPP module can greatly improve the receptive field, separating out contextual features while maintaining speed. Domain-specific fine-tuning is then performed to significantly improve performance [24]. In addition, FPN captures strong semantic features and PAN conveys strong localization features, which can accomplish target localization more effectively [25]. As the images of drivers' shoes that may be different in type are captured by the camera at different rays of light and different angles, strong features are required to ensure detection and identification.

As for the detection head (Head) of the network, YOLO V4 also improved the loss function. Based on the loss function IOU of YOLO V3, the CIOU-Loss function was proposed in YOLO V4:

$$CIOU = IOU - \frac{\rho^2}{c^2} - \frac{v^2}{1 - IOU + v} \tag{2}$$

$$v = \frac{4}{\pi^2}(arctan\frac{w^{gt}}{h^{gt}} - arctan\frac{w}{h})^2 \tag{3}$$

$$LOSS_{CIOU} = 1 - CIOU \tag{4}$$

Because of the symmetry of human feet, the side-looking and down-looking characteristics of shoes are also very similar. For the images of drivers' shoes captured by the camera, loss function calculation by IOU only will lead to a serious loss of accuracy. For the loss function based on IOU, when a detection result does not intersect with the ground truth, or when multiple detection results have the same size but different positions, the calculation of the loss function will be inaccurate, which will make the weighting parameters obtained by training unreliable. However, the loss function based on CIOU can well avoid the above problems. CIOU considers the Euclidean distance between the detection result and the center of the ground truth so that different loss function values can be obtained at different positions of the detection result, making the weighting parameters obtained by training more reliable.

4 Experimental Method

4.1 Data Set Setting

Due to the wide variety of shoes, the experiment divided the shoe-wearing behaviors of drivers into five categories: high-heeled shoes, platform shoes, slippers, barefoot and flat shoes. Among them, wearing high-heeled shoes, platform shoes, slippers, and barefoot are abnormal shoe-wearing behaviors, while flat shoes are standard shoe-wearing behaviors.

The experiment collected 300 images of feet of different types at different angles for training. Among them, there are 60 images of high-heeled shoes, 60 platform shoes, 60 slippers, 60 bare feet, and 60 flat shoes.

4.2 Parameter Settings

In this paper, five deep learning models based on YOLO V4, YOLO V3, YOLO V2, Faster-RCNN and Fast-RCNN were verified through comparison with the traditional SVM model. According to the network structures of different models, corresponding parameters were set respectively to ensure the optimal detection speed and accuracy of each model. Then, the model with the best comprehensive performance was selected as the supporting framework of the method of detecting drivers' abnormal wearing of shoes proposed in this paper.

The basic parameter settings of this experiment are shown in Table 1 below:

Table 1. Basic Parameter Settings of the Experiment

Learning Model / Parameter Setting	YOLO v4	YOLO v3	YOLO v2	Faster-RCNN	Fast-RCNN	SVM
weight	608	416	416	1000	1000	1000
height	608	416	416	1000	1000	1000
batch_size	64	16	64	1	1	
learning_rate	0.00261	0.001	0.001	0.00001	0.00001	
momentum	0.949	0.9	0.9			
decay	0.0005	0.0005	0.0005	0.8	0.8	

4.3 Evaluation Standard

The method proposed in this paper divides drivers' shoe-wearing behaviors into abnormal shoe-wearing behavior including wearing high-heeled shoes, platform shoes, slippers, and barefoot, and normal shoe-wearing behavior such as wearing flat shoes, which is a typical classification problem. Hence, the experiment adopted: recall rate (Recall), precision rate (Precision), average precision rate (AP), and Intersection-over-Union (IoU) as evaluation indicators. The calculation formula of the above evaluation indicators is as follows:

$$recall = \frac{TP}{(TP + FN)} = \frac{TP}{P} \tag{5}$$

$$Precision = \frac{TP}{TP + FP} \tag{6}$$

$$AP = \int_0^1 p(r)dr \approx \sum_{k=1}^N P(k)\Delta r(k), \tag{7}$$

where, P\p is precision rate and r is recall rate

$$IoU = \frac{DR \cap GT}{DR \cup GT} \tag{8}$$

In formula (8), DR is the detection result, and GT is the ground truth, as shown in Fig. 5:

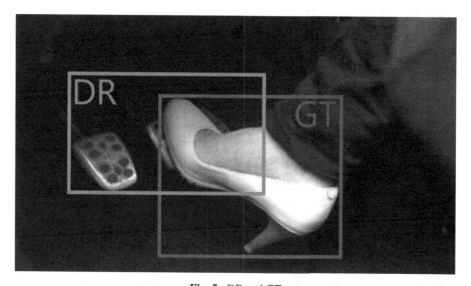

Fig. 5. DR and GT

4.4 Experiment Effect

The sample images collected in the experiment were trained by YOLO v4, YOLO v3, YOLO v2, Faster-RCNN, Fast-RCNN deep learning models and traditional SVM.

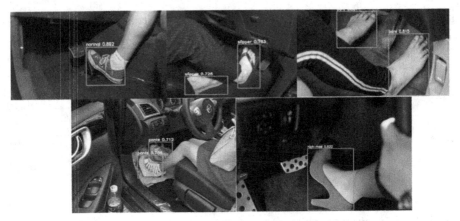

Fig. 6. Samples of Detection Results

All these models could meet the basic requirements for classification of drivers' shoe-wearing behaviors to realize detection and identification of them. Samples of detection results are shown in Fig. 6.

On this basis, the evaluation indicators of each learning model were also calculated in the experiment, as shown in Table 2 below:

Table 2. Comparison of Performance Parameters of Learning Models in the Experiment

Learning Model / Evaluation Indicators	YOLO v4	YOLO v3	YOLO v2	Faster-RCNN	Fast-RCNN	SVM
Recall	0.912	0.884	0.853	0.887	0.866	0.750
Precision	0.920	0.860	0.840	0.915	0.885	0.792
AP	0.922	0.857	0.832	0.912	0.879	0.814
IoU	0.825	0.768	0.729	0.792	0.771	0.701
FPS	75	45	48	15	12	5

As shown in Table 2 above, the four indicators of recall rates (Recall), precision rate (Precision), average precision rate (AP) and Intersection-over-Union (IoU) comprehensively reflect the accuracy of these learning models. Among the six models, YOLO V4 has the highest accuracy. YOLO retains context information when performing target recognition, which enables it to effectively avoid background misrecognition in the complex environment of the cab. The parameter FPS in Table 2 is a standard to measure target detection rate. FPS records the number of images that can be processed per second. According to the data in Table 2, the detection speed of YOLO V4 is faster than the other five models. The efficiency of YOLO V4 ensures that it will give timely feedback to the driver before driving. To sum up, YOLO V4 deep learning model is significantly better than the other five models in performance, and all the performance parameters of the traditional SVM learning model are far lower than that of the deep learning models. Therefore, the YOLO V4 algorithm was selected as the supporting framework of the method of detecting drivers' abnormal wearing of shoes proposed in this paper.

5 Summary and Outlook

5.1 Summary

The shoe-wearing behaviors of drivers are related to the life and property safety of everyone, so an efficient and accurate detection and identification network are essential. Based on the above introduction to deep learning models and the comparison of performance among multiple learning models obtained through the experiment, it can be shown that YOLO V4 has the best comprehensive performance among all the models, proving that it is reasonable to adopt YOLO V4 algorithm as the supporting framework of the method of detecting drivers' abnormal wearing of shoes proposed in this paper. For the goal of detecting abnormal shoe-wearing behaviors of drivers, the characteristics of deep learning allow the neural network to capture more fine-grained features of each type of shoe, and the structure of YOLO V4 helps the neural network to complete feature enhancement more quickly and accurately. Based on these advantages, the neural network can classify the images of drivers' shoes captured under different rays of light and angles with high accuracy.

5.2 Future Prospects

In the experiment described in this paper, high-heeled shoes, platform shoes, slippers, barefoot and flat shoes were used for training and detection. In the future, we will continue to add new shoe types, improve the training data set, and make the neural network more universal. Moreover, in addition to the detection of drivers' shoe-wearing behaviors before driving, we will further study the detection of drivers' abnormal behaviors during driving. There are also standards of safe behaviors for drivers during driving. By training the neural network and using the deep learning model to capture and enhance the corresponding features of normal driving behaviors, theoretically, the abnormal driving behaviors of drivers can be detected and identified in the course of their driving.

References

1. Car Home. Pay attention to safety, pay attention to your feet [EB/OL] (2009). https://club.aut ohome.com.cn/bbs/threadowner/59ac783ba8317616/2161861-1.html
2. Yang, K., Zhang, D., Yang, L.: Vehicle driver safety belt detection based on deep learning. J. China Univ. Metrol. **3**, 326–333 (2017)
3. Xiong, Q., Lin, J., Yue, W.: A deep learning-based method for detecting driver's calling behavior. Control Inf. Technol. (6), 53–56, 62 (2019)
4. Turk, M.: Eigenfaces for recognition. J. Cogn. Neurosci. 3 (1991)
5. Chen, D., Cao, X., Wang, L., Wen, F., Sun, J.: Bayesian face revisited: a joint formulation. In: Fitzgibbon, A., Lazebnik, S., Perona, P., Sato, Y., Schmid, C. (eds.) ECCV 2012. LNCS, vol. 7574, pp. 566–579. Springer, Heidelberg (2012). https://doi.org/10.1007/978-3-642-33712-3_41

6. Darui, S., Lenan, W., et al.: Face recognition based on nonlinear feature extraction and SVM. J. Electron. Inf. Technol. **26**(2), 307–311 (2004)

7. Omerustaoglu, F., Okan Sakar, C., Kar, G.: Distracted driver detection by combining in-vehicle and image data using deep learning. Appl. Soft Comput. **96**, 106657 (2020)

8. Lu, W., Hu, H., Wang, J., Wang, L., Deng, Y.: Tractor driver fatigue detection based on convolution neural network and facial image recognition. Trans. Chin. Soc. Agricul. Eng. **34**(7), 192–199 (2018)

9. Liu, Z., Peng, Y., Hu, W.: Driver fatigue detection based on deeply-learned facial expression representation. J. Vis. Commun. Image Represent. **71**, 102723 (2020)

10. Nojiri, N., Kong, X., Meng, L., Shimakawa, H.: Discussion on machine learning and deep learning based makeup considered eye status recognition for driver drowsiness. Procedia Comput. Sci. **147**, P264-270 (2019)

11. Wang, X., Zhang, W.: Anti-occlusion face recognition algorithm based on a deep convolutional neural network. Comput. Electr. Eng. **96**, Part A (2021)

12. Zhao, C.H., Zhang, B.L., Zhang, X.Z., Zhao, S.Q., Li, H.X.: Recognition of driving postures by combined features and random subspace ensemble of multilayer perceptron classifiers. Neural Comput. Appl. **22**(1), 175–184 (2013)

13. Xing, Y., Lv, C., Cao, D., Velenis, E.: Multi-scale driver behavior modeling based on deep spatial-temporal representation for intelligent vehicles. Transp. Res. Part C: Emerg. Technol. **130** (2021)

14. Lafuente-Arroyo, S., Martin-Martin, P., Iglesias, C., Maldonado-Bascon, S., Acevedo-Rodriguez, F.J.: RGB camera-based fallen person detection system embedded on a mobile platform. Expert Syst. Appl. **197**, 116715 (2022)

15. Naveed, H., Jafri, F., Javed, K., Babri, H.A.: Driver activity recognition by learning spatiotemporal features of pose and human object interaction

16. Wang, C., Fu, Z.: Traffic sign detection algorithm based on YOLO v2 model. Comput. Appl. **38**(S2), 276–278 (2018)

17. Shahverdy, M., Fathy, M., Berangi, R., Sabokrou, M.: Driver behavior detection and classification using deep convolutional neural networks. Expert Syst. Appl. **149**(1), 113240 (2020)

18. Xu, M., Fang, H., Lv, P., Cui, L., Zhang, S., Zhou, B.: D-STC: deep learning with spatiotemporal constraints for train drivers detection from videos. Pattern Recogn. Lett. **119**(1), 222–228 (2019)

19. Xiao, W., Liu, H., Ma, Z., Chen, W.: Attention-based deep neural network for driver behavior recognition. Future Gener. Comput. Syst. **132**, 152–161 (2022)

A Learning-Based Driving Style Classification Approach for Intelligent Vehicles

Peng Mei[1], Hamid Reza Karimi[2(✉)], Cong Huang[3], Shichun Yang[1(✉)], and Fei Chen[1]

[1] School of Transportation Science and Engineering, Beihang University, Beijing, China
yangshichun@buaa.edu.cn
[2] Department of Mechanical Engineering, Politecnico di Milano, Milan, Italy
hamidreza.karimi@polimi.it
[3] School of Transportation and Civil Engineering, Nantong University, Nantong, China

Abstract. Driving behavior is crucial to the energy consumption analysis of electric vehicles. This paper proposes an unsupervised learning method to classify driving behavior for three typical road conditions. First, three specific road conditions are selected from the open access data, including characteristic information such as speed and acceleration. Besides, the characteristic data is processed, so each distinct value has the same weight. Second, two unsupervised learning clustering algorithms are introduced and compared in typical working conditions. Finally, the clustering results under three working conditions are obtained. Specifically, we can classify driving styles in high-speed conditions into aggressive, standard, and calm; besides, the classification method of K-medoids is more advantageous. In intersection conditions, driving styles are usually divided into standard and calm. Considering the calculation time and other factors, the K-means algorithm shows superior effects compared to the K-medoids algorithm. The driving style can be divided into standard and calm in campus conditions. In this case, K-medoids have a more significant advantage. The research results have implications for the classification of driving styles under different road conditions.

Keywords: Driving style classification · unsupervised learning · intelligent vehicles

1 Introduction

Electric vehicles (EVs) are the most widely used carrier of intelligent network technology in the automotive industry [1]. Still, their shortcomings, such as short driving range and long charging time, have become the bottleneck for developing pure electric vehicles. Under the existing technical background, combining the advantages of network technology, developing estimation algorithms with practical value, and improving the prediction accuracy of the driving range are the primary means to alleviate the "range anxiety". Many scholars and researchers have conducted in-depth research on the "range anxiety" problem caused by the poor accuracy of EV's cruising range estimation. Many factors affect the driving range, among which the main elements are the state estimation of the power battery, the driver's driving style, and future driving conditions.

H. R. Karimi and N. Wang (Eds.): S-Cube 2022, LNICST 487, pp. 179–190, 2023.
https://doi.org/10.1007/978-3-031-34899-0_12

Driving style is an inherent attribute accumulated by drivers when driving on the road for a long time, and different drivers have similarities and differences in their driving styles [2]. Elassad et al. [3] proposed the "driver-vehicle-environment" framework, which can explain the factors affecting driving behavior. First, the driver's age, gender, and personality directly impact driving style. Second, external environmental factors such as road type, traffic conditions, and weather can also indirectly impact driving behavior. Finally, car features such as head-up displays and in-vehicle aids can also affect driving behavior. These effects ultimately fall into three categories: driving events (turning or following), physiological states (fatigue and distraction), and psychological states.

Much experimental research have been carried out on driving styles, and the classification methods can be divided into rule-based, model-based, and machine-learning methods [2]. The principle of the rule-based method is to artificially give a threshold for the factors that affect the determination of driving behavior. When the value of an indicator exceeds the point, the driving style can be determined as a specific category. First, the acceleration information of the experimental vehicle was recorded, and the more frequent the longitudinal or lateral acceleration changes were obtained from the experimental data, the more aggressive the driving behavior style. Then the acceleration probability was used as the driving style. The style classification indicator divides driving styles into three categories: calm, moderate, and aggressive, with an overall accuracy rate of 68.49% [7]. Bejani et al. [8] proposed a driving style evaluation system based on environment perception and designed a rule-based fuzzy controller to classify the driving style, which proved the experiment's reliability. The fuzzy controller becomes the first choice for rule-based classification when there are many input characteristic parameters. Filev et al. [9] used fuzzy logic to evaluate factors such as acceleration change rate, speed change rate, and steering angle as cautious and moderate, more radical and radical. However, the fuzzy control logic mostly depends on the driver's experience, can only cover some of the situations well, and the accuracy rate needs to be improved.

Vaitkus et al. [4] used the supervised learning algorithm of KNN to extract five main features from all the data. In a specific route, the classification accuracy rate was as high as 100%; extracting three main parts, the classification accuracy rate also reached 98%. Since supervised learning methods usually need to label the training data accurately, these labels are difficult to obtain in practical applications, making applying supervised learning difficult, and it takes much time to mark the data manually. To solve the above problems, Wang et al. [5] proposed an SVM method for semi-supervised learning, which divides driving styles into aggressive and standard types according to several labels. Mohammadnazar et al. [6] used the relevant information generated by the Internet of Vehicles technology to measure the instantaneous driving behavior and used unsupervised learning to classify the driving styles of different types of roads.

Meanwhile, to quantify the driving style, information such as speed, longitudinal acceleration, and lateral acceleration are extracted while the car is driving. K-means and K-medoid methods classify drivers into aggressive, regular, and calm types. The study shows that the thresholds of the evaluation indicators for drivers of different road types are also different, and the proportion of vehicles driving in urban areas is higher than that of drivers in high-speed road conditions.

To accurately predict the subsequent driving range, the content of this paper is mainly aimed at the driving style clustering problem of unsupervised learning organized as follows; the second section introduces the data sources and the eigenvalues of the data in different scenarios. In Sect. 3, the unsupervised learning approach, containing k-means and k-medoids, is presented. The two different methods are compared in the different conditions in Sect. 4. In the last section, all work is summarized.

2   Data

The classification results of driving styles are different under different road conditions. A driver who behaves aggressively in high-speed road conditions is likely to act as an average driver in an urban environment full of light traffic intersections. Therefore, this chapter conducts a driving style analysis for three typical driving conditions, including highways, campus conditions, and urban hubs. Many scholars have shared open access data online to study better driving characteristics analysis, such as Next Generation Simulation, the Highway Drone Dataset, and the Interaction dataset. Nevertheless, most datasets are based on highway conditions and are not universal. Therefore, the data set selected in this paper includes data sets such as high-speed, intersection, and intersection, given in Fig. 1 [10, 11].

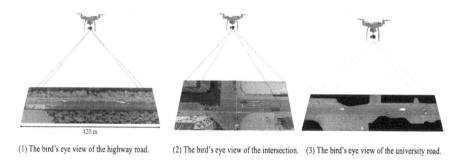

(1) The bird's eye view of the highway road.   (2) The bird's eye view of the intersection.   (3) The bird's eye view of the university road.

Fig. 1. The bird's eye view of three typical driving road.

The highD dataset is a new dataset of natural vehicle trajectories recorded on German highways [11]. Traffic flows were recorded at six locations, including more than 110500 cars. The course of each vehicle is extracted, including vehicle type, size, and maneuverability. Because the dataset includes different kinds of vehicles, such as cars and trucks, and the dataset is huge. Therefore, it is necessary to filter the data first and select the car's driving data recorded at the exact high-speed location. Since the length of the expressway is 410 m and records about 13 s, the amount of information on each vehicle is limited, which is conducive to analyzing driving behavior.

The inD dataset is a new dataset of natural vehicle trajectories recorded at German intersections [10]. The data type of the intersection is different from that of the expressway. The data on bicycles and pedestrians are added, and the working conditions are more complicated. The maximum speed limit on the road is 13.8 m/s. We first filter out the car's data and then process the data to obtain the vehicle's average speed, lateral acceleration, and longitudinal acceleration during the drone shooting process, and then comprehensively analyze the driving style. Similarly, the UniD dataset is a new dataset of natural road user trajectories recorded on the campus of RWTH Aachen University, and we apply the same approach.

3 Methodology

Since the above data has no labels, it is a challenge to classify the trajectory data of cars by traditional methods; we need to use the clustering algorithm to organize the data. As a typical algorithm in unsupervised learning, the clustering algorithm can divide similar sample data into a specific category; the common ones are K-means and K-medoids, and the two algorithms will be introduced.

3.1 K-means

The main idea of the K-means algorithm [12] is that given the K value and K initial cluster center points, each data point is divided into clusters represented by the nearest cluster center point. After all the points are allocated, recalculate the center point of the group according to all the points in the cluster. Then iteratively performs the steps of assigning points and updating the cluster center points until the change of the cluster center points is minimal or the specified number of iterations is reached. The flow of the K-means algorithm is shown in Table 1. The minimize error function is defined as follows:

$$E = \sum_{i=1}^{k} \sum_{x \in C_i} d(x, \mu(C_i)) \tag{1}$$

where $C_1, \ldots, C_K$ mean the k clusters, $\mu(C_i)$ is the centroid of cluster C_i, and $d(x, \mu(C_i))$ represents the distance between the observation x and $\mu(C_i)$. The Euclidean Distance d from x to μ is calculated using the equation below:

$$d = \sqrt{\sum_{k=1}^{n} (x_k - \mu_k)^2} \tag{2}$$

3.2 K-medoids

Since the center point of K-means is located at an arbitrary value in the continuous space, it is sensitive to noise. Unlike K-means, K-medoids can only take a particular data point in the dataset as the center point [13]. The flow of the K-medoids algorithm is shown in Table 2. The error function of K-medoids is as follows:

$$E = \sum_{i=1}^{k} \sum_{x \in C_i} (x - m(C_i)) \tag{3}$$

The silhouette coefficient is an effective index proposed to solve the validity of the clustering results, and the following formula can express it [14]:

$$s(i) = \frac{b(i) - a(i)}{\max\{a(i), b(i)\}} \tag{4}$$

$$s(i) = \begin{cases} 1 - \frac{a(i)}{b(i)} & a(i) < b(i) \\ 0 & a(i) < b(i) \\ \frac{b(i)}{a(i)} - 1 & a(i) < b(i) \end{cases} \tag{5}$$

where $a(i)$ represents the average distance from sample i to other samples; $b(i)$ means the average distance from sample i to other clusters C. As the silhouette coefficient approaches 1, the sample clustering becomes more reliable.

In addition, among the selected eigenvalues, the average velocity value is much larger than the acceleration. Therefore, in the cluster analysis, the weight of the speed will account for a higher weight by default. In this case, we need to normalize the extracted eigenvalues with the following formula [15]:

$$x_{scale} = \frac{x - x_{min}}{x_{max} - x_{min}} \tag{6}$$

where x_{scale} means the normalized value, x denotes the original feature data; x_{min} and x_{max} are the minimum and maximum values of the original feature data, respectively.

Table 1. The flow of the K-means algorithm.

Input: dataset D=$\{x_1, x_2, ..., x_n\}$
Step 1: Randomly select k initial center points in D;
Step 2: Divide other data points into clusters with the smallest distance from a center point;
Step 3: Recalculate the center point according to the distance from the data point in each cluster to the center point;
Step 4: Reassign data points to the closest clusters according to the obtained center points;
Step 5: Repeat (3) and (4) until the data points for each cluster no longer change;
Output: Clusters C=$\{C_1, C_2, ..., C_k\}$

Table 2. The flow of the K-medoids algorithm.

Input: dataset D=$\{x_1, x_2, ..., x_n\}$

Step 1: Randomly select k initial center points in D;
Step 2: Divide other data points into clusters with the smallest distance from a center point;
Step 3: Calculate the error function of formula (3);
Step 4: Randomly select a non-center point data point from D, and compute the error function each time, assuming that one of the current center points is exchanged for the selected non-center point data;
Step 5: Repeat (3) and (4) until the data points for each cluster no longer change;

Output: Clusters C=$\{C_1, C_2, ..., C_k\}$

4 Results and Discussion

4.1 Highway Road

We screened characteristic data for high-speed driving, including average vehicle speed, lateral acceleration, and average lateral acceleration. The original data points are shown in Fig. 2, the average speed ranges from 20 m/s to 50 m/s in the highway condition. We apply K-means and K-medoids approaches to divide the data points into clusters, and the results are given in Fig. 3. To select the optimal number of clusters, we choose the K value with the highest SC value as the clustering; the comparison chart is depicted in Fig. 4, where the SC value of K-means is 0.7584, and the SC value of K-medoids is 0.7616. Following our assessment, the K-medoids method is the optimal choice for

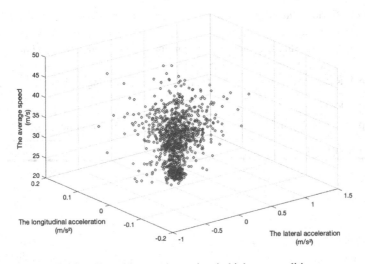

Fig. 2. Filtered feature data points in highway condition.

high-velocity operations. In this case, it makes more sense to divide driving styles into three categories.

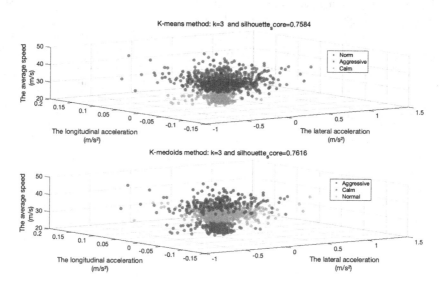

Fig. 3. Cluster analysis comparison in highway condition.

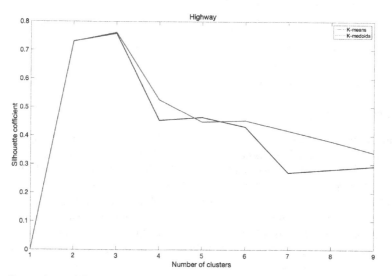

Fig. 4. Comparison of K-means and K-medoids clustering performance using SC in highway condition. (Color figure online)

4.2 Intersection Road

Unlike highways, vehicles at intersections are more cautious; the data points are shown in Fig. 5. Using the same method, we get that when k = 2, the SC value is the highest. The clustering results are given in Fig. 6, the red dots in the graph indicate a standard driving style, and the blue ones show a cautious driving style. The comparison results are depicted in Fig. 7; the red line indicates the relationship between the silhouette coefficient and the number of clusters using the K-medoids method; the blue line indicates the K-means method. It can be seen that when the number of groups is 2, the silhouette factors of the two ways reach the highest value. Moreover, the K-means method is more suitable for driving style cluster analysis in the intersection road.

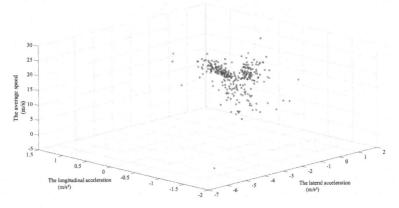

Fig. 5. Filtered feature data points in intersection condition.

4.3 University Road

The campus road conditions have more pedestrians and bicycles and relatively few motor vehicles. The data distribution is depicted in Fig. 8. Similarly, when k = 2, the SC value is the highest, the clustering results are shown in Fig. 9. It can be seen from the figure that the classification effect of the K-means method is different from that of the K-medoids method. Blue dots indicate a calm driving style, and red dots indicate a regular driving style. The comparison results are given in Fig. 10; the silhouette factors of the two ways reach the highest value in the two cluster conditions. Moreover, the K-medoids method is more suitable for driving style cluster analysis on the university road.

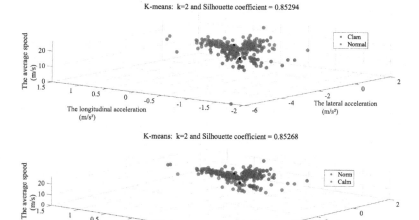

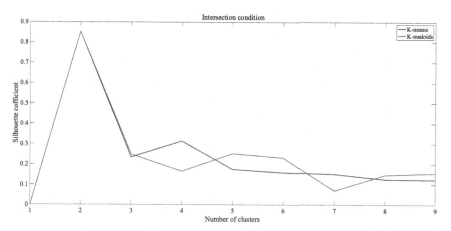

Fig. 6. Cluster analysis comparison in intersection condition. (Color figure online)

Fig. 7. Comparison of K-means and K-medoids clustering performance using SC in intersection condition. (Color figure online)

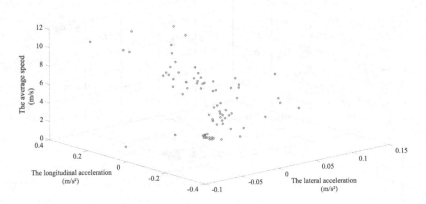

Fig. 8. Filtered feature data points in campus condition.

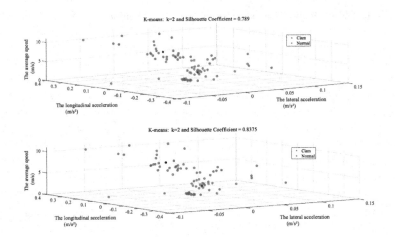

Fig. 9. Cluster analysis comparison in campus condition.

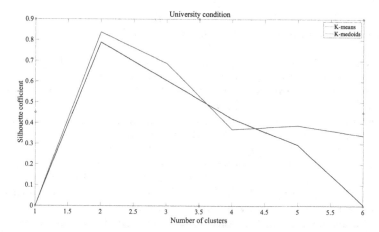

Fig. 10. Comparison of K-means and K-medoids clustering performance using SC in campus condition. (Color figure online)

5 Conclusion

Due to different road conditions, the classification methods of driving styles are also different. Based on the experimental data of three road conditions, this paper uses different unsupervised learning algorithms to cluster and analyze them. We can classify driving styles in high-speed conditions into aggressive, standard, and calm. The classification method of K-medoids is more advantageous; its silhouette factor is 0.7616. In intersection conditions, driving styles are usually divided into standard and calm. The effects of K-means and K-medoids are not much different; both silhouette factors are nearly 0.853. Considering the calculation time and other factors, we recommend the K-means algorithm. In campus conditions, the driving style can be divided into two categories: standard and calm, and in this case. The K-medoids approach has a more significant advantage; its silhouette factor is 0.8375. The research results have implications for the classification of driving styles under different road conditions. In the follow-up research, we will use supervised learning to identify driving behaviors based on the labeled data classified by unsupervised learning.

Acknowledgements. This work is supported by the National Key Research and Development Program of China (2021YFB2501705), partly by the Natural Science Foundation of the Higher Education Institutions of Jiangsu Province (Grant No. 22KJB510040), and the Basic Science Research Program of NanTong City (Grant No. JC12022028).

References

1. Mei, P., et al.: An adaptive fuzzy sliding-mode control for regenerative braking system of electric vehicles. Int. J. Adapt. Control Signal Process. **36**(2), 391–410 (2022)

2. Martinez, C.M., Heucke, M., Wang, F.Y., et al.: Driving style recognition for intelligent vehicle control and advanced driver assistance: a survey. IEEE Trans. Intell. Transp. Syst. **19**(3), 666–676 (2017)

3. Abou Elassad, Z.E., Mousannif, H., Al Moatassime, H., et al.: The application of machine learning techniques for driving behavior analysis: a conceptual framework and a systematic literature review. Eng. Appl. Artif. Intell. **87**, 103312 (2020)

4. Vaitkus, V., Lengvenis, P., Žylius, G.: Driving style classification using long-term accelerometer information. In: 2014 19th International Conference on Methods and Models in Automation and Robotics (MMAR), pp. 641–644. IEEE (2014)

5. Wang, W., Xi, J., Chong, A., et al.: Driving style classification using a semisupervised support vector machine. IEEE Trans. Human-Mach. Syst. **47**(5), 650–660 (2017)

6. Mohammadnazar, A., Arvin, R., Khattak, A.J.: Classifying travelers' driving style using basic safety messages generated by connected vehicles: application of unsupervised machine learning. Transp. Res. Part C: Emerg. Technol. **122**, 102917 (2021)

7. Jardin, P., Moisidis, I., Zetina, S.S., et al.: Rule-based driving style classification using acceleration data profiles. In: 2020 IEEE 23rd International Conference on Intelligent Transportation Systems (ITSC), pp. 1–6. IEEE (2020)

8. Bejani, M.M., Ghatee, M.: A context aware system for driving style evaluation by an ensemble learning on smartphone sensors data. Transp. Res. Part C: Emerg. Technol. **89**, 303–320 (2018)

9. Filev, D., Lu, J., Prakah-Asante, K., et al.: Real-time driving behavior identification based on driver-in-the-loop vehicle dynamics and control. In: 2009 IEEE International Conference on Systems, Man and Cybernetics, pp. 2020–2025. IEEE (2009)

10. Bock, J., Krajewski, R., Moers, T., et al.: The ind dataset: a drone dataset of naturalistic road user trajectories at German intersections. In: 2020 IEEE Intelligent Vehicles Symposium (IV), pp. 1929–1934. IEEE (2020)

11. Krajewski, R., Bock, J., Kloeker, L., et al.: The highd dataset: a drone dataset of naturalistic vehicle trajectories on German highways for validation of highly automated driving systems. In: 2018 21st International Conference on Intelligent Transportation Systems (ITSC), pp. 2118–2125. IEEE (2018)

12. Krishna, K., Murty, M.N.: Genetic K-means algorithm. IEEE Trans. Syst. Man Cyber. Part B (Cyber.) **29**(3), 433–439 (1999)

13. Park, H.S., Jun, C.H.: A simple and fast algorithm for K-medoids clustering. Expert Syst. Appl. **36**(2), 3336–3341 (2009)

14. Aranganayagi, S., Thangavel, K.: Clustering categorical data using silhouette coefficient as a relocating measure. Int. Conf. Comput. Intell. Multimedia Appl. (ICCIMA 2007) IEEE **2**, 13–17 (2007)

15. Eck, N.J., Waltman, L.: How to normalize cooccurrence data? An analysis of some well-known similarity measures. J. Am. Soc. Inform. Sci. Technol. **60**(8), 1635–1651 (2009)

CADM: Confusion Model-Based Detection Method for Real-Drift in Chunk Data Stream

Songqiao Hu[1], Zeyi Liu[2], and Xiao He[2(✉)]

[1] School of Automation, Beijing Institute of Technology, Beijing 100081, China
1120193091@bit.edu.cn
[2] Department of Automation, Tsinghua University, Beijing 100084, China
liuzy21@mails.tsinghua.edu.cn, hexiao@tsinghua.edu.cn

Abstract. Concept drift detection has attracted considerable attention due to its importance in many real-world applications such as health monitoring and fault diagnosis. Conventionally, most advanced approaches will be of poor performance when the evaluation criteria of the environment has changed (i.e. concept drift), either can only detect and adapt to virtual drift. In this paper, we propose a new approach to detect real-drift in the chunk data stream with limited annotations based on concept confusion. When a new data chunk arrives, we use both real labels and pseudo labels to update the model after prediction and drift detection. In this context, the model will be confused and yields prediction difference once drift occurs. We then adopt cosine similarity to measure the difference. And an adaptive threshold method is proposed to find the abnormal value. Experiments show that our method has a low false alarm rate and false negative rate with the utilization of different classifiers.

Keywords: Concept drift · Confusion model · Chunk data stream · Similarity

1 Introduction

Concept drift is a nonnegligible factor in data analysis of dynamic systems. For example, much data is collected by sensors, but the sensors' output is vulnerable to its structure and the surrounding environment, of which temperature is the most influential. Under different temperatures, the distribution range of the collected data and even their categories will change. If the monitor system fails to detect the change, it will be difficult to provide correct decision-making suggestions when risks happen [1].

In the literature, several advanced studies have been proposed for solving this problem. Gama *et al.* [2] proposed Drift Detection Method (DDM) to detect whether the overall online error rate increased greatly, which was used to judge whether the warning level or the drift level was reached. [3] proposed

© ICST Institute for Computer Sciences, Social Informatics and Telecommunications Engineering 2023
Published by Springer Nature Switzerland AG 2023. All Rights Reserved
H. R. Karimi and N. Wang (Eds.): S-Cube 2022, LNICST 487, pp. 191–201, 2023.
https://doi.org/10.1007/978-3-031-34899-0_13

a two-time window-based drift detection algorithm named ADaptive WINdow-ing (ADWIN). ADWIN indicates that concept drift occurs if the means of data in two windows differ significantly. In [4], conformal prediction was introduced to detect concept drift. Concept drift was confirmed if the conformal predic-tion result in the two data chunks showed a great difference. Otherwise, pseudo labels were used to update the model. Lu et al. [5] adopted ensemble learning and adjusted each base classifier's weight according to their performance. Once a base classifier was dropped out and a new classifier needed to generate, the size of the train data chunk increased continuously until the variance stopped rising. Using the selected size data chunk to train a new base classifier could adapt to concept drift. DSPOT proposed by Siffer et al. [7] believed that anomalies are usually extreme values and utilized extreme theory to fit the extreme value distributions for calculating the dynamic concept drift threshold. Sethi et al. [8] proposed the GC3 framework, which uses grid density clustering and a unified grid density sampling mechanism to achieve better performance with a lower label rate. The concept drift was then detected, which is the idea of feedback.

Generally, there are two main types of concept drift: real concept drift changes in $P(y|x)$, and virtual concept drift changes in $P(x)$. Nevertheless, many of the above methods can only detect virtual drift but do nothing for real drift. [3] only considers the mean of the data but is unconcerned about the labels of the data. So it can just handle virtual drift in principle. [4] seems to be put forward for real concept drift. However, judging whether two data chunks have significant distribution differences only uses the pseudo labels predicted by the same classifier. Therefore, it cannot find the change in the labels. In [7], only the case of one-dimensional time series is taken into account, and whether it is an outlier is given according to the value of the feature, and the samples do not have labels at all. So the method is similar to judging concept drift from $P(x)$. Another typical problem in data mining and concept drift is label cost. In real situations, obtaining actual data labels usually requires a lot of time and energy, especially in the case of a high-speed data stream. Therefore, it is unrealistic to regard the concept drift as a supervised learning problem [2] [5] [6]. [8] is one of the few methods that consider both actual drift and labeling cost. The main framework is based on the idea of feedback. Namely, some samples are selected for annotations after the prediction. Then, the classifier is adjusted according to the difference between the prediction and labeling results.

In this paper, we propose a novel chunk-based confusion model method called Confusion And Detection Method (CADM) to deal with real concept drift with limited annotations. The main contribution of this paper can be summarized as follows: (1) A novel method is provided to detect real concept drift with limited labels in chunk data streams; (2) To the best of our knowledge, it is the first method that requires labels after concept drift detection. The drift detection results can then be used to guide the annotation costs; (3) The effectiveness is verified based on numerous experiments.

The rest of the paper is organized as follows. Section 2 introduces the method and datasets adopted in this study. Section 3 describes and discusses some exper-imental results and Sect. 4 presents the conclusions.

2   Proposed Method

2.1   Motivation

The main idea is generated from the confusion model, which refers to a model that has a low degree of certainty in the classification judgment of samples. Generally, it can be caused by different concepts contained in training data. An example can be shown in Fig. 1.

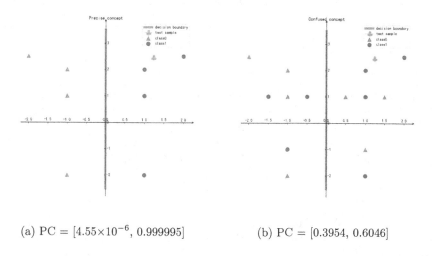

(a) PC = [4.55×10⁻⁶, 0.999995]   (b) PC = [0.3954, 0.6046]

Fig. 1. The prediction confidence (PC) for different training data by Naive Bayes model. (a) The training data is from the same concept. PC is then completely certain. (b) Add another batch of data with a different concept on the basis of (a). PC becomes uncertain. Such a model is called the confusion model.

In general, incremental learning models [9] have greater advantages to serve as the confusion model compared to common models due to the ability to update the model without storing historical data. In the case of the chunk data stream, the model can predict and select some samples to update when each data chunk arrives. To detect drift and improve the prediction performance of the model, we provide some samples with hard pseudo labels according to the prediction and annotate some samples manually. The purpose of pseudo labels is to increase training samples, improve prediction performance and adapt to virtual drift. While the purpose of manual annotations is to confuse the model when the real drift occurs, which makes the difference in prediction.

2.2   Difference Measurement

Difference measurement aims to measure the prediction difference in the new data chunk after the incremental update. Let $U_0=\{x_1, x_2, ..., x_n\}$ be the set of n unlabeled samples in new chunk, h_{t-1} denote the model before update, h_t represent the model after update, $h(\cdot)=[p_1, ..., p_m]^T$ be the confidence probability vector for m classes. In this case, we define the matrix $H_{t-1}=[h_{t-1}(x_1), ..., h_{t-1}(x_n)]$ and $H_t=[h_t(x_1), ..., h_t(x_n)]$ as shown in Eqs. (1) and (2).

$$H_{t-1} = [h_{t-1}(x_1), ..., h_{t-1}(x_n)] = [\alpha_{t-1,1}^T, ..., \alpha_{t-1,m}^T]^T \tag{1}$$

$$H_t = [h_t(x_1), ..., h_t(x_n)] = [\alpha_{t,1}^T, ..., \alpha_{t,m}^T]^T \tag{2}$$

In this context, the function $Sim(\cdot)$ can be defined with the utilization of model similarity as:

$$Sim(H_{t-1}, H_t) = \frac{1}{m}\sum_{i=1}^{m} \frac{\alpha_{t-1,i}^T \cdot \alpha_{t,i}}{||\alpha_{t-1,i}|| \cdot ||\alpha_{t,i}||}. \tag{3}$$

In Eq. (3), the cosine similarity between $\alpha_{t-1,i}$ and $\alpha_{t,i}$ is calculated for each class. The mean of cosine similarity of m classes is used to denote the cosine similarity of two models. Clearly, $Sim(h_{t-1}, h_t) \in [-1, 1]$ is always valid. The smaller the value is from 1, the more different the predictions of the two models are, which indicates that more likely concept drift occurs.

2.3 Adaptive Threshold

For drifting samples of the same number, the difference degree of the models after updating varies with the number of samples that have been trained. The more samples have been trained, the smaller the impact of new samples on the model. Therefore, it is necessary to adopt the adaptive threshold.

Given that the model changes greatly when updates at the beginning, the oscillation of cosine similarity will be large at first and then gradually decrease. To this end, we propose *Deviation-Adaptive Threshold* (DAT) which considers the statistical features such as mean and variance. A fixed-size window is adopted to store latest cosine similarity values. At each time stamp, the current average level of cosine similarity is judged according to the mean of the values in the window. The current oscillation level can then be obtained according to the standard deviation. Then the abnormal cosine similarity value can be obtained with such an average level and oscillation level. To understand the whole procedure, the pseudo-code is shown in Algorithm 1.

2.4 Drift Detection

When the new data chunk arrives, it is needed to calculate the cosine similarity between the model updated by the last data chunk and the non-updated model. The window and threshold can then be updated. If the cosine similarity is lower than the threshold, the drift can then be judged to occur. The details of the algorithm can then be summarized in Algorithm 2. And the overall flow chart is summarized as shown in Fig. 2.

Algorithm 1. DAT (Deviation-Adaptive Threshold)

Input: New data $\mathbf{C}_{new}$, previous window $\mathbf{W}_{pre}$, the size of window l, deviation coefficient k.
Output: Threshold $\mathbf{t}$, new window $\mathbf{W}_{new}$.
1: **if** length($\mathbf{W}_{pre}$)$<l$ **then**
2:     Add $\mathbf{C}_{new}{\rightarrow}\mathbf{W}_{pre}$
3: **else**
4:     Pop($\mathbf{W}_{pre}$,0)   //delete the first element
5:     Add $\mathbf{C}_{new}{\rightarrow}\mathbf{W}_{pre}$
6: $\mathbf{W}_{pre}{\rightarrow}\mathbf{W}_{new}$
7: mean($\mathbf{W}_{new}$)${\rightarrow}\overline{x}$
8: std($\mathbf{W}_{new}$)${\rightarrow}\sigma$
9: $\overline{x}$ - $k\sigma{\rightarrow}\mathbf{t}$
10: **return** $\mathbf{t}$, $\mathbf{W}_{new}$

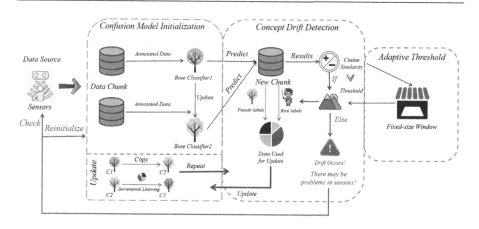

Fig. 2. The overall flow chart.

3   Experimental Analysis

In this section, we empirically compare the proposed method with other state-of-the-art (SOTA) methods for chunk data streams with various concept drifts. The effectiveness of the adaptive threshold setting method in CADM and how it changes with cosine similarity are also illustrated.

3.1   Experimental Settings

Four simulation datasets with decision boundaries of different shapes are selected, which generally contain two variables .The extreme concept drift, i.e. labels of all samples are reversed, is simply introduced (see Fig. 3, 4). Several advanced methods (DWM [10], ARF [11], HT [12], NB [13], CPSSDS [4], OSELM

Algorithm 2. CADM (Confusion And Detection Method)

Input: Data chunk $\boldsymbol{stream}=\{D_i$, i=1,...,N,$D_i = \{\boldsymbol{x}_j{\in}\mathcal{X}$, j=1,...,$|D_i|\}\}$, classifier type $\mathcal{C}$, label ratio λ, the size of window $\boldsymbol{l}$, deviation coefficient $\boldsymbol{k}$.

Output: Drift points list $\boldsymbol{L}_{drift}$.

1: //Confusion model initialization.
2: $\mathcal{C}_1, \mathcal{C}_2 = \mathcal{C}()$
3: $D = \boldsymbol{stream}.\text{next\_chunk}()$
4: $\boldsymbol{x}_{labeled} = \text{Random}(D, \lambda{\cdot}|D|)$
5: $\boldsymbol{y}_{labeled} = \text{Give\_label}(\boldsymbol{x}_{labeled})$
6: $\mathcal{C}_1.\text{fit}(\boldsymbol{x}_{labeled}, \boldsymbol{y}_{labeled})$
7: $\mathcal{C}_2.\text{fit}(\boldsymbol{x}_{labeled}, \boldsymbol{y}_{labeled})$
8: $\boldsymbol{W} = [\,]$
9: $\boldsymbol{L}_{drift} = [\,]$
10: **while** $(D = \boldsymbol{stream}.\text{next\_chunk}()){\neq}\emptyset$ **do**
11:      $\boldsymbol{H}_{t-1} = \mathcal{C}_1.\text{predict\_prob}(D)$
12:      $\boldsymbol{H}_t = \mathcal{C}_2.\text{predict\_prob}(D)$
13:      $\boldsymbol{cos} = Sim(H_{t-1},H_t)$
14:      $\boldsymbol{t}, \boldsymbol{W} = \textbf{DAT}(\boldsymbol{cos}, \boldsymbol{W}, \boldsymbol{l}, \boldsymbol{k})$ //calculate the threshold and update the window
15:      **if** $\boldsymbol{cos} < \boldsymbol{t}$ **then**
16:          Add chunk_index $\rightarrow \boldsymbol{L}_{drift}$
17:          $\boldsymbol{W} = [\,]$
18:          $\mathcal{C}_1, \mathcal{C}_2 = \mathcal{C}()$
19:          $\boldsymbol{x}_{labeled} = \text{Random}(D, \lambda{\cdot}|D|)$
20:          $\boldsymbol{y}_{labeled} = \text{Give\_label}(\boldsymbol{x}_{labeled})$
21:          $\mathcal{C}_1.\text{fit}(\boldsymbol{x}_{labeled}, \boldsymbol{y}_{labeled})$
22:          $\mathcal{C}_2.\text{fit}(\boldsymbol{x}_{labeled}, \boldsymbol{y}_{labeled})$ //drift occurs and reinitialize the models
23:      **else**
24:          $\boldsymbol{x}_{labeled} = \text{Random}(D, \lambda{\cdot}|D|)$
25:          $\boldsymbol{y}_{labeled} = \text{Give\_label}(\boldsymbol{x}_{labeled})$
26:          $\boldsymbol{x}_{pseudo} = \text{Random}(D{-}\{\boldsymbol{x}_{labeled}\}, \lambda{\cdot}|D|)$
27:          $\boldsymbol{y}_{pseudo} = \text{Hard\_pseudo\_label}(\boldsymbol{x}_{pseudo}, \mathcal{C}_2)$
28:          $\mathcal{C}_1 = \mathcal{C}_2$
29:          $\mathcal{C}_2.\text{partial\_fit}([\boldsymbol{x}_{labeled}, \boldsymbol{x}_{pseudo}], [\boldsymbol{y}_{labeled},\boldsymbol{y}_{pseudo}])$
        return $\boldsymbol{L}_{drift}$

---

[14], BLS [15]) are selected to be compared, which are implemented by *skmultiflow*[1].

For the parameters of CADM, the size of the window is set at 10, the label ratio is set at 0.2, and the size of the chunk is 200. We set k as 2 by analogy to the probability criterion of Gaussian distribution[2]

3.2   Experimental Results

Drift Detection and Threshold Change. In four simulation datasets, we set an extreme real drift at every 25 chunks, respectively. Naive Bayes [11] is used

---

[1] https://scikit-multiflow.github.io/.
[2] The code is available at https://github.com/songqiaohu/CADM-Confusion-Model.

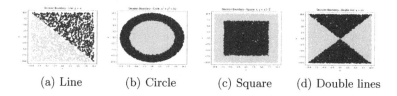

(a) Line   (b) Circle   (c) Square   (d) Double lines

Fig. 3. Simulation datasets with different shape-decision boundaries.

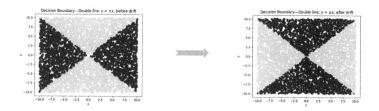

Fig. 4. Distribution of samples and labels before and after drifts.

in CADM for this experiment, where the default parameters provided by *scikit-multiflow* library in Python are considered. The change in cosine similarity and threshold are shown in Fig. 5. The effect of drift detection is reported in Table 1. Clearly, *drift chunk* refers to the chunk where drift begins, *FA* refers to *False Alarm*, and the table content is the position where drift is detected.

Table 1. Drift detection of CADM in different datasets.

Dataset	Drift chunk																			
	26	51	76	101	126	151	176	201	226	251	276	301	326	351	376	401	426	451	476	FA
Line	27	52	77	102	127	152	178	202	227	251	×	×	327	352	377	403	427	452	477	–
Circle	27	×	×	103	127	152	177	202	227	252	277	302	327	352	377	402	427	452	477	–
Square	27	52	77	102	×	×	179	202	227	252	279	302	327	352	377	402	427	452	477	–
Doubleline	27	52	78	102	127	153	177	203	226	252	277	302	327	352	377	402	427	452	477	–

From this experiment, it can be verified that the proposed method has great advantages against false alarms. However, each drift detection has a certain delay, which is caused by two reasons: one is the principle of the method itself. The model should need to be confused before drift can be detected; the other is the randomness of samples. More samples are needed if a small number of samples cannot sufficiently confuse the model.

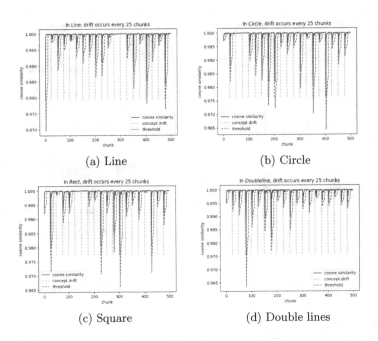

Fig. 5. Cosine similarity and threshold varies with chunk.

Prediction Accuracy. In this experiment, we compare the performance of the previously mentioned algorithms and their combination with CADM in prediction accuracy. The adjustable parameters of all methods are identical, including training data, label ratio, etc. The dataset used is *Doubleline*, where the decision boundary is nonlinear.

From Fig. 6 and Table 2, the following conclusions can be drawn: **i)**Drifts in simulation datasets frequently occur. Without drift detection, the updating and adaptation speed of *NB, HT, BLS* and *OSELM* is slower than that of drift change, especially in the environment with few labels. Therefore, the accuracy curve almost changes following the drifts as shown in Fig. 6 (a)-(d); **ii)**After combining with *CADM*, all methods can quickly detect and adapt to the drifts. Hence, the accuracy curve can rapidly rise to a high position after a sharp fall. The overall accuracy improves significantly, as shown in Fig. 6 (e)-(h), which also shows the scalability and applicability of *CADM*; **iii)**Among all methods,

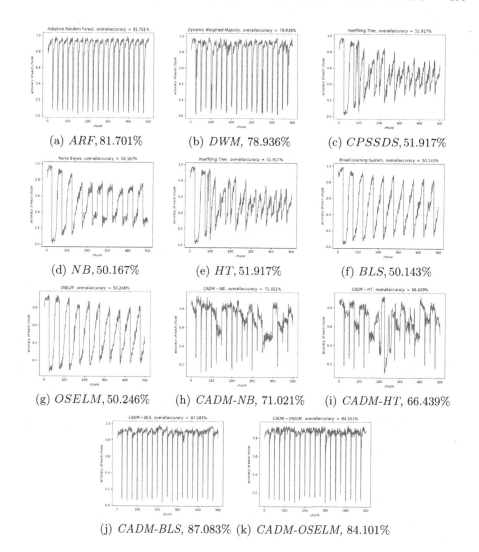

Fig. 6. Prediction accuracy of different methods.

CADM-BLS achieves the highest accuracy, which is higher than *ARF* and *DWM*. *CADM-OSELM* is also higher than *DWM*, which shows that the combinations of *CADM* and some base classifiers outperform the current mainstream algorithms with drift detection in *scikit-multiflow*. **iv)** For *CPSSDS* shown in Fig. 6 (k), its performance is similar to the methods without drift detection. As mentioned in the first section, it can only detect virtual drift rather than real drift.

Table 2. Overall accuracy for all methods in *Doubleline* (over ten runs).

Methods		Accuracy ± std(%)
Methods with drift detection	ARF	**81.164 ± 0.215**
	DWM	**78.973 ± 0.872**
	$CPSSDS$	51.917 ± 0.000
Methods without drift detection	NB	49.846 ± 0.297
	HT	51.969 ± 0.590
	BLS	49.780 ± 0.134
	$OSELM$	49.801 ± 0.193
Methods with $CADM$	$CADM-NB$	65.773 ± 4.338
	$CADM-HT$	64.893 ± 3.881
	$CADM-BLS$	**86.851 ± 1.156**
	$CADM-OSELM$	**79.293 ± 5.780**

4   Conclusion

In this paper, we have proposed the $CADM$ to deal with real concept drift with limited annotations. $CADM$ updates the model with manually annotated samples and pseudo-label-samples predicted by the model simultaneously, which can improve the performance of the model when there is no drift and cause confusion when there is drift. Then, cosine similarity and adaptive threshold have also been proposed to judge whether drift occurs. We have verified its effectiveness and superiority in extreme-drifting simulation datasets by combining CADM with different classifiers.

Acknowledgment. This work was supported by National Natural Science Foundation of China under Grant 61733009, National Key Research and Development Program of China under Grant 2017YFA0700300, and Huaneng Group science and technology research project.

References

1. Liu, Z., Deng, Y., Zhang, Y., Ding, Z., He, X.: Safety assessment of dynamic systems: an evidential group interaction-based fusion design. IEEE Trans. Instrum Measur. **70**, 1–14 (2021)
2. Gama, J., Medas, P., Castillo, G., Rodrigues, P.: Learning with drift detection. In: Proceedings of the 17th Brazilian Symposium On Artificial Intelligence, pp. 286–295 (2004)
3. Bifet, A., Gavalda, R.: Learning from time-changing data with adaptive windowing. In: Proceedings of the 2007 SIAM International Conference on Data Mining. Society for Industrial and Applied Mathematics, pp. 443–448 (2007)

4. Tanha, J., Samadi, N., Abdi, Y., et al.: CPSSDS: conformal prediction for semi-supervised classification on data streams. Inf. Sci. **584**, 212–234 (2022)
5. Lu, Y., Cheung, Y.M., Tang, Y.Y.: Adaptive chunk-based dynamic weighted majority for imbalanced data streams with concept drift. IEEE Trans. Neural Netw. Learn. Syst. **31**(8), 2764–2778 (2019)
6. Liu, Z., Zhang, Y., Ding, Z., He, X.: An online active broad learning approach for real-time safety assessment of dynamic systems in nonstationary environments. IEEE Trans. Neural Netw. Learn. Syst., (2022)
7. Siffer, A., Fouque, P.A., Termier, A., et al.: Anomaly detection in streams with extreme value theory. In: Proceedings of the 23rd ACM SIGKDD International Conference on Knowledge Discovery and Data Mining, pp. 1067–1075 (2017)
8. Sethi, T.S., Kantardzic, M., Hu, H.: A grid density based framework for classifying streaming data in the presence of concept drift. J. Intell. Inf. Syst. **46**(1), 179–211 (2016)
9. Losing, V., Hammer, B., Wersing, H.: Incremental on-line learning: a review and comparison of state of the art algorithms. Neurocomputing **275**, 1261–1274 (2018)
10. Kolter, J.Z., Maloof, M.A.: Dynamic weighted majority: an ensemble method for drifting concepts. J. Mach. Learn. Res. **8**, 2755–2790, December (2007). ISSN 1532–4435
11. Gomes, H.M., et al.: Adaptive random forests for evolving data stream classification. Mach. Learn. **106**(9), 1469–1495 (2017). https://doi.org/10.1007/s10994-017-5642-8
12. Hulten, G., Spencer, L., Domingos, P.: Mining time-changing data streams. In: KDD'01, pp. 97–106. ACM Press, San Francisco, CA (2001)
13. Murphy, K.P.: Naive Bayes classifiers. Univ. British Columbia **18**(60), 1–8 (2006)
14. Ding, S., Zhao, H., Zhang, Y., et al.: Extreme learning machine: algorithm, theory and applications. Artif. Intell. Rev. **44**(1), 103–115 (2015)
15. Chen, C.L.P., Liu, Z.: Broad learning system: an effective and efficient incremental learning system without the need for deep architecture. IEEE Trans. Neural Netw. Learn. Syst. **29**(1), 10–24 (2017)

Research on Reading Comfort of Office Light Environment Based on Subjective Evaluation

Manqun Zhang, Zhisheng Wang[⊠], Yue Feng, and Xinjing Qin

School of Information Science and Engineering, Dalian Polytechnic University, Dalian, China
wangzs@dlpu.edu.cn

Abstract. People's requirements for office lighting environment are becoming higher and higher, not only for its comfortable and healthy, but also to ensure that people's work efficiency. Aiming at the problem of visual comfort of office light environment, this study carried out subjective and objective evaluation experiment of lighting comfort of office reading environment. This paper studies the coupling influence of lighting elements on paper reading and VDT reading in the office light environment, conducts experiments on the fixed brightness of the screen, and analyzes and discusses the influence of lighting source on visual fatigue degree of reading. In this study, the visual comfort of paper reading and VDT reading was discussed from the perspective of correlation analysis and multiple regression analysis based on the psychophysical data of 30 observers. The experimental results show that visual comfort of paper reading and VDT reading is significantly correlated with illumination and color temperature. The development of this study will provide effective theoretical reference for the design of the current office light environment and has certain guiding significance for the design of light source in various office places.

Keywords: Visual fatigue · Office lighting · Subjective evaluation

1 Introduction

In the rapid development of China's economic construction, people not only have a higher level of material life requirements, but also gradually pay attention to the spiritual needs. Because of the need to use a lot of eyes, if the long-term work in an uncomfortable light environment is easy to cause visual deterioration and other physiological problems [1]. At the same time, it can cause psychological problems and reduce work efficiency. Comfortable lighting environment can not only ensure good eyesight health, but also provide safeguard for the safe and efficient work and activities. It can not only beautify the office environment, but also ensure people's psychological and physical comfort.

At present, domestic and foreign researchers have explored the influence of lighting source on visual fatigue degree of staff in office. Wu Hong et al. found that eye fatigue is related to light environment [2]. Sivaji et al. conducted an experiment on office lighting with eye tracker, and the results showed that illumination and color temperature

H. R. Karimi and N. Wang (Eds.): S-Cube 2022, LNICST 487, pp. 202–216, 2023.
https://doi.org/10.1007/978-3-031-34899-0_14

had a certain influence on reading comfort [3]. Liu Gang et al. conducted an evaluation experiment based on subjective questionnaire. They conducted multivariate nonlinear regression analysis using SPSS software to study the influence of illumination, relative color temperature and illumination uniformity on environmental comfort. The results show that the intermediate color temperature light source and 200–300 lx light environment are more comfortable [4]. Taptagaporn et al. found that reading comfort is better when the horizontal illumination is 500 lx and the computer screen is bright through experiments [5]. Wu Tongyao et al. found that VDT reading comfort of human eyes increased first and then decreased with the increase of illumination through experimental research [6]. Through visual acuity test and heart rate test, Han Zeyang et al. found that color temperature had different effects on visual fatigue under different reading modes [7].

The above studies on the office light environment have mainly focused on the influence of illumination, color temperature and other lighting indicators on the comfort level of one of them. However, the current office materials are a combination of paper and electronic, and the previous studies were only limited to one of them, which does not meet the needs of today.

In view of the above problems, this study combins paper reading and electronic reading, studies the coupling effects of lighting elements on paper reading and electronic reading in the office light environment through subjective evaluation experiment, and analyzed and discusses the impact of lighting source on reading visual fatigue. To provide some technical reference for the design of office light environment under the current epidemic situation.

2 Experimental Design

2.1 Control Variables

Illumination (300 lx, 400 lx, 500 lx) and color temperature (4500 K, 5600 K) were selected as experimental variables in the evaluation experiment of visual comfort of office light environment[8, 9]. In addition, all other lighting parameters are in line with the national standard GB50034–2013[10]. In the experimental process, the illumination and color temperature were arranged and combined according to the experimental purpose. The following 6 experimental conditions of artificial light environment were respectively: 1.300 lx 4500 K; 2.300 lx 5600 K; 3.400 lx 4500 K; 4.400 lx 5600 K; 5.500 lx 4500 K; 6.500 lx 5600 K.

2.2 Lighting Environment Design

The experiment was carried out in a dark, enclosed laboratory. A set of tables and chairs, lighting equipment, illuminometer, VDT equipment (laptop computer) and reading materials required for the experiment are placed in the laboratory, as shown in Fig. 1. The lighting device used a Huawei desk lamp, which can adjust the required illumination and color temperature through mobile phone software. Before the experiment, the illumination, color temperature and color rendering index of the subjects were measured with a color illuminance meter. After the lamp was turned on and stable for 30 s, the lighting parameters in each light environment met the requirements of the experimental design. Record debugging data for debugging in formal experiments. The measurement results of lighting parameters in six light environments are shown in Table 1.

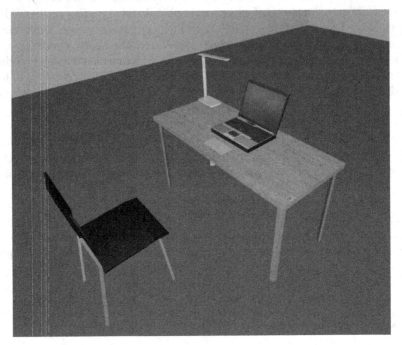

Fig. 1. Simulated experimental environment

Table 1. Test results of lighting parameters in six light environments

Number	Color rendering index	Illumination	Color temperature
1	95	296 lx	4487 K
2	95	302 lx	5624 K
3	95	407 lx	4499 K
4	95	399 lx	5612 K
5	95	502 lx	4505 K
6	95	499 lx	5602 K

2.3 The Experimental Method

A total of 30 college students were invited to participate in this experiment, including 18 males and 12 females. Thirty subjects had normal visual acuity, no ocular diseases, and no ocular acid, dry eye, dizziness and blurred vision before participating in the experiment. Because the experimental space was limited, two people in a group participated in the experiment and filled in the questionnaire. The content of the questionnaire is about the degree of visual fatigue scale and record of the reading time of the subjects. The visual fatigue scale scores the degree of eye acid, eye dryness, blurred vision, dizziness and inattention to judge the degree of visual fatigue of subjects. The questionnaire is divided into five grades according to their degree, of which the first grade is not at all, the second grade is low, the third grade is moderate, the fourth grade is deep, and the fifth grade is the deepest.In this study, the effects of illumination and color temperature on visual comfort of paper reading and electronic reading were studied by recording reading time and subjective evaluation results[11, 12]. Electronic reading comfort was evaluated by typing speed and subjective questionnaire.

At the beginning of the experiment, the parameters of the light environment were modulated by software according to the data recorded in the dimming process. After each adjustment of the light environment parameters, one of the subjects was asked to apply the light environment 30 s later and fill in the questionnaire. After finishing the paper reading, the other subject was switched to the paper reading experiment, and the other subject took a rest during this period.After resting, the first participant read electronically and completed the questionnaire after completing the typing task. Then, the second participant was given the electronic reading experiment. After all experiments in each light environment were completed, turned off the experimental light source and turned on the basic lighting to prevent glare caused by dark adaptation which was caused by turning on the light source after rest. Since it was an evaluation experiment on visual comfort, in order to avoid the effects of long-term reading on visual fatigue[13], two people took a rest for 2 min after the experiment in each light environment. Two subjects rested for 20 min after completing the three light environment experiments, and then completed the follow-up experiments.After the experiment, SPSS software was used for statistical analysis of reading time and questionnaire results.

The experiment was divided into two parts, one for paper reading and the other for electronic reading. Prepare a text for each light environment with the same number of words for each text. Before starting the experiment, arrange the reading material and the cell phone used for timing. Then, the subjects got used to the light.When the subjects are ready, they can click the start timer button and start reading the material. After finishing, click the timing button and record the reading time on the questionnaire. Finally, fill in the subjective questionnaire and score the content according to the reading experience. After taking a break from paper reading, start e-reading. For the same reading text content in the same light environment, use a laptop to edit the text printed on A4 paper with song Type-4 character on Word, and punctuation marks also need to be edited. Just like paper reading, subjects clicked the start timing button and began to edit the text. After finishing, they recorded the editing time and scored the content of the questionnaire. The same operation is performed in all six light environments.

3 Analysis of Experimental Data

3.1 Reliability Analysis

The data obtained from the subjective evaluation experiment were summarized and sorted out by Office Excel software, and one-way analysis of variance and multiple linear regression analysis were conducted by IBM SPSS software.

At the end of the experiment, the reliability of the questionnaire was analyzed by SPSS software to test the reliability of the questionnaire. Reliability is used to verify the stability of the definition of the evaluation scale and ensure the reliability of subsequent data analysis. In the reliability analysis of SPSS software, Cronbach's Alpha coefficient was used to evaluate the internal consistency of the whole visual fatigue scale.Its calculation formula is as follows:

$$r_{tt} = \frac{n}{n-1} \left[1 \frac{\sum_{i=1}^{n} (SD_i^2)}{SD_t^2} \right] \tag{1}$$

where, r_{tt} is the reliability coefficient of evaluation scale; is the number of items on the scale; SD_i^2 is the variance of the score of item i; SD_t^2 is the variance of the total score of the scale[14]. When Cronbach's Alpha coefficient is greater than 0.8, the reliability of the experimental scale is high.

The Cronbach's Alpha coefficient of the experimental data in this study was 0.868 for paper reading and 0.892 for electronic reading, which showed high internal consistency, and the experimental data could be further analyzed and processed.

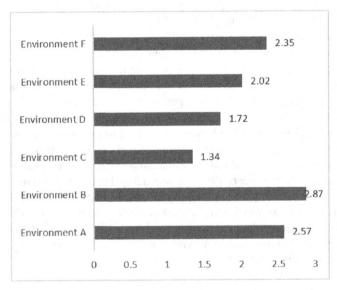

Fig. 2. Average score of paper reading for the six lighting schemes

3.2 Data Summary

The data obtained from the summary of experimental results were sorted out, and the average scores of the subjective questionnaire under six light environments were obtained by Office Excel software, as shown in Fig. 2 and Fig. 3. In the figure: Environment A. 300 lx,4500 K; Environment B. 300 lx,5600 K; Environment C. 400 lx, 4500 K; Environment D. 400 lx, 5600 K; Environment E. 500 lx, 4500 K; Environment F.500 lx, 5600 K.

It can be seen from Fig. 2 that the average score of Environment B in paper reading is the highest (AVG = 2.87), while the average score of Environment C is the lowest (AVG = 1.34). The average scores of Environment C and Environment D were lower than 2 (1.34 and 1.72, respectively), and the illuminance of these two environments was 400 lx.. The average scores of Environment A and Environment B and the average scores of Environment E and Environment F were more than 2 points, which were 2.57, 2.87, 2.02 and 2.35 respectively. The illuminance of Environment A and Environment B was 300 lx, and the illuminance of Environment E and Environment F was 500 lx.At the same time, it can be seen that the average scores of Environment A, Environment C and Environment E are smaller than those of Environment B, Environment D and Environment F. It can be seen that the scores under light environment of 4500 K color temperature are significantly lower than those under light environment of 5600 K color temperature, but the difference between the average scores of the two color temperatures is small, and the best environment is 400 lx 4500 K.

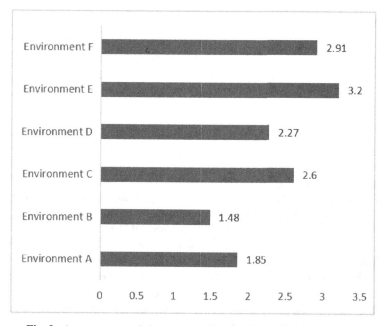

Fig. 3. Average score of electronic reading for the six lighting schemes

It can be seen from Fig. 3 that the average score of Environment E in electronic reading is the highest (AVG = 2.87), while the average score of Environment B is the lowest (AVG = 1.34). The average scores of Environment A and Environment B were lower than 2, which were 1.85 and 1.48 respectively. The illuminance of these two environments was 300 lx. The average scores of Environment C, Environment D and Environment F were all more than 2 points, which were 2.6, 2.27 and 2.91 respectively. The two environmental illuminance of Environment C and Environmen D was 400 lx, and the environmental illuminance of Environment F was 500 lx. At the same time, it can be seen that the average values of Environment A, Environment C and Environment E are higher than those of Environment B, Environment D and Environment F. It can be seen that the scores under light environment of 4500 K color temperature are significantly higher than those under light environment of 5600 K color temperature, and the average scores of the two color temperatures differ greatly, and the best feedback is the environment of 300 lx 5600 K.

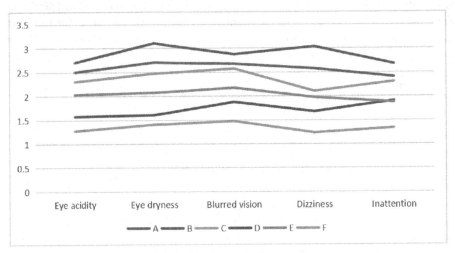

Fig. 4. Average score of five degree words in different light environments of paper reading

As can be seen from Fig. 4, in paper reading, the average scores of the five degree words of Environment C are the lowest, and the scores of each word pair of Environment B are the highest. Among them, six environments showed significant differences in the degree of inattention, with Environment C, Environment D and Environment F showing significant increases, while the other three environments showed decreases. The curves under different light environments differ greatly.

As can be seen from Fig. 5, the average score of five degree words of Environment B in electronic reading is the lowest, and the score of each word pair of Environment E is the highest. Among them, in the degree of dizziness, the average scores of the six light environments were significantly different, and the scores of Environment C and Environment E were significantly different from those of the other four environments. The scores of Environment F and Environment A are very similar.

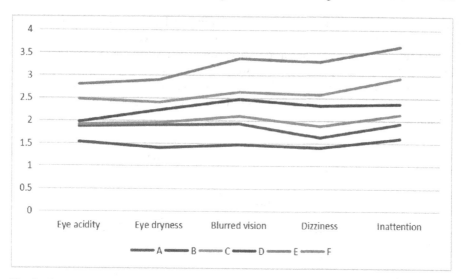

Fig. 5. Average score of five degree words in different light environments of electronic reading

3.3 Correlation Analysis

SPSS software was used to analyze the correlation between illumination and color temperature of electronic reading and paper reading and the degree of eye acidity, eye dryness, blurred vision, dizziness and inattention. The analysis results of Pearson correlation coefficient are shown in Table 1 and Table 2.

3.3.1 Correlation Analysis of Paper Reading

The results showed that the degree of eye acid, dry eye, blurred vision, dizziness and inattention were negatively correlated with illumination ($P < 0.05$), and positively correlated with color temperature ($P < 0.05$). The Pearson correlation coefficient between the degree of dizziness and illuminance was $r = -.366^{**}$, and the closer its value was to -1, the more significant the negative correlation was, and the change of illuminance had the greatest impact on the degree of dizziness. However, the absolute values of Pearson's correlation coefficients of the five words were all greater than 0.2 and less than 0.4, so the degree of eye acid, dry eye, blurred vision, dizziness and inattention were weakly correlated with the degree of illumination. There was a significant negative correlation between the five visual fatigue degree quantifiers and illuminance, and the significance was the degree of dizziness > the degree of dry eye > the degree of inattention > the degree of acid > the degree of blurred vision.

The Pearson correlation coefficient between the degree of inattention and color temperature is $r = .285^{**}$. The closer its value is to 1, the more significant the positive correlation is, and the change of color temperature has the greatest impact on the degree of inattention. Among them, the Pearson correlation coefficient of the degree of blurred vision, the degree of dizziness and the degree of inattention was greater than 0.2 and less than 0.4, so the degree of visual blur, the degree of dizziness and the degree of inattention showed significant weak correlation with color temperature. However, the correlation coefficient of the degree of eye acid and the degree of eye dryness was less than 0.2 but close to 0.2, showing a very weak correlation with color temperature. There was a significant positive correlation between the five visual fatigue degree quantifiers and the color temperature, the significance of which was the degree of inattention > the degree of blurred vision > the degree of dizziness > the degree of dry eye > the degree of acid.

Table 2. The Pearson correlation coefficient between illumination and color temperature and visual fatigue degree in paper reading

		The degree of eye acidity	The degree of eye dryness	The degree of blurred vision	The degree of dizziness	The degree of inattention
Illumlnation	Pearson correlation	-.222**	-.301**	-.204**	-.366**	-.248**
	Significance (two tails)	.003	.000	.006	.000	.001
	The case number	180	180	180	180	180
Color temperature	Pearson correlation	.160*	.194**	.208**	.202**	.285**

Continue to Table 2:

		The degree of eye acidity	The degree of eye dryness	The degree of blurred vision	The degree of dizziness	The degree of inattention
	Significance (two tails)	.032	.009	.005	.007	.000
	The case number	180	180	180	180	180

3.3.2 Correlation Analysis of Electronic Reading

In electronic reading, the degree of eye acid, dry eye, blurred vision, dizziness and inattention were positively correlated with illuminance ($P < 0.05$), and negatively correlated with color temperature ($P < 0.05$). The Pearson correlation coefficient between the degree of dizziness and inattention and illumination was r = .637**, and the change of illumination had the greatest effect on the degree of dizziness and inattention. The Pearson correlation coefficient of the degree of visual blur, dizziness and inattention was greater than 0.6, which was strongly correlated with the color temperature. The Pearson correlation coefficients of the degree of eye acid, dry eye and visual blur were greater than 0.4 and less than 0.6, which were moderately correlated with color temperature. There was a significant positive correlation between the five visual fatigue degree quantifiers and illuminance, the significance of which was the degree of dizziness = the degree of inattention > the degree of blurred vision > the degree of eye acid > the degree of dry eye.

The Pearson correlation coefficient between the degree of eye acid and color temperature was r = −.1.97**, and the change of color temperature had the greatest effect on the degree of eye acid. The Pearson correlation coefficient of the degree of visual blur, dizziness and inattention was less than 0.2 but close to 0.2, showing very weak correlation. There was a significant negative correlation between the five visual fatigue degree quantifiers and color temperature, and the significance was the degree of eye acid > the degree of inattention > the degree of dizziness > the degree of dry eye > the degree of blurred vision.

According to Pearson correlation value of data analyzed by SPSS software, multiple factors in visual fatigue degree have certain correlation with illumination and color temperature. Therefore, the reading comfort of paper and electronic reading can be improved by adjusting the illumination and color temperature (Table 3).

Table 3. Pearson correlation coefficient between illumination and color temperature and visual fatigue degree in electronic reading

		the degree of eye acidity	the degree of eye dryness	the degree of blurred vision	the degree of dizziness	the degree of inattention
IllumInation	Pearson correlation	.515**	.504**	.621**	.637**	.637**
	Significance (two tails)	.000	.000	.000	.000	.000
	The case number	180	180	180	180	180
Color temperature	Pearson correlation	−.197**	−.163*	−.149*	−.171*	−.182*
	Significance (two tails)	.008	.028	.046	.021	.015
	The case number	180	180	180	180	180

3.4 The Analysis of Multiple Linear Regression

Firstly, illumination and color temperature have significant differences with he degree of eye acidity, eye dryness, blurred vision, dizziness and inattention, and there is a significant relationship through the correlation analysis. Then, the overall visual fatigue of the subjects was defined as the average score of each subject's five visual fatigue states.

SPSS software was used to process the dummy variables of the sorted experimental effective data. Then, the scores of visual fatigue degree were analyzed by multiple linear regression to test whether the different levels of illumination and color temperature had an effect on the degree of visual fatigue[15].

3.4.1 The Analysis of Multiple Linear Regression in Paper Reading

It can be seen from Table 4 that the visual fatigue degree at 400 lx and 500 lx in paper reading is significantly lower than that at 300 lx (P < 0.05). The visual fatigue degree at 500 lx was significantly higher than that at 400 lx. Since the higher the score of visual fatigue,the deeper the degree of visual fatigue, paper reading under 400 lx light environment has the highest visual comfort. It can be observed from Table 5 that the visual fatigue degree of paper reading at 5600 K is significantly higher than that at 4500 K (P < 0.05), so the visual comfort degree of paper reading at 4500 K is the highest.

Table 4. Multiple linear regression analysis results of illumination in paper reading

Model		Unnormalized coefficient		Normalization coefficient	t	Significance
		B	Standard error	Beta		
1	(Constant)	2.720	.044		61.542	.000
	400 lx	−1.190	.063	−.945	−19.039	.000
	500 lx	−.537	.063	−.426	−8.586	.000
2	(Constant)	1.530	.044		34.617	.000
	500 lx	.653	.063	.519	10.453	.000
	300 lx	1.190	.063	.945	19.039	.000

a. Dependent variable: degree of visual fatigue

Table 5. Multiple linear regression analysis results of color temperature in paper reading

Model		Unnormalized coefficient		Normalization coefficient	t	Significance
		B	Standard error	Beta		
1	(Constant)	1.976	.060		32.768	.000
	5600 K	.338	.085	.285	3.962	.000

a.Dependent variable: degree of visual fatigue

It can be observed from Table 6 that the visual fatigue degree at 400 lx and 500 lx in electronic reading is significantly higher than that at 300 lx(P < 0.05). The visual fatigue degree at 500 lx was significantly higher than that at 400 lx. Therefore, the visual comfort of 300 lx is the highest for electronic reading.It can be seen from Table 7 that the visual fatigue degree at 5600 K in paper reading is significantly lower than that at 4500 K (P < 0.05), so the visual comfort degree at 5600 K in paper reading is the highest.

Table 6. Results of multiple linear regression analysis of illumination in electronic reading

Model		Unnormalized coefficient		Normalization coefficient	t	Significance
		B	Standard error	Beta		
1	(Constant)	1.667	.063		26.552	.000
	400 lx	.770	.089	.488	8.674	.000
	500 lx	1.387	.089	.878	15.621	.000
2	(Constant)	2.437	.063		38.820	.000
	500 lx	.617	.089	.390	6.947	.000
	300 lx	−.770	.089	−.488	−8.674	.000

a.Dependent variable: degree of visual fatigue

Table 7. Multiple linear regression analysis results of color temperature in electronic reading

Model		Unnormalized coefficient		Normalization coefficient	t	Significance
		B	Standard error	Beta		
1	(Constant)	2.551	.077		33.158	.000
	5600 K	−.331	.109	−.222	−3.042	.003

a.Dependent variable: degree of visual fatigue

3.5 Analysis of Reading Efficiency

Through statistical analysis of reading time of 30 samples in two modes and six light environments, the average value is calculated, and the results are shown in Fig. 6 and Fig. 7.

The shorter the reading time is, the higher the reading efficiency is, that is, the higher the reading comfort is, the longer the reading time is, the lower the reading efficiency is due to the influence of fatigue, the lower the reading comfort is. As can be seen from Fig. 2, from the perspective of color temperature analysis, the reading time of paper at 4500 K between 300 lx and 500 lx is shorter than that at 5600 K, and the difference in reading time at 400 lx is larger than that at 300 lx and 500 lx, indicating that paper reading under the condition of the same illumination, The reading comfort is higher when the

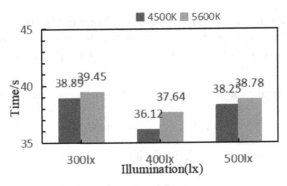

Fig. 6. Average reading time of paper reading

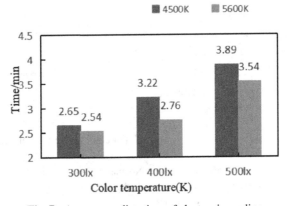

Fig. 7. Average reading time of electronic reading

light environment is 4500 K. From the perspective of illumination, at 4500 K and 5600 K, the reading time under 400 lx electronic environment is shorter than that under 300 lx and 500 lx environment, and the reading time drops significantly between 300 lx and 400 lx, while the change between 400 lx and 500 lx is little, indicating that paper reading under the same color temperature, When the light environment is 400 lx, the reading comfort is the highest, followed by 500 lx and 300 lx. Therefore, the lighting design applied to office needs can choose a light source with a color temperature of 4500 K under the condition of uniform illumination. When the color temperature increases, the change of visual comfort of reading is not obvious. Therefore, from the perspective of green, environmental protection and energy saving, the intermediate color temperature light source can be selected and the intermediate illumination applied to the paper reading office needs.

As can be seen from Fig. 3, from the perspective of color temperature, the e-reading time between 300 lx and 500 lx at 5600 K is slightly shorter than that at 4500 K, and the difference is small. Especially when the illumination is 300 lx, the electronic reading time at the two color temperatures is basically the same, indicating that the electronic reading time at the same illumination level is similar. The reading comfort is slightly higher than 4500 K when the light environment is 5600 K. According to the analysis from the perspective of illumination, at 4500 K and 5600 K, the reading time under 300 lx electronic environment is shorter than that under 400 lx and 500 lx, and the difference is obvious, indicating that the reading comfort of electronic reading under low illumination is the highest under the same color temperature, and the reading time increases slightly at 400 lx. The reading time was significantly different from that at 500 lx. Therefore, in the need to complete electronic reading tasks such as typing, low color temperature and light source can be selected to meet people's visual comfort needs. Because the comfort gap between the intermediate color temperature and light source and the high color temperature and light source is not obvious, so from the perspective of energy conservation, you can also choose the medium color temperature and light source. However, due to the limited text content and short reading time, the reading time is relatively close, which may have a certain impact on the result.

4 Conclusion

A psychophysical experiment was carried out using a subjective questionnaire to obtain the subjective evaluation data of reading time and reading feeling in paper and electronic reading under six light environments.

Through experiments, it can be found that illuminance and color temperature can have a certain impact on people's reading comfort, and the effects are different in paper reading and electronic reading. Whether it is paper reading or electronic reading, reading in a medium-color temperature light environment is more comfortable.At the same time, considering factors such as green energy saving, it is recommended to use an intermediate color temperature light source.It can also be found that the higher the illuminance, the higher the visual comfort of paper reading is, while the lower the visual comfort of electronic reading.From the analysis of the influencing factors of illuminance, people's needs for the light environment in different reading modes are significantly different.

Funding. Department of Social Sciences, Ministry of Education, Ministryof Education Humanities and Social Science Research(21YJC740036).

References

1. Zhu, C.H.: Study on indoor environment comfort evaluation and grey theory analysis. Hunan University, Changsha (2012)
2. Wu, H.: Light pollution and light civilization. In: Proceedings of the National Symposium on Electric Light Source Science and Technology, pp. 577–580 (2005)
3. Sivaji, A., et al. Lighting does matter: preliminary assessment on office workers. Procedia-Soc. J. Behav. Sci. **97**(1), 638–647 (2013)
4. Liu, G., Liu, M.L., Luo, C., et al.: Research on comfort of office light environment based on evaluation experiment. J. Light. Eng. **28**(6), 48–51,69 (2017)
5. Taptagaporn, S., Sotoyama, M., Saito, S., et al.: Visual comfort in VDT workstation design. J. Hum. Ergol. **24**(1), 84–88 (1995)
6. Wu, T.Y., Wang, L.X., Yu, J., et al.: Subjective evaluation of reading comfort of mobile phone under artificial lighting environment. J. Light. Eng. **29**(6), 28–32 (2018)

7. Han, Z.Y., Su, X.M., Hao, Z.G.: Comparison of visual fatigue between VDT and paper reading under different color temperature illumination. J. Light. Eng. **31**(06), 56–60 (2020)

8. Guo, X.Y., Shang, X.R., Tian, J.G., et al.: Effect of lighting environment on reading efficiency of electronic paper book at night. Pack. Eng. **40**(18), 171–175 (2019)

9. Hu, J.B., Lu, D.Q.: Research on reading fatigue of mobile phone under low light environment and related product development. Ind. De. **9**, 61–62 (2019)

10. Building lighting Design Standard:GB50034--2013. China Architecture and Architecture Press, Beijing (2014)

11. Huang, H.P., Wu, L.C., Yuan, Y.: Effects of age and ambient illuminance on visual comfort for reading on a Mobile Device. Color. Res. Appl. **42**(3), 352–361 (2017)

12. Ye, X.Q., Chen, Y.M., Sang, X.Z., et al.: An optimization method for parameters configuration of the light field display based on subjective evaluation. Displays 101945 (2020)

13. Cai, D.D., Pan, Y.Q., Huang, Z.Z.: Research on subjective evaluation index of office light environment comfort. Build. Energy Conser. **41**(12), 62–67 (2013)

14. Gao, H.W., Wang, Z.S., Zhu, D., et al.: Research on the influence of lighting mode and CCT on the lighting design of art museum based on subjective experiment. AIP Adv. **10**(12), 1–11 (2020)

15. Bao, F.D., Weng, X.Z.: Software solution and case analysis of multiple regression analysis. Data Stat. Manage **5**, 56–61 (2000)

Illuminance Affecting Factors Analysis
for Classroom Environments

Zihang Wei[1], Nianyu Zou[1(✉)], Yingjie Zhang[1], JiayuanLin[1], Fan Cao[1], Kai Liu[1],
and Min Cheng[2]

[1] Research Institute of Photonics, Dalian Polytechnic University, Dalian 116034, China
n_y_zou@dlpu.edu.cn
[2] CQC Standard (Shanghai) Testing Technology Co., LTD., Shanghai 200233, China

Abstract. The reasonable placement of lamps in the classroom will play a vital role in the classroom lighting environment of the classroom, in which the classroom lights and blackboard lights, as the two most important parts of the classroom lighting environment, their importance is self-evident. The illumination level in the classroom can be improved by adjusting the position of the blackboard lights and the classroom lights. At the same time, the influence of the lamps on the illumination level in the classroom is analyzed, and the best parameters are selected by changing the installation position and rotation Angle of the lamps, so as to put forward optimization suggestions for improving the illumination level in the classroom.

Keywords: Classroom lighting environment · Analog simulation

1 Introduction

As one of the important elements of human living environment, light provides a bright and comfortable living environment for human living life. Normal people get more than 87% of the external information through vision [1]. A good indoor lighting environment can effectively reduce eye fatigue, ensure the health of visual organs, and improve learning or labor efficiency. However, according to a number of scholars and institutions carrying out a lot of tests on the lighting environment of the local classroom, it is found that the illumination level and glare of the desktop and blackboard surface do not meet the existing relevant standards, among which the factors affecting students' vision include lighting environment deviation, learning pressure, unsanitary use of eyes, etc [2–5]. At the same time, it is also found that it can improve the visual comfort of students when illumination and reduce the glare of lamps, and improve their learning ability [6].

The placement of lamps in the classroom plays a very important role in the level of illumination in the classroom. The reasonable layout of lamps can improve the uniformity of illumination in the classroom. At the same time, there should not be too strong contrast between light and shade in the classroom. When the light and shade in the field of vision change sharply, the human eye can't adapt well, which will cause the decline in the city. If the eyes need to frequently adapt to a variety of different brightness, it is easy to produce visual fatigue [7].

H. R. Karimi and N. Wang (Eds.): S-Cube 2022, LNICST 487, pp. 217–226, 2023.
https://doi.org/10.1007/978-3-031-34899-0_15

2 Classroom Environment Design

2.1 Build a Classroom Model

The DIALux EVO software is used to establish a classroom space of 9.00 m long, 7.40 m wide and 3.50 m high. The blackboard in the classroom is 4.00 m long, 1.20 m wide, 0.20 m thick, and the bottom of the blackboard is 1.00 m from the ground. According to the relevant standards of the surface reflectivity in the classroom, the ceiling reflectivity is set at 0.70, the front wall reflectivity is set at 0.50, the side wall and rear wall reflectivity is set at 0.70, the ground reflectivity is set at 0.20, the blackboard surface reflectivity is 0.20 [10]. Items in the classroom include projector, multimedia curtain, lockers, curtains and so on. There are 30 desks in the classroom, available for 30 students. Figure 1 shows the simulation diagram of the classroom.

Fig. 1. Classroom simulation diagram.

2.2 Lamps Selection

The blackboard lamps and the classroom lamps in the classroom are installed by the boom rod. Three sets of blackboard lamps and eight sets of classroom lamps are selected. Figure 2 shows the arrangement of the lamps.

Blackboard lamps select LED lamps with grille and reflector, whose power is 36W, color temperature is 5000K, Luminous flux is 2880 lm, and color rendering index is 90. Classroom lamps select LED lamps with transparent cover, whose power is 36W, color temperature is 5000K, Luminous flux is 3000lm, and color rendering index is 90. The detailed parameters of the lamps are shown in Table 1.

The classroom area is 66.60 m^2, with 11 sets of lighting fixtures, including 3 sets of blackboard lamps and 8 sets of classroom lamps. The total power is 396 W, and the power density is 5.95 W/m^2. It meets the requirements that the classroom block lighting power density shall not be higher than 9 W/m^2 [10].

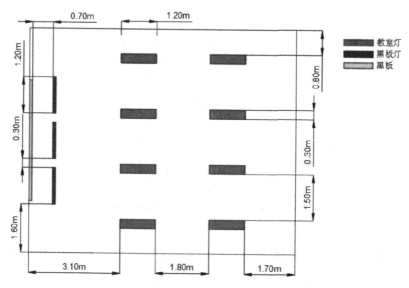

Fig. 2. Lamps layout.

Table 1. Lamps parameters

Types of lamps	Light source type	Parameter	Quantity	Distribution curve flux
Blackboard lights	LED	Power: 36W Color temperature: 5000K Luminous flux: 2880lm Color rendering index: 90 Levels of protection: IP20	3	
Classroom lights	LED	Power: 36W Color temperature: 5000K Luminous flux: 3000lm Color rendering index: 90 Levels of protection: IP20	8	

2.3 Judgment Criteria

The desktop illumination will be judged by the level illumination of the 0.75 m high desktop area. The blackboard illumination will be judged by the vertical illumination of the blackboard surface area. The UGR measurement point is at the center of the rear wall 1.10 m away from the rear wall [8].

The final simulation results are evaluated based on the relevant criteria, judged as follows:

(1) The maintenance average illumination of the class desktop should not be less than 300 lx, and the illumination uniformity should not be less than 0.70.
(2) The maintenance average illumination of the blackboard surface should not be less than 500 lx, and the illumination uniformity should not be less than 0.80.
(3) The uniform glare value at the position of the student observation point should not be higher than 16.0 [10].

3 Factors Affecting the Illuminance of Classroom Environment

3.1 Effect of Classroom Lamps Installation Height on Illumination

The height of the simulation surface of the desktop illumination is 0.75 m, GB 7793-2010 stipulates that the vertical distance between the classroom lamps and the desktop should not be less than 1.7 m [11]. In this simulated data collection, the installation height of classroom lamps is 2.6 m–3.3 m, which tries to comply with the actual use. In this simulation, the desktop illumination and illumination uniformity of the classroom lamps are collected at the installation height of every 0.10 m. The changes of the illumination and illumination uniformity in the simulation are shown in Fig. 3.

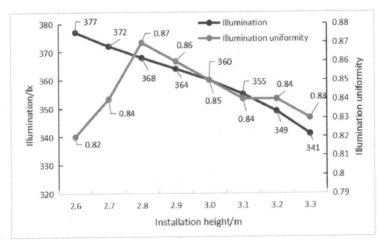

Fig. 3. Effect of installation height on illumination.

As can be seen from Fig. 3, when the installation height of the classroom lamps increase, the average illumination of the desktop is gradually reduced from 377 lx to 341 lx. The highest illumination uniformity is achieved at the installation height of 2.80 m. At this time, the desktop maintains the average illumination is 368 lx, and the illumination uniformity is 0.87. Meet the requirement of maintaining average illumination not less than 300 lx, and the uniformity of illumination also meets the requirement of no less than 0.7.

3.2 Influence of Classroom Lamps Distribution on Illuminance

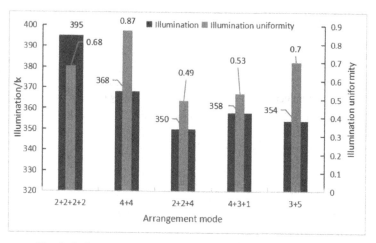

Fig. 4. Influence of classroom lamp distribution on illuminance.

As shown in Fig. 4, five different classroom lamps distributions are selected. Different lamps create different lighting environment. Among the five permutations, although the average desktop illumination maintenance meets the requirement of no less than 300 lx, only two groups of desktop illumination uniformity meet the requirement of no less than 0.7. That is, the second group on the left and the first set on the right in the figure. The data of the second group on the left is much better than that of the first group on the right. Considering that the arrangement of the lamps in the classroom needs to be neat, the arrangement of the second group on the left is selected.

3.3 The Influence of the Blackboard Lamps Spacing on the Illuminance

As shown in Fig. 5, the influence of blackboard lamps on the level of blackboard illumination when the distance between blackboard lamps changes. As you can see from the figure, when the spacing is 0.30 m. When the spacing is 0.70 m, the illumination and illumination uniformity are the lowest. Therefore, the data is optimal when the blackboard lamp spacing is 0.30 m.

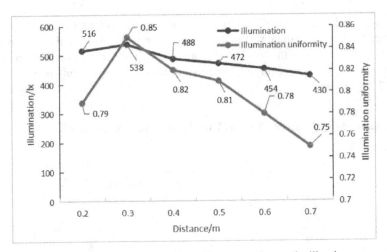

Fig. 5. The influence of the blackboard lamps spacing on the illuminance.

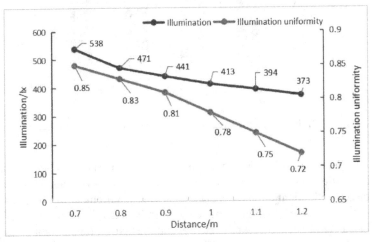

Fig. 6. Effect of the horizontal distance between the blackboard lamps and the blackboard on the illuminance.

3.4 Effect of the Horizontal Distance Between the Blackboard Lamps and the Blackboard on the Illuminance

As shown in Fig. 6, when the horizontal distance between the blackboard lamps and the blackboard surface is between 0.70 m and 1.20 m, the illuminance and illumination uniformity of the blackboard surface also decrease. Only when the distance is 0.70 m, the average illumination and illumination uniformity of the blackboard surface meet the requirements of 2.3 above. Therefore, the horizontal distance between the blackboard lamps and the blackboard surface will be selected as 0.70 m.

3.5 The Influence of Vertical Distance Between Blackboard Lamps and Upper Edge on Illumination

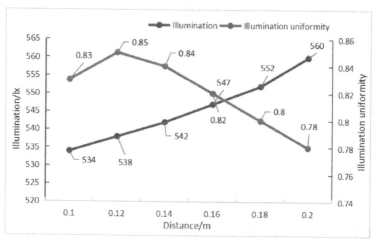

Fig. 7. The influence of vertical distance between blackboard lamps and upper edge on illumination.

As shown in Fig. 7, the vertical distance between the blackboard lamps and the upper edge affects the blackboard. It can be seen that as the distance increases from 0.10 m to 0.20 m, the illumination keeps increasing. The minimum value of 534 lx meets the requirement of maintaining the average illumination in 2.3. When the distance is 0.12 m, the uniformity of illuminance is 0.85, and the requirement of uniformity of illuminance is not less than 0.80 in 2.3 above. Since the illumination meets the above requirements, the distance between the lamp with the highest illumination uniformity and the upper edge of the blackboard, that is, 0.12 m. At this time, the average illumination of the blackboard surface is 538 lx and the illumination uniformity is 0.85.

3.6 Effect of Blackboard Lamps Rotation Angle on Illuminance

As shown in Fig. 8, the illuminance and illumination uniformity of the blackboard surface are analyzed for different rotation angles of the blackboard lamp to determine its influence on the illuminance level of the blackboard surface. With the increasing rotation angle, the illumination increases first and then decreases, with a minimum of only 356 lx and a maximum of 972 lx. In terms of illumination uniformity, with the increase of rotation angle, illumination uniformity decreases and then increases, with the lowest only 0.33 and the highest 0.85. When the rotation Angle is 0° and 15° respectively, the average illumination and illumination uniformity of the blackboard surface meet the requirements of 2.3 above. However, when the rotation angle is 0, the illumination uniformity is higher. Considering that the illumination gap between the blackboard surface and the desktop is too large, resulting in students' eyes switching between light and shade repeatedly, resulting in visual fatigue [7], so the rotation angle is 0°.

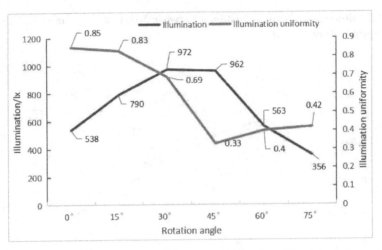

Fig. 8. Effect of blackboard lamps rotation angle on illuminance.

4 Simulation Optimization Results

As can be seen from the previous chapter, the installation height of classroom lamps is 2.8 m, and the arrangement mode is evenly distributed in two rows, with 4 lamps in each row. The distance between the blackboard lamps is 0.30 m, the horizontal distance between the blackboard lamp and the blackboard surface is 0.70 m, the vertical distance between the blackboard lamp and the upper edge of the blackboard is 0.12 m, and the rotation angle is 0°.

According to the above conclusions, the optimization simulation of the classroom lighting environment is carried out. In the simulation process, the central point distribution method is applied to collect the data of the illuminance and illuminance uniformity of the blackboard and desktop. The data are shown in Table 2.

Table 2. Simulation result

Parameter name	Technology	Optimize the results
Maintain average illumination on the desktop	≥300 (lx)	368.0
Table illumination uniformity	≥0.7	0.87
Blackboard maintains average illumination	≥500 (lx)	538.0
Blackboard illumination uniformity	≥0.8	0.85
UGR	≤16	13.1
Lighting power density	≤9(W/m^2)	5.95

According to the above optimization results, all parameters meet the requirements of 2.3 above. At the same time, the isoilluminance diagrams of class desktop and blackboard surface are obtained, as shown in Figs. 9 and 10.

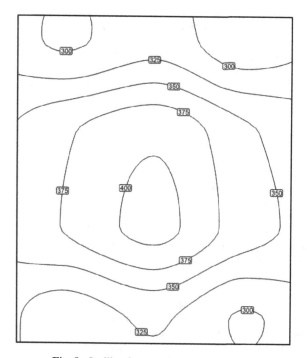

Fig. 9. Isoilluminance diagram of desktop.

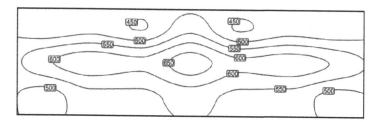

Fig. 10. Isoilluminance diagram of blackboard surface.

5   Conclusion

Through the simulation of Dialux Evo software, this paper analyzes in detail the installation height and distribution of classroom lights, as well as the influence of the position and rotation angle of blackboard lights on the illumination of classroom environment.

The results show that among the environmental illumination factors in the classroom. The installation height and distribution of the classroom lights, the position and rotation Angle of the blackboard lights relative to the blackboard all have a certain impact on the environmental illuminance in the classroom. In the optimization of classroom environmental illumination, it is necessary to optimize the classroom simulation, so as to achieve a better classroom environmental illumination level.

Acknowledgement. This work was supported by the following: 2019 Industry Standardization Project of the Ministry of Culture and Tourism (Grant No. WH2019–19), Cooperation research project between Dalian Polytechnic University and CQC Standard (Shanghai) Testing Technology Co., Ltd.

References

1. Yang, G.: Visual and Visual Environment. Tongji University Press (2002)
2. Duan, J., et al.: Analysis of lighting status and influencing factors in Primary and secondary schools in Beijing, Health in Chinese schools (2012)
3. Yang, J., Zhai, X., Li, J., Wu, L., Guo, X.; Research on the classroom lighting current situation of primary and secondary schools in a district and county in Beijing. J. Light. Eng. (2016)
4. Ye, S., Liu, S., Cao, Y., Wang, Q., Zhang, X.: Correlation between classroom lighting status of students and eyesight in primary and secondary schools in Tianjin, School Health in China (2018)
5. Liu, J., Mijie: Change trend of the health level of primary and middle school students in Beijing since 1985. Chinese Journal of Evidence-based Pediatrics (2011)
6. Hua, W.-J., Jin, J.-X., Wu, X.-Y., et al.: Elevated light levels in schools have a protective effect on myopia. Ophthal. Physiol. Opt. J. Br. College Ophthal. Optic. (Optometrists) (2015)
7. Allen, Xue, P., He, Z.: Effect of light environment on vision of teachers and students. China Education Technology and Equipment (2010)
8. GB 50034—2013"Architectural lighting design standards"
9. Wang, Y., Tang, X., Yue, F., et al.: Study on the revision of the height standard of school desks and chairs. Chinese School Health (2000)
10. T/CEEIA365—2019 "Specification for optical environment design and test evaluation in primary and secondary schools"
11. GB 7793–2010 "Standards for Lighting and Lighting in Primary and Secondary"

Virtual Simulation Measurement of Lamp Intensity Distribution Based on Near Field Goniophotometer

Shasha Liu, Xia Huang, Kexin Hao, Fan Cao[✉], and Nianyu Zou[✉]

Research Institute of Photonics, Dalian Polytechnic University, Dalian 116034, China
caoqianfan@163.com, n_y_zou@dlpu.edu.cn

Abstract. In order to solve the problems of not mastering the experimental process and not knowing the results clearly when using the full space distribution photometer for near-field measurement of lamps, a virtual simulation measurement of lamp intensity distribution based on near field Goniophotometer is proposed. The virtual simulation system builds the experimental platform and simulates the basic process of near-field measurement of lamps by the full-field Goniophotometer. The scheme includes the use of 3D Max and Blender to build models, unity 3D to simulate animation and scene development. According to the light intensity distribution of different types of lamps, the IES file is used to draw the light distribution curve of different lamps. The design results also prove that the system has good operability, interactivity and stability, realizes low-cost, safer and more convenient experiments, and improves the efficiency of lamp experiment of near field Goniophotometer.

Keywords: Unity 3D · Goniophotometer · Light distribution curve · near field measurement

1 Introduction

The Full-field Goniophotometer is an instrument used to measure the photometer spatial distribution characteristics of light sources or lamp. It is widely used in measurement equipment such as lighting product production enterprises, research institutions, testing laboratories, etc. [1–3]. In addition, it has an important status and role in the teaching of lighting and photoelectric instruments. However, due to the lack of equipment and the COVID-19 in traditional teaching and training, students do not fully understand the equipment. At the same time, the near-field measurement of the Full-field Goniophotometer can meet the needs of high-precision measurement at a short distance, and is suitable for the light intensity distribution of lamps and light sources with small luminous surface [4–8]. Therefore, an open network virtual experiment teaching system based on virtual reality technology is proposed to solve the above problems.

© ICST Institute for Computer Sciences, Social Informatics and Telecommunications Engineering 2023
Published by Springer Nature Switzerland AG 2023. All Rights Reserved
H. R. Karimi and N. Wang (Eds.): S-Cube 2022, LNICST 487, pp. 227–238, 2023.
https://doi.org/10.1007/978-3-031-34899-0_16

With the rapid development of virtual reality technology, the research on virtual laboratory simulation is gradually carried out. First, Poland uses virtual reconfigurable manufacturing systems to improve students' cognition and practice ability; what is more, Norway also uses virtual environment to cultivate navigation professional students at sea deck operation capacity. At the same time, China's Ministry of Education opened the "Demonstrative Virtual Simulation Experiment Teaching Project" for higher education in 2018. The project was published through the ILAB platform. At present, the platform has been included in 2079 professional experimental projects. Virtual reality technology is continuously applied to teaching experiment training, further improve students' learning cognition and practical hands-on ability, and further contribute to occupational overall quality [8–11].

Great achievements have been made in virtual laboratories at home and abroad, but the construction of the virtual simulation laboratory of lighting projects is still in its infancy in China. In 2018, Dalian University of Technology has developed lighting construction and distribution virtual simulation experimental system based on mixed realistic technology. The feasibility of the virtual simulation platform constructed of the Full-field Goniophotometer measuring system began in 2020. There is no research report on other research teams in this area [12–15].

In view of this, this paper intends to carry out the virtual simulation measurement of lamp intensity distribution based on near field Goniophotometer. The measurement of near field Goniophotometer is based on virtual reality technology, which does not take up real laboratory resources and t is a detached from the real scenario. In the virtual lab, it can provide students with a variety of experimental equipment, so that students can more understand the working principle of the instrument, thereby saving the expensive funds required to purchase equipment; and real-time distance education, to solve the special reasons for the school can not provide a safe experimental environment. Virtual simulation measurement of lamp intensity distribution based on near field Goniophotometer is detached from the real scene, and compared to the physical apparatus of the experiment cost is lower, it will not occupy real laboratory resources, better interactivity, and better stimulate the autonomy of student learning.

2   Overall System Design

The near-field measurement system of the Full-field Goniophotometer is a complex virtual operating system. The system structure is designed to take into account the environmental simulation, operational simulation and other aspects. Using unity 3D, 3D max and Blender to build the virtual measurement of the Full-field Goniophotometer is mainly divided into the Full-field Goniophotometer information display and spatial light intensity distribution measurement process simulation, as shown in Fig. 1 below, the system is applied to optical to different lamps or light sources for light intensity distribution and 3D display of its results.

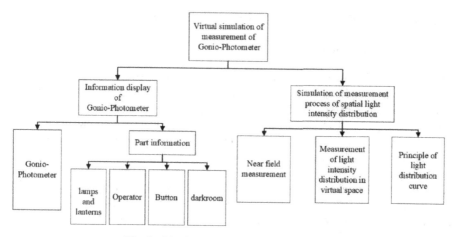

Fig. 1. Block Diagram of the system design

The experimental platform of the virtual near-field measurement simulation system first collates and analyzes the components of the Full-field Goniophotometer, the measurement principle and operation process of the Full-field Goniophotometer, and analyzes the mathematical model required for the system design combined with the experimental data. It is mainly composed of laboratory (darkroom), the Full-field Goniophotometer instrument, lamp model, operating table, button and other components. Among them, the darkroom is a model established by using the three-dimensional modeling software Blender and imported into unity's measurement scene in FBX format as a game object type. The model of the full space distribution meter mainly composed of control cabinet, turntable base, fixed mirror, vertical axis is made in 3D max and imported into Unity 3D to handle the necessary texturing, rendering, baking and animation settings for the model. The model of road lamps is established in blender, and the FBX format file is used as the game object type to import the measurement scene. Add a light source component to the game object's road lamps, and set the intensity of the light source component to 1. At the same time, set the whole space distribution photometer model and lamp model at the specified position inside the darkroom in unity.

The Unity 3D editing platform edits, adjusts and refines the imported 3D model and then renders a virtual scene of the full-space distribution photometer measurement system using Shader. After entering the virtual experiment platform, the user will enter the predefined full-space distribution photometer lab, and there will be a prearranged virtual experimenter for the user to operate in order to facilitate the user's operation. By operating the virtual experimenter, the user can perform basic movement, jumping, acceleration, perspective movement, and interaction with objects in the surrounding environment such as the lamp model and the photometer. By moving the virtual experimenter, the user can achieve the basic operation function in the virtual laboratory, so as to complete the steps of installing the lamp and getting the lamp parameters. At the same time, the design functions such as lamp measurement with full spatial distribution luminometer are realized by C# script, Finally, the virtual measurement simulation platform of lamps based on near-field Goniophotometer is released.

3 Simulation of Spatial Light Intensity Distribution Measurement

3.1 Near Field Measurement

The virtual near-field measurement is based on a full spatial distribution photometer with virtual near-field made by 3D Max, as shown in Fig. 2(b) below, which mainly consists of a rotating arm (Y axis), a lamp arm, a near-field detector, a luminaire and a rotatable reflector covered by black fleece. The principle of near-field measurement is to cover the rotatable reflector with black fleece so that the light from the measured light source or luminaire is directly received by the near-field detector.

When the measurement is started, the vertical axis starts to rotate around the gamma axis to measure the light intensity of the measured light source or lamp at various angles in a certain plane; At the same time, when the vertical axis rotates for one circle, the lamp can rotate around the C-axis to switch between different measurement planes, as shown in Fig. 2 (a) below.

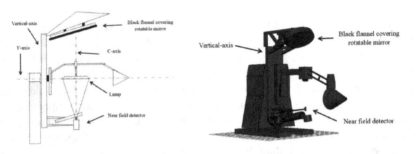

(a) A schematic diagram of near field measurement   (b)A virtual near field measurement model

Fig. 2. Measurement of the near field

In Unity, the horizontal angle of the vertical axis rotation and the vertical angle of the lamp are put into the rotation script. When the lamp is installed and turned on, click Start Measurement. The vertical axis starts to rotate around the gamma axis. When the rotation angle does not exceed 360°, continue to rotate. When the rotation angle exceeds 360°, reset its angle to 0°. At the same time, the angle of the lamp around the C-axis mechanical arm can be increased by 5° each time in this simulation design, then check whether the angle of the axis of the lamp around axis C exceeds 360°. If not, continue to work and output parameters in real time. If it exceeds, stop output, as shown in Fig. 3 below.

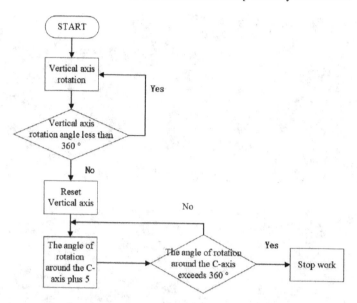

Fig. 3. The rotation principle for near field measurement

3.2 Measurement of Virtual Light Power Distribution

When entering the virtual light power distribution measurement experimental platform, a virtual experimenter will be controlled from a first-person perspective, by manipulating the virtual experimenter to the distribution photometer luminaire measurement experimental platform. Control the virtual experimenter to the distribution luminometer at the nearby installation of lamps, as shown in Fig. 4 (a); then turn on the light switch, as shown in Fig. 4 (b); to the operating table click to start measuring, as shown in Fig. 4 (c), at this time began to run the pre-designed full-space distribution luminometer animation script, the user can intuitively see the full-space distribution luminometer robot arm began to rotate, while relying on the robot arm rotation Angle parameters and has been entered to set the corresponding lamp parameters for comparison, the user can intuitively watch the three-dimensional dynamic formation of the light distribution curve on the operating table; at the end of the experiment, the light distribution curve is no longer drawn, click to end the measurement, as shown in Fig. 4 (d).

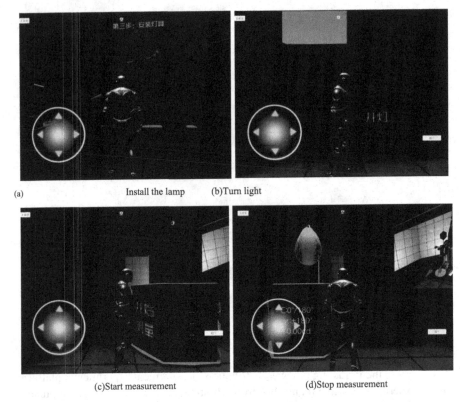

(a)   Install the lamp   (b)Turn light

(c)Start measurement   (d)Stop measurement

Fig. 4. Virtual light intensity measurement

3.3 Principle of Light Distribution Curve

The light intensity distribution curve are used in virtual near-field light intensity distribution measurements to represent the light intensity distribution in all directions in space. There are two types of light distribution curves: the right-angle coordinate system method and the polar coordinate method. Here, the polar coordinate method is chosen to describe the light intensity distribution of the luminaire, which is more intuitive to show the light distribution curve in three dimensions.

In the virtual light distribution curve drawing, the light distribution curve is drawn by calling the IES file. The initial stationary angle of the mechanical arm is 90°, and the vertical axis mechanical arm rotates between 90° to 360° and 0° to 90°. At the same time, due to the spatial light intensity distribution characteristics of Lambert light source, its light intensity between 180° and 360° is zero, so the rotation angle will be detected during the rotation of the vertical axis mechanical arm, and the data between 180° and 360° will not be displayed and output. In addition, when the program detects that the rotation of the vertical axis manipulator has exceeded 360°, it will reset the rotation angle of the vertical axis manipulator to 90°.

The light distribution curve is mainly derived from the three-dimensional coordinate formula of the ball, as shown in Fig. 5 (a), and the φ (PHI) and θ (theta) mainly based on the data processing of the IES file of the lamp, select some data of the IES file of a certain lamp, as shown in Fig. 5 (b). It is mainly composed of horizontal angle, vertical angle and data of the luminaire, etc.

First, assign a value to the horizontal angle according to the horizontal angle in the IES file, and then a different assignment is made to Phi by comparing the size of the horizontal angle with 180°. If it is less than 180°, the horizontal angle in the IES file is assigned to Phi, and because the data in the IES is placed upside down, theta is given to output the value in the IES upside down; if it is greater than 180°, the negative of the horizontal angle in the IES file is assigned to Phi, and theta is given to output the negative of the number in the IES positively. Finally, Phi is then taken as a remainder, so that the angle is controlled between 270°–360°(0°)–90°, thus satisfying the distribution characteristics of the spatial light intensity of the Lambert light source. Next, the angle values of Phi and theta are converted into radian values to obtain φ and θ, and import the data into the spatial light intensity parameter table, as shown in Fig. 5(c) below. Finally, the radius is normalized so that the size of the drawn curve can be controlled, and then the real-time 3D coordinate map of the light distribution curve is obtained through the spherical coordinate system, and the flow chart of the light distribution curve is shown in Fig. 5(d) below.

The light distribution curves of different lamps are also different. If the lamp has a rotational axis of symmetry, the distribution of light intensity in its space can be expressed only through the light intensity distribution curve on one metering surface of the axis. In the measurement of virtual distribution photometer, a lamp with a rotational axis of symmetry is selected [16–19]. Figure 5 (a) is the light distribution curve measured by the instrument, the red line is the initial measured light distribution curve, and the blue line is the final measured light distribution curve, Because they are symmetrical lamps, they are overlapped together. Figure 6 (b) is the C0 surface drawn on the virtual near-field measurement light distribution curve, which is the same as the initial light distribution curve in Fig. 6 (a). Fig. 6(c) and Fig. 6(d) are the C90 and C360 surfaces drawn on the virtual near-field measurement light distribution curve of the lamp respectively, and the drawn light distribution curve is the same as the actual measured light distribution curve.

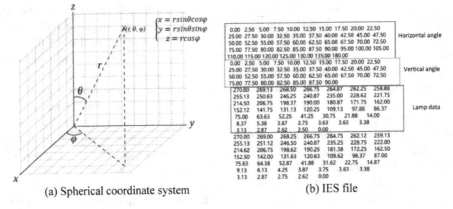

(a) Spherical coordinate system

(b) IES file

	A	B	C	D	E	F	G	H
1	RHO	THETA	INTENSITY	THETA RAD	COS	SIN	X	Y
2	int	float	float	float	float	float	float	float
3	1000	0	270	0	1	0	0	270
4	1000	2.5	269.13	0.043633231	0.999048222	0.043619387	11.73928572	268.8738479
5	1000	5	268.5	0.087266463	0.996194698	0.087155743	23.40131693	267.4782764
6	1000	7.5	266.75	0.130899694	0.991444861	0.130526192	34.81786177	264.4679168
7	1000	10	264.87	0.174532925	0.984807753	0.173648178	45.99419282	260.8460295
8	1000	12.5	262.25	0.218166156	0.976296007	0.216439614	56.76128876	256.0336279
9	1000	15	258.88	0.261799388	0.965925826	0.258819045	67.0030744	250.0688779
10	1000	17.5	255.13	0.305432619	0.953716951	0.3007058	76.71907063	243.3218056
11	1000	20	250.63	0.34906585	0.939692621	0.342020143	85.72050852	235.5151615
12	1000	22.5	246.25	0.392699082	0.923879533	0.382683432	94.23579522	227.5053349
13	1000	25	240.87	0.436332313	0.906307787	0.422618262	101.7960607	218.3023567
14	1000	27.5	235	0.479965544	0.887010833	0.461748613	108.5109241	208.4475458
15	1000	30	228.62	0.523598776	0.866025404	0.5	114.31	197.9907278
16	1000	32.5	221.75	0.567232007	0.843391446	0.537299608	119.1461882	187.0220531
17	1000	35	214.5	0.610865238	0.819152044	0.573576436	123.0321456	175.7081135
18	1000	37.5	206.75	0.654498469	0.79335334	0.608761429	125.8614254	164.0258031
19	1000	40	198.37	0.698131701	0.766044443	0.64278761	127.5097781	151.9602362
20	1000	42.5	190	0.741764932	0.737277337	0.675590208	128.3621394	140.082694
21	1000	45	180.87	0.785398163	0.707106781	0.707106781	127.8944035	127.8944035
22	1000	47.5	171.75	0.829031395	0.675590208	0.737277337	126.6273826	116.0326182
23	1000	50	162	0.872664626	0.64278761	0.766044443	124.0991998	104.1315928

(c) Data sheet of spatial light intensity

Fig. 5. Principle of light distribution curve

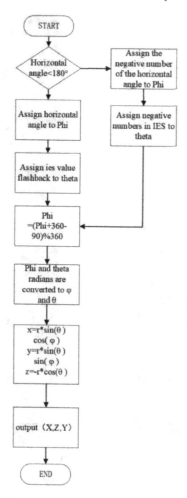

（d）Flow chart of light distribution curve

Fig. 5. (*continued*)

Light distribution in space is asymmetric, then the spatial distribution of light intensity needs a number of light intensity distribution curve of the measurement plane to indicate, so from a variety of asymmetric lamps and lanterns to choose a typical lamp, as shown in Fig. 7. Figure 7(a) below shows the asymmetric light distribution curve of the lamp measured by the instrument, red indicates the initial light measurement plane and blue indicates the final light measurement plane showing different light distribution curves, Fig. 7(b), 7(c) and Fig. 7(d) below show the C0, C90 and C360 surfaces of the lamp in the virtual near-field measurement light distribution curve, respectively, each light measurement plane showing different light distribution curves.

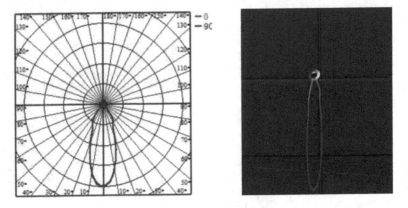

(a) The light distribution curve of the lamps   (b) Virtual light distribution curve at C0°

(c) Virtual light distribution curve at C90°   (d) Virtual light distribution curve at C360°

Fig. 6. The light distribution curve of symmetrical lamps

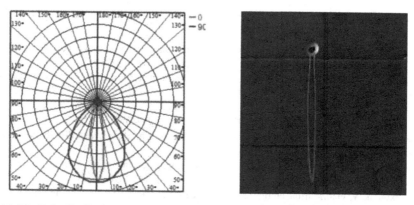

(a) The light distribution curve of the lamps   (b) Virtual light distribution curve at C0°

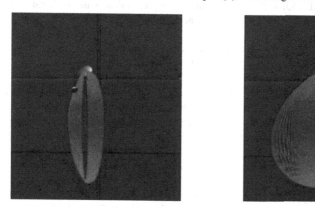

(c) Virtual light distribution curve at C90°   (d) Virtual light distribution curve at C360°

Fig. 7. The light distribution curve of asymmetrical lamps

4   Conclusion

The system combines virtual reality technology and light intensity near-field measurement of full-space distribution photometer lamps, and completes a virtual simulation system for near-field measurement of full-space distribution photometer lamps through unity 3D. The system is a study of light intensity measurement, combining 3Dmax, Blender and C#, and realizes the simulation of full-space distribution photometer and the construction of dark room and the drawing of light distribution curve. This system makes the project closer to the actual experiment through program simulation, and provides a good training platform for those who learn remotely.

Acknowledgements. This work was supported by Joint cooperation research project between Dalian Polytechnic University and CQC Standard (Shanghai) Testing Technology Co., Ltd.

References

1. Cao, F., Wang, B., He, X., Zou, N.: Design of gonio-photometer virtual experiment platform. Nanjing: Electr. Electron. Teach. Newspaper **43**(2), 144–147 (2021)
2. Wang, Y.: Research on LED spatial chromaticity measurement. Hangzhou: Zhejiang University (2011)
3. Yao, P., Chen, Z., Tong, J., Qian, L.: Virtual simulation system of cutter suction dredger based on unity3D. Beijing: J. Syst. Simul. **28**(9), 2069–2084 (2016)
4. Pan, J., Li, Q.: High precision measurement method of light color spatial distribution of light source and lamp. Jinan: J. Light. Eng. (2007)
5. Reeves, S.M., et al.: Virtual laboratories in undergraduate science and engineering courses: a systematic review, 2009–2019. J. Sci. Educ. Technol. 1–15 (2020)
6. Potkonjak, V., et al.: Virtual laboratories for education in science, technology, and engineering: a review. Comput. Educ. **95**, 309–327 (2016)
7. Huang, H.M., Rauch, U., Liaw, S.S.: Investigating learners' attitudes toward virtual reality learning environments: based on a constructivist approach. Comput. Educ. **55**(3), 1171–1182 (2010)
8. Wang, K., Li, A., Ma, C., et al.: Design of digital circuit 3D virtual laboratory based on simulation technology. Beijing: Exp. Technol. Manag. **34**(2), 11–15 (2017)
9. Yan, L.: Research on the construction and application of situational teaching mode based on virtual simulation training platform -- taking computer assembly and maintenance course in secondary vocational school as an example. Dalian: Liaoning Normal University (2021)
10. Zhang, Y., Cao, G., Zou, N., et al.: Construction and research of experimental teaching platform for light source and lighting specialty. Shijiazhuang: Educ. Teach. Forum **000**(010), 251–252 (2016)
11. Jin, Y.: Research on near field distribution photometric measurement technology. Zhejiang: Zhejiang University (2017)
12. Jan, A., Paula, C., et al.: Practical limitation of near-field goniophotometer measurements imposed by a dynamic range mismatch. Opt. Express **23**(3), 2240 (2015)
13. Schmähling, F., Wübbeler, G., Lopez, M., et al.: Virutal experiment for near-field goniophotometric measurements. Apple Opt. **53**(7), 1481–1487 (2014)
14. López, M., Bredemeier, K., Rohrbeck, N., et al.: LED near-field goniophotometer at PTB. Metrologia **49**(2), S141–S145(5) (2012)
15. Lautzenheiser, T., Weller, G., Stannard, S.: Photometry for near field applications. J. Illum. Eng. Soc. **19**(2), 103–112 (1990)
16. Leloup, F.B., Audenaert, J., Hanselaer, P.: Practical limitations of near-field goniophotometer measurements imposed by a dynamic range mismatch. Newrad (2014)
17. Fan, H., Cao, M., Li, S., et al.: Application and research of light source near-field measurement in LED optical design. J. Opt. **32**(12), 222–226 (2012)
18. Li, X., Chen, C., Lv, J., et al.: Near field photometric measurement technology and its application example analysis. China Light. Appliance **402**(09), 32–36 (2018)
19. Bergen, A.: A practical method of comparing luminous intensity distributions. Light. Res. Technol. **44**(1), 27–36 (2022)

Author Index

© ICST Institute for Computer Sciences, Social Informatics and Telecommunications Engineering 2023
Published by Springer Nature Switzerland AG 2023. All Rights Reserved
H. R. Karimi and N. Wang (Eds.): S-Cube 2022, LNICST 487, p. 239, 2023.
https://doi.org/10.1007/978-3-031-34899-0

Printed in the United States
by Baker & Taylor Publisher Services